Cary's new and correct English atlas: being a new set of county maps from actual surveys. Exhibiting all the ... roads, cities, towns, ... Preceded by a general map of South Britain, ...

John Cary

Cary's new and correct English atlas: being a new set of county maps from actual surveys. Exhibiting all the ... roads, cities, towns, ... Preceded by a general map of South Britain, ...
Cary, John
ESTCID: T198229
Reproduction from Trinity College Library Watkinson Collection
The titlepage and dedication are engraved. Each map is followed by a leaf of letterpress explanation. With a list of subscribers. Issued in 12 parts. In this setting the first column of the contents page ends: "Shropshire" and the four columns on p. 9 ('The market and borough towns') end: "Narboth", "Pickering", "Shelford" and "Tetbury". In some copies the preliminary and final letterpress leaves may be bound in different orders and one of the maps may bound in as the fontispiece.
London : printed for John Cary. Published as the act directs Septr. 1st, 1787.
[104],17,[1]p.,plates : maps ; 4°

Eighteenth Century
Collections Online
Print Editions

Gale ECCO Print Editions

Relive history with *Eighteenth Century Collections Online*, now available in print for the independent historian and collector. This series includes the most significant English-language and foreign-language works printed in Great Britain during the eighteenth century, and is organized in seven different subject areas including literature and language; medicine, science, and technology; and religion and philosophy. The collection also includes thousands of important works from the Americas.

The eighteenth century has been called "The Age of Enlightenment." It was a period of rapid advance in print culture and publishing, in world exploration, and in the rapid growth of science and technology – all of which had a profound impact on the political and cultural landscape. At the end of the century the American Revolution, French Revolution and Industrial Revolution, perhaps three of the most significant events in modern history, set in motion developments that eventually dominated world political, economic, and social life.

In a groundbreaking effort, Gale initiated a revolution of its own: digitization of epic proportions to preserve these invaluable works in the largest online archive of its kind. Contributions from major world libraries constitute over 175,000 original printed works. Scanned images of the actual pages, rather than transcriptions, recreate the works *as they first appeared.*

Now for the first time, these high-quality digital scans of original works are available via print-on-demand, making them readily accessible to libraries, students, independent scholars, and readers of all ages.

For our initial release we have created seven robust collections to form one the world's most comprehensive catalogs of 18th century works.

Initial Gale ECCO Print Editions collections include:

History and Geography
Rich in titles on English life and social history, this collection spans the world as it was known to eighteenth-century historians and explorers. Titles include a wealth of travel accounts and diaries, histories of nations from throughout the world, and maps and charts of a world that was still being discovered. Students of the War of American Independence will find fascinating accounts from the British side of conflict.

Social Science
Delve into what it was like to live during the eighteenth century by reading the first-hand accounts of everyday people, including city dwellers and farmers, businessmen and bankers, artisans and merchants, artists and their patrons, politicians and their constituents. Original texts make the American, French, and Industrial revolutions vividly contemporary.

Medicine, Science and Technology
Medical theory and practice of the 1700s developed rapidly, as is evidenced by the extensive collection, which includes descriptions of diseases, their conditions, and treatments. Books on science and technology, agriculture, military technology, natural philosophy, even cookbooks, are all contained here.

Literature and Language
Western literary study flows out of eighteenth-century works by Alexander Pope, Daniel Defoe, Henry Fielding, Frances Burney, Denis Diderot, Johann Gottfried Herder, Johann Wolfgang von Goethe, and others. Experience the birth of the modern novel, or compare the development of language using dictionaries and grammar discourses.

Religion and Philosophy
The Age of Enlightenment profoundly enriched religious and philosophical understanding and continues to influence present-day thinking. Works collected here include masterpieces by David Hume, Immanuel Kant, and Jean-Jacques Rousseau, as well as religious sermons and moral debates on the issues of the day, such as the slave trade. The Age of Reason saw conflict between Protestantism and Catholicism transformed into one between faith and logic -- a debate that continues in the twenty-first century.

Law and Reference
This collection reveals the history of English common law and Empire law in a vastly changing world of British expansion. Dominating the legal field is the *Commentaries of the Law of England* by Sir William Blackstone, which first appeared in 1765. Reference works such as almanacs and catalogues continue to educate us by revealing the day-to-day workings of society.

Fine Arts
The eighteenth-century fascination with Greek and Roman antiquity followed the systematic excavation of the ruins at Pompeii and Herculaneum in southern Italy; and after 1750 a neoclassical style dominated all artistic fields. The titles here trace developments in mostly English-language works on painting, sculpture, architecture, music, theater, and other disciplines. Instructional works on musical instruments, catalogs of art objects, comic operas, and more are also included.

The BiblioLife Network

This project was made possible in part by the BiblioLife Network (BLN), a project aimed at addressing some of the huge challenges facing book preservationists around the world. The BLN includes libraries, library networks, archives, subject matter experts, online communities and library service providers. We believe every book ever published should be available as a high-quality print reproduction; printed on-demand anywhere in the world. This insures the ongoing accessibility of the content and helps generate sustainable revenue for the libraries and organizations that work to preserve these important materials.

The following book is in the "public domain" and represents an authentic reproduction of the text as printed by the original publisher. While we have attempted to accurately maintain the integrity of the original work, there are sometimes problems with the original work or the micro-film from which the books were digitized. This can result in minor errors in reproduction. Possible imperfections include missing and blurred pages, poor pictures, markings and other reproduction issues beyond our control. Because this work is culturally important, we have made it available as part of our commitment to protecting, preserving, and promoting the world's literature.

GUIDE TO FOLD-OUTS MAPS and OVERSIZED IMAGES

The book you are reading was digitized from microfilm captured over the past thirty to forty years. Years after the creation of the original microfilm, the book was converted to digital files and made available in an online database.

In an online database, page images do not need to conform to the size restrictions found in a printed book. When converting these images back into a printed bound book, the page sizes are standardized in ways that maintain the detail of the original. For large images, such as fold-out maps, the original page image is split into two or more pages

Guidelines used to determine how to split the page image follows:

- Some images are split vertically; large images require vertical and horizontal splits.
- For horizontal splits, the content is split left to right.
- For vertical splits, the content is split from top to bottom.
- For both vertical and horizontal splits, the image is processed from top left to bottom right.

CARY'S
NEW and CORRECT
ENGLISH ATLAS;
BEING
A New Set of County Maps
FROM
ACTUAL SURVEYS
EXHIBITING

All the Direct & principal Cross Roads, Cities, Towns, and most considerable Villages, Parks, Rivers,

NAVIGABLE CANALS &c.

Preceded by a General MAP of South Britain,

SHEWING

The Connexion of one Map with another

ALSO

A General Description of each County,

AND

Directions for the junction of the Roads from one County to

ANOTHER

LONDON

Printed for JOHN CARY, Engraver, Map and Print seller, the corner of Arundel Street Strand.

Published as the Act directs Sept'r 1 1787

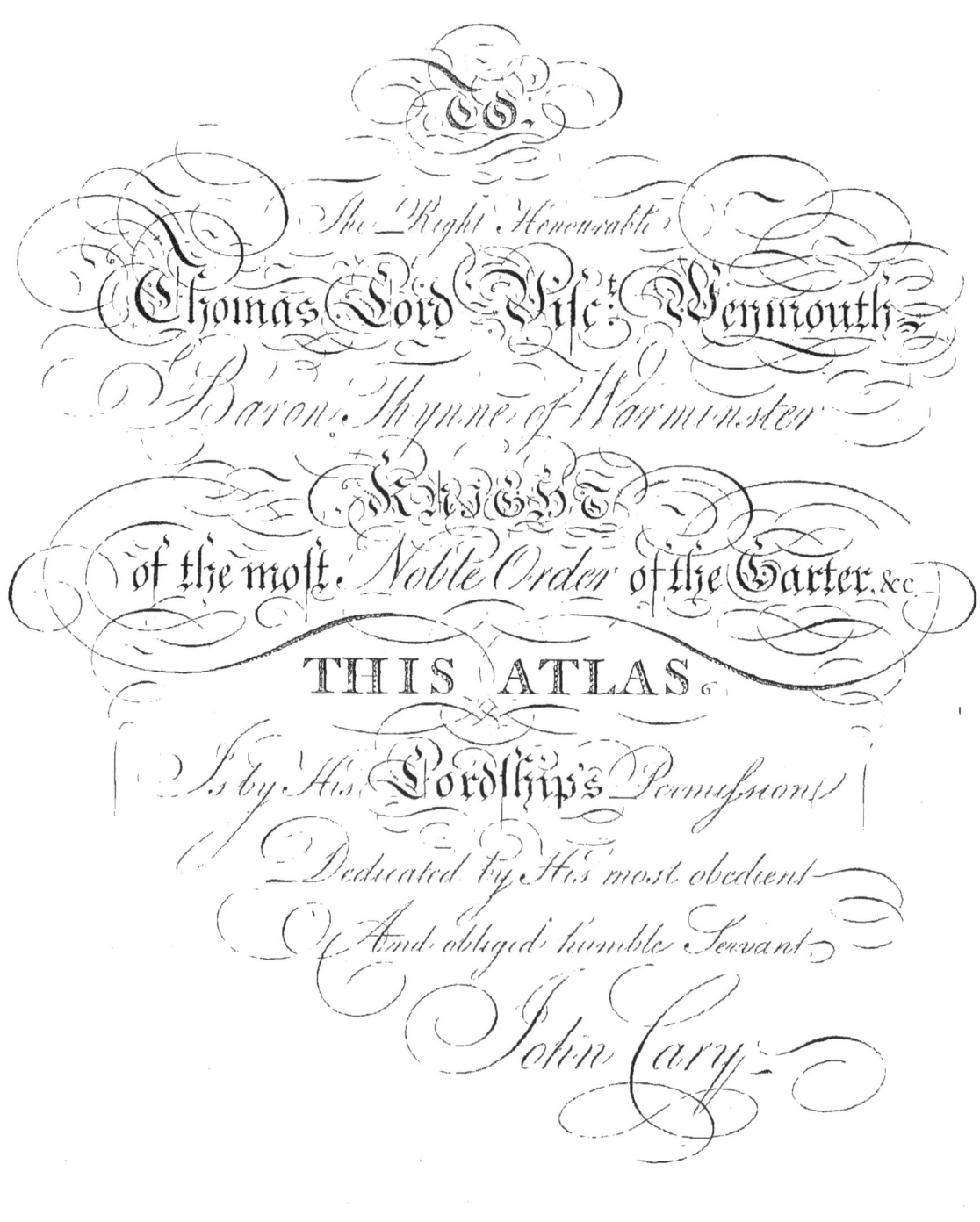

ADVERTISEMENT.

THE liberal encouragement which the Public are always ready in shewing to works where utility and improvement have been a principal object, induced the Proprietor to undertake the present Publication, full of the idea that his labours, in proportion to its merit, would find its reward; possessed of that opinion, he determined that no exertion on his part should be wanting to render the ENGLISH ATLAS as complete as the size of it could possibly admit; that it is more so than any other work of this kind now extant, he thinks himself warranted in asserting, from having recourse to better materials than hitherto used for a work of this Nature. The kind encouragement already shewn to this publication, by a very numerous and respectable subscription, has been a flattering testimony of the approbation of the Public, to whom the Proprietor begs leave to tender his sincerest acknowledgements for the partiality they have shewn him.

Added to the Descriptions of the Counties, with Directions for the Junction of the Roads (which was all that was at first intended to accompany the Maps) a complete Alphabetical List of the Market Towns is given, with the days on which their Markets are held, and their Distance from the metropolis; to which is subjoined, a Correct List of all the Post and Sub-Post Towns with the Receiving Houses under each, throughout England and Wales, shewing the Rates of Postage, the Time of Arrival of the Post in the Country, and its Dispatch for London.—For which Information, as well as other Material Assistance in the completion of this work, the Proprietor is indebted to the liberal permission he was honoured with by the Comptroller General of the Post Office, to resort to such official documents as enables him to vouch for the correctness and accuracy of these important articles.

Sanctioned by the kind protection the Public have shewn him, he presumes to offer to their notice a large MAP OF ENGLAND AND WALES, which he is now engraving, upon a scale of five miles to an inch, a size which enables him to lay down every Parish, (those excepted which are situated in large Towns) with the principal Gentlemen's Seats, Roads, Rivers, and Navigable Canals, as well as other useful matter; and a particular attention will be paid to the Orthography of this Map, a circumstance so frequently complained of, (owing to the difference of pronunciation from the locality of situation) and which experience only can obviate.

N. B. *A Specimen of the Work may be seen at* J. CARY's, *Strand.*

CONTENTS.

GENERAL MAP OF SOUTH-BRITAIN AND WALES.

Bedfordshire.
Berkshire
Buckinghamshire.
Cambridgeshire.
Cheshire.
Cornwall.
Cumberland.
Derbyshire.
Devonshire.
Dorsetshire.
Durham.
Essex
Glocestershire.
Hampshire.
Herefordshire
Hertfordshire.
Huntingdonshire.
Kent.
Lancashire.
Leicestershire.
Lincolnshire.
Middlesex
Monmouthshire;
Norfolk
Northamptonshire.
Northumberland.
Nottinghamshire.
Oxfordshire.
Rutlandshire.
Shropshire.

Somersetshire.
Staffordshire.
Suffolk.
Surry.
Sussex
Warwickshire.
Westmoreland.
Wiltshire.
Worcestershire.
Yorkshire, a General Map.
Ditto, North Riding.
Ditto, East Riding
Ditto, West Riding.

North Wales, including the Counties of
Anglesey.
Carnarvon;
Denbigh.
Flint.
Merioneth, and
Montgomery.

South Wales, including the Counties of
Brecknock.
Carmarthen.
Cardigan.
Glamorgan,
Pembroke, and
Radnor.

DIRECTIONS
FOR
THE JUNCTION OF THE ROADS
OF
ENGLAND AND WALES
THROUGH ALL THE COUNTIES.

ROUTE 1
From LONDON to the LAND's END in Cornwall

See the Map of	Towns, &c. passed through
Middlesex	Kensington
	Brentford
	Hounslow
	Staines
Surry	Egham
	Bagshot
Hampshire	Blackwater
	Murrel Green
	Basingstoke
	Whitchurch
	Andover
Wilts	Lapcombe's Corner
	Salisbury
	Vernditch Chace
Dorset	Woodyates Inn
	Blandford
	Piddleton
	Dorchester
	Winterborn Abbas
	Bridport
	Chidiock
	Charmouth
Devonshire	Axminster
	Honiton
	Exeter
	Chudleigh
	Ashburton
	Brent
	Ivybridge
	Plympton Earl
	Plymouth
Cornwall	Saltash
	Liskard
	Lostwithiel
	St Blazey
	St Austle
	Grampond
	Truro
	Penryn
	Falmouth
	Helston
	Marazion or Market Jew
	Penzance
	Land's End

ROUTE 2
LONDON to TRURO through LAUNCESTON

See the Map of	Towns, &c. passed through
Hampshire	Basingstoke, as in Route 1
	Popham Lane
	Stockbridge
Wiltshire	Lapcombe's Corner
	Salisbury
	Tippet
Dorsetshire	Shaftesbury
Somersetshire	Milborn Port
Dorsetshire	Sherborne
Somersetshire	Yeovil
	Crewkerne
	Chard
Devonshire	Honiton
	Exeter
	Cheriton Bishop's Cross
	South Zeal
	Okehampton
	Bridistow
	Lifton
Dorset	Launceston
	Bodmin
	St Michael
	Truro

ROUTE 3
LONDON to WINCHESTER, POOL, and WEYMOUTH

See the Map of	Towns, &c. passed through
Surry	Bagshot, as in Route 1
Hampshire	Farnley Bridge
Surry	Farnham
Hampshire	Alton
	Alresford
	Winchester
	Rumsey
	Ringwood
	Palmer's Ford
Dorset	Pool
	Lytchet Minster
	Wareham
	Melcomb Regis
	Weymouth

ROUTE 4
LONDON to SOUTHAMPTON

See the Map of	Towns, &c. passed through
Hampshire	Winchester, as in Route 3
	Otterborne
	South Stoneham
	Southampton

ROUTE 5
LONDON to GOSPORT

Hampshire	Alton, as in Route 3
	West Meon
	Wickham
	Fareham
	Gosport

ROUTE 6
LONDON to PORTSMOUTH

Hampshire	Alton, as in Route 3
	Tisted
	Petersfield
	Horndean
	Portsdown
	Portsmouth

ROUTE 7
LONDON to WELLS, BRIDGEWATER, and MINEHEAD

Hampshire	Andover, as in Route 1
	Wevhill
	Quarley
Wiltshire	Amesbury
	Shrewton
	Heytesbury
	Warminster
Somersetshire	Frome
	Whatley
	Shepton Mallet
	Wells
	Glastonbury
	Bridgewater
	Nether Stowey
	Watchet
	Minehead

[2]

ROUTE 8.
LONDON to EXETER by TAUNTON, continued to DARTMOUTH

See the Map of	Towns, &c. passed through.
Wiltshire	Salisbury, as in Route 2
	Wilton
	Chilmark
	Hindon
	Stourhead
Somersetshire	Castle Cary
	Somerton
	Langport
	Taunton
	Wellington
Devonshire	Redhill
	Collumpton
	Bidnich
	Exeter
	Newton Bushel
	Dartmouth

ROUTE 9
LONDON to BARNSTAPLE and ILFRACOMB

Somersetshire	Wellington, as in Route 8
Devonshire	Stampford Peverell
	Tiverton
	South Molton
	Barnstaple
	Ilfracomb

ROUTE 10
LONDON to STRATTON.

Devonshire	Exeter, as in Route 1.
	Crediton
	Hatherly
	Holdsworthy
Cornwall	Stratton

ROUTE 11
LONDON to PORTSMOUTH, through GUILDFORD

Surry	Wandsworth
	Kingston
	Esher
	Guildford
	Godalming
	Devil's Punch Bowl
Hampshire	Liphook
	Petersfield
	Horndean
	Portsmouth

ROUTE 12
LONDON to CHICHESTER, through GUILDFORD

Surry	Godalming, as in Route 11
	Haslemere
Sussex	Sussex Bells
	Midhurst
	Chichester

ROUTE 13
LONDON to ARUNDEL, through DORKING

See the Map of	Towns, &c. passed through
Surry	Clapham
	Upper Tooting
	Tooting
	Morden
	Leatherhead
	Mickleham
	Dorking
	Ockley
Sussex	Slingford
	Billinghurst
	Pulborough
	Arundel

ROUTE 14
LONDON to NEW SHOREHAM and BRIGHTHELMSTONE

Surry	Dorking, as in Route 13
Sussex	Capel
	Warnham
	Horsham
	West Grinstead
	Steyning
	Bramber
	Shoreham
	Brighthelmstone

ROUTE 15
LONDON to BRIGHTHELMSTONE, through DORKING

Sussex	Horsham, as in Route 14
	Hendfield
	Poynings
	Brighthelmstone

ROUTE 16
LONDON to BRIGHTHELMSTONE, through RYEGATE

Surry	Clapham
	Tooting
	Mitcham
	Sutton
	Ryegate
	Povy Cross
Sussex	Crawley
	Cuckfield
	Clayton
	Brighthelmstone

ROUTE 17
LONDON to BRIGHTHELMSTONE, through CROYDON and LINDFIELD

Surry	Streatham
	Croydon
	Godstone Green
	Felbridge
Sussex	Lindfield
	Ditchling
	Brighthelmstone

ROUTE 18
LONDON to LEWES and BRIGHT-HELMSTONE

See the Map of	Towns, &c. passed through
Surry	Felbridge, as in Route 17.
Sussex	East Grinstead
	Sheffield Bridge
	Lewes
	Falmer
	Brighthelmstone

ROUTE 19
LONDON to LEWES, through SEVENOAKS

Surry	New Cross
Kent	Lewisham
	Bromley
	Sevenoaks
	Tunbridge
	Tunbridge Wells
Sussex	Crowborow Beacon
	Uckfield
	Lewes

ROUTE 20
LONDON to EAST BOURNE

Kent	Tunbridge Wells, as in Route 19
Sussex	Frant
	Mayfield
	Hailsham
	Willington
	East Bourne

ROUTE 21
LONDON to HASTINGS

Kent	Tunbridge, as in Route 19.
	Lamberhurst
Sussex	Hurst Green
	Battel
	Hastings

ROUTE 22
LONDON to DOVER

Surry	New Cross
Kent	Dartford
	Northfleet
	Rochester
	Feversham
	Canterbury
	Dover

ROUTE 23
LONDON to MARGATE

Kent	Canterbury, as in Route 22.
	St Irry
	Sarr
	Acol
	Margate

ROUTE

ROUTE 24.
LONDON to HYTHE and FOLKSTONE.

See the Map of	Towns, &c. passed through
Surry	New Cross
Kent	Eltham
	Farningham
	Wrotham
	Maidstone
	Busted
	Harrietsham
	Ashford
	Hythe
	Folkstone

ROUTE 25.
LONDON to NEW ROMNEY.

Kent	Tunbridge, as in Route 19
	Brenchley
	Goudhurst
	Cranbrook
	Tenterden
	Appledore
	New Romney

ROUTE 26.
LONDON to BATH, BRISTOL, and MILFORD HAVEN.

Middlesex	Hounflow, as in Route 1
	Longford
Buck.	Colnbrook
	Slough
	Maidenhead Bridge
Berks	Maidenhead
	Reading
	Newbury
	Hungerford
Wiltshire	Foxfield
	Marlborough
	Fifield
	Beckhampton House
	Calne
	Chippenham
	Box
Somersetshire	Barthford
	Bathaston
	Bath
	Keynsham
	Bristol
	Henbury
Glocestershire	Redwick Green
	New Passage
Monmouthshire	St. Pier
	Caerwent
	Newport
	St. Mellons
	Rumney Bridge
Glamorganshire	Rumney Bridge
	Cardiff
	Cowbridge
	Neath
	Swansea
	Pontardulais

See the Map of	Towns, &c. passed through
Caermarthenshire	Llanethy
	Kidwelly
	Caermarthen
Pembrokeshire	Llanguido
	Haverfordwest
	Milford Haven

ROUTE 27.
LONDON to BATH, through DEVIZES.

Wiltshire	Beckhampton House, as in Route 26
	Shepherd's Shore
	Devizes
	Seend
	Milksham
Somersetshire	Bathford
	Bath

ROUTE 28.
LONDON to WELLS, thro' MARLBOROUGH.

Wiltshire	Beckhampton House, as in Route 26
	Devizes
	Seend
	Trowbridge
Somersetshire	Rode
	Frome
	Shepton Mallet
	Wells

ROUTE 29.
LONDON to GLOCESTER and ST DAVID's.

Berks	Maidenhead, as in Route 26
Oxfordshire	Henley
	Nettlebed
	Turners Court
Berkshire	Wallingford
	Wantage
	Faringdon
Glocestershire	Lechlade
	Fairford
	Cirencester
	Birdlip
	Glocester
	Bulley
	Michael Dean
	Coleford
Monmouthshire	Monmouth
	Rockfield
	Landirly
	Abergavenny
Brecknockshire	Crickhowel
	Brecon
	Trecastle
Caermarthenshire	Llandovery
	New Radnor
	Caermarthen
	Whitland
Pembrokeshire	Haverfordwest
	St David's

ROUTE 30.
LONDON to BRISTOL, thro' ABINGDON.

See the Map of	Towns, &c. passed through
Oxfordshire	Huntercomb End, as in Route 29
	Benfington
	Dorchester
	Bircot
	Clifton
Berkshire	Abingdon
	Fifield
	Faringdon
Wiltshire	Highworth
	Purton
	Malmsbury
	Luckington
Glocestershire	Acton Turville
	Bristol

ROUTE 31.
LONDON to GLOCESTER, HEREFORD, NEW RADNOR, and CARDIGAN, through OXFORD.

Oxfordshire	Huntercomb End, as in Route 29
	Benfington
	Dorchester
	Oxford
Berkshire	Botley
Oxfordshire	Ensham
	Whitney
	Burford
Glocestershire	Little Barrington
	Northleach
	Frogmill
	Little Whitcomb
	Glocester
	Bulley
Herefordshire	Riford
	Weston
	Ross
	Peterstow
	Llandinabo
	Hereford
	Weobley
	Kyneton
	The Whetstone
Brecknockshire	Builth
	Tavern y Pryd
Caermarthenshire	Ludovach
	Llanymdovry
Cardiganshire	Llanbeder
	Rheed Owen
	Newcastle
	Caruigan

ROUTE 32.
LONDON to OXFORD, WORCESTER, and ABERISTWITH.

Middlesex	Bayswater
	Acton
	Uxbridge
	Beaconsfield

Buck-

[4]

See the Map of	Towns, &c. passed through	See the Map of	Towns, &c. passed through	See the Map of	Towns, &c. passed through
Buckinghamshire	Loudwater	Buckinghamshire	Chalfont St Giles	Shropshire	Wellington
	High Wycomb		Amersham		Shrewsbury
Oxfordshire	Stoken Church		Wendover		Aborighton
	Tetsworth		Aylesbury		Illesmere
	Wheatley		Wendon	Flintshire	Overton
	Oxford		Winslow	Denbighshire	Wrexham
	Wolvercot		Buckingham		Ruthin
	Woodstock		Tingwick		Denbigh
	Over Kiddington	Oxfordshire	Finmore	Caermarthenshire	Abercorway
	Chapel House		Mixbury		Bangor
	Little Rolwright	Northamptonshire	Barley Mow		Holyhead or
Glocestershire	Four Shire Stone		Croughton	Anglesea	Beaumaris
	Morton in the Marsh		Aynhoe		Holyhead
Worcestershire	Broadway Street	Oxfordshire	Nell Bridge		
	Evesham		Adderbury		ROUTE 36
	Pershore		Banbury		LONDON to HOLYHEAD, through
	Worcester		Drayton		CHESTER
	Dodenham		Wroxton		
Herefordshire	Bromyard	Warwickshire	Upton	Middlesex	Islington
	Docklow		Lower Pulerton		Highgate
	Leominster	Worcestershire	Goldicot	Hertfordshire	Chipping Barnet
	Kingsland	Warwickshire	Stratford upon Avon	Middlesex	South Mim
	Shoodon		Lasfelt	Hertfordshire	S Albans
Radnorshire	Comb		Alcester		Redburn
	Presteign		Coughton	Bedfordshire	Dunstable
	Ditcoyd		Beoley		Hockliffe
	Cascob	Worcestershire	Crab's Cross	Bucks.	Fenny Stratford
	Llanybangle Chap		Headless Cross		Stony Stratford
	Rhydergowy	Warwickshire	Tudebig	Northamptonshire	Towcester
Montgomeryshire	Taley Brook	Worcestershire	Bromsgrove		Daventry
Cardiganshire	Eomsturh Brook		Chaddesley Corbet		Brownston
	Mowen Glowth		Winterford	Warwickshire	Willoughby
	Llanbadern Vawr		Kidderminster		Dunchurch
	Aberistwith	Staffordshire	Turnpike		Coventry
			Shatterford		Meriden
	ROUTE 33	Shropshire	Quat		Coleshill
	LONDON to HOLYHEAD, thro' WORCESTER		Quatford		Moxhull
			Bridgenorth		Lingley Hall
Worcestershire	Worcester, as in Route 32.		Morvill		Sutton
	Hallow		Much Wenlock	Staffordshire	Sutton Colefield
	Great Whitley		Harley		Watling Street
	Stockton		Shrewsbury		Weston under Lizard
	Tenbury		Montford Bridge	Shropshire	Woodcot Hall
Shropshire	Burford		Oswestry		Church Aston
Herefordshire	Little Hereford		Salatin		Newport
Shropshire	Ashford Boulder	Denbighshire	Llangollen		Chetwynd
	Ludlow	Merionethshire	Corwen		Ternhill
	Onnybury	Denbighshire	Llanroft		Bletchly
	Basfod Gate	Caernarvon	Bangor		Whitchurch
	Bishop's Castle	Anglesea	Holyhead	Cheshire	Cum Grindley
Montgomeryshire	Montgomery				Chester
	Welchpool		ROUTE 35	Flintshire	St Asaph
	Llanvilling		LONDON to HOLYHEAD, through	Denbighshire	Abergely
Merionethshire	Bala		BIRMINGHAM	Caermarthenshire	Abercorway
	Llanroft				Beaumaris or
Denbigh	Conway	Warwickshire	Stratford upon Avon, as in		Bangor
Caernarvonshire	Bangor		Route 34	Anglesea	Holyhead
Anglesea	Holyhead		Henley		
			Birmingham		ROUTE 37
	ROUTE 34	Staffordshire	Hockley Brook		LONDON to CHESTER, through
	LONDON to HOLYHEAD, through BUCK-		Wolverhampton		BIRMINGHAM
	INGHAM and SHREWSBURY	Shropshire	Tetterhall		
			Boningale	Warwickshire	Birmingham, as in Route 35
Middlesex	Uxbridge, as in Route 32		Shefnal	Staffordshire	Walsal
Buckinghamshire	Chalfont St Peter		Wombridge		Bloxwich

Stafford-

[5]

See the Map of	Towns, &c. passed through
Staffordshire	Cannock
	Stafford
	Fedlefhall
	Ashley Heath
	Muckleston
Shropshire	Dormoton
	Woore
Cheshire	Namptwich
	Tarperley
	Chester

ROUTE 38
LONDON to AYLESBURY, BICESTER, and OXFORD, through TRING

Middlesex	Paddington
	Edgware
	Stanmore
Hertfordshire	Bufhy Heath
	Watford
	Berkhamsted
	Tring
Buckinghamshire	Aylesbury
	Fleetmarston
Oxfordshire	Bicester
	Oxford

ROUTE 39
LONDON to WARRINGTON, LANCASTER, and CARLISLE

Warwickshire	Meriden, as in Route 36
	Coleshill
	Moxhull
Staffordshire	Baffet's Crofs
	Weeford
	Litchfield
	Longdon
	Colwich
	Stone
	Newcastle
	Talk
Cheshire	Lawton
	Smallwood
	Holm's Chapel
	Change Hill
	Knutsford
Lancashire	Warrington
	Newton
	Wigan
	Standish
	Preston
	Lancaster
	Bolton
Westmorland	Burton
	Kendal
	Patton
	Garsdale
	Birbeck Fells
Cumberland	Penrith
	Petruia
	Carlisle

ROUTE 40
LONDON to PRESTON and MANCHESTER, through DERBY and NORTHAMPTON

See the Map of	Towns, &c. passed through
Bedfordshire	Dunstable, as in Route 36
	Woodburn
Buckinghamshire	Waveton
	Newport Pagnel
	Stoke Colington
Northamptonshire	Horton
	Northampton
	Kingsthorpe
	Brixworth
Leicestershire	Kernath
	Harborough
	Gren Magna
	Leicester
	Mount Soriel
	Loughborough
	Kegworth
Derbyshire	Cavendish Bridge
	Shardlowe
	Derby
	Makworth
	Ashborne
	Red House
	Alfon
	New Haven
	Buxton
	Elner Lane
Cheshire	Whaly Bridge
	Difley
	Stockport
Lancashire	Manchester
	Bolton in the Moors
	Chorley
	Preston

ROUTE 41
LONDON to SHEFFIELD, SETTLE, KIRBY LONSDALE, and WHITEHAVEN, through DERBY

Derbyshire	Derby, as in Route 40
	Duffield
	Hoge
	Chesterfield
	Dronfield
Yorkshire	Sheffield
	Chapel Town
	Barnfley
	Wakefield
	Leeds
	Cookridge
	Otley
	Skipton
	Settle
	Clapham
	Ingleton
	West Houfe
Westmorland	Kirby Lonsdale
	Crofs Lands
	Kendal
	Staveley
	Amblefide

See the Map of	Towns, &c. passed through
Cumberland	Townhead
	Winburn
	Kefwick
	Crofthwaite
	Cockermouth
	Little Clifton
	Whitehaven

ROUTE 42
LONDON to HALIFAX and CLITHERO, through BEDFORD, NOTTINGHAM, and ROTHERHAM

Hertfordshire	St Alban's, as in Route 36
	Harpden
Bedfordshire	Luton
	Silfoe
	Williamfted
	Elftow
	Bedford
	Blefoe
Northamptonshire	Higham Ferrars
	Kettering
	Rockingham
Rutlandshire	Uppingham
	Oakham
	Langham
Leicestershire	Melton Mowbray
	Nether Boughton
Nottinghamshire	Over Boughton
	Nottingham
	Mansheld
Yorkshire	Rotherham
	Chapel Town
	Worley Chapel
	Peniston
	Huddersfield
	Halifax
Lancashire	Burnley
	Clithero

ROUTE 43
LONDON to MANCHESTER and CLITHERO, through LEFY, UTTOXETER, and HINCKLEY

Northamptonshire	Northampton, as in Route 40
	Welford
Leicestershire	Kilworth
	Lutterworth
	Hinckley
	Atherston
	Tamworth
Staffordshire	Buxton
	Uttoxeter
	Cheadle
	Leek
Cheshire	Macclesfield
	Stockport
Lancashire	Manchester
	Bury
	Haslingdon
	Clithero

ROUTE 44.
LONDON to BERWICK, through YORK.

See the Map of	Towns, &c passed through
Middlesex	Highgate
	Barnet
Herts	Hatfield
	Welwyn
	Baldock
	Biggleswade
	Sandy
	Eaton Socon
Huntingdon	Buckden
	Alconbury
	Stilton
	Walmsford
Lincolnshire	Stamford
Rutlandshire	Bridge Casterton
	Colsterworth
	Grantham
Nottinghamshire	Newark
	Tuxford
	East Retford
Yorkshire	Bawtry
	Doncaster
	Pontefract
	Sherborne
	Tadcaster
	York
	Easingwold
	Thirsk
	North Allerton
	Croft
Durham	Darlington
	Aycliffe
	Durham
	Chester le Street
Northumberland	Newcastle
	Morpeth
	Alnwick
	Belford
Durham	Berwick

ROUTE 45
LONDON to PENRITH, through BOROUGH-BRIDGE and APPLEBY.

Yorkshire	Pontefract, as in Route 44
	Wetherby
	Borough bridge
	Leeming
	Catterick
	Gretta Bridge
	Bowes
Westmorland	Brough
	Appleby
Cumberland	Penrith

ROUTE 46
LONDON to SCARBOROUGH, through LINCOLN and HUNTINGDON.

Middlesex	Stoke Newington
	Tottenham
	Enfield Wash

See the Map of	Towns, &c passed through
Herts	Cheshunt
	Ware
	Puckeridge
	Buntingford
Cambridge	Royston
	Kneesworth
	Caxton
Huntingdonshire	Godmanchester
	Huntingdon
	Stilton
	Yaxley
Northamptonshire	Peterborough
	Glinton
Lincolnshire	Market Deeping
	Bourne
	Folkingham
	Sleaford
	Lincoln
	Spittle
	Rethorne
	Glanford Bridge
	Barton
Yorkshire	Kingston upon Hull
	Beverley
	Great Driffield
	Langtoft
	Foxholes
	Scarborough

ROUTE 47.
LONDON to LYNN REGIS, through CAMBRIDGE

Hertfordshire	Puckeridge, as in Route 46
	Barkway
	Bailey
Cambridgeshire	Foulmere
	Cambridge
	Ely
	Littleport
Norfolk	Southery
	Downham
	Lynn Regis

ROUTE 48
LONDON to NORWICH, through NEW MARKET.

Middlesex	Hackney
	Clapton
Essex	Walthamstow
	Epping
	Harlow
Herts	Sawbridgeworth
	Bishop's Stortford
Essex	Saffron Walden
Cambridgeshire	Chesterford
	Abington
	New Market
Suffolk	Mildenhall
	Thetford
Norfolk	Attleborough
	Wyndham
	Norwich

ROUTE 49
LONDON to NORWICH, through IPSWICH

See the Map of	Towns, &c passed through
Middlesex	Bow
Essex	Stratford
	Romford
	Brentwood
	Ingatestone
	Chelmsford
	Witham
	Colchester
Suffolk	Stratford
	Ipswich
	Twaite
Norfolk	Scole Inn
	Norwich

ROUTE 50.
LONDON to NORWICH, through SUDBURY

Essex	Chelmsford, as in Route 49
	Braintree
	Halsted
	Sudbury
Suffolk	Lavenham
	Bildeston
	Stow Market
	Mendlesham
Norfolk	Diss
	Buckenham
	Norwich

ROUTE 51
LONDON to LYNN REGIS, through BRANDON and NEW MARKET

Cambridgeshire	New Market, as in Route 48
Suffolk	Brandon
Norfolk	Methwold
	Stething
	Lynn Regis

ROUTE 52
LONDON to YARMOUTH, through IPSWICH

Suffolk	Ipswich, as in Route 49
	Woodbridge
	Saxmundham
	Blithborough
	Beccles
Norfolk	Haddiscoe
Suffolk	Bradwell
Norfolk	Yarmouth

THE MARKET AND BOROUGH TOWNS IN ENGLAND AND WALES

With the DAYS their MARKETS are held, and their DISTANCE from LONDON.

N B The Borough Towns are distinguished by being in Italic, and their Number of Representatives by *, and the Cities and Universities in Small Capitals.

ABBOTSBURY, *Dorsetshire*, Th 128
Aberconway, *Carnar* F 231
Aberford, *York* W 184
Abergaveny, *Monm* T 140
Aberystwith, *Card* M 204
* *Abingdon*, Berks M F 57
* *St Albans*, Hertf W S 21
* *Aldborough*, York. W 205
* *Aldborough*, Suff W S 95
Alford, *Linc* T 140
Alfreton, *Darby* M 139
Alnwick, *Northumb* S 306
Alresford, *Hamp* Th 57
Alston Moor, *Cumb* S 206
Alton, Hants S 48
Altringham, *Ches* F 184
Amesbury, *Wilts* F 78
Ambleside, *Westm* W 271
* *Amersham*, Bucks, T 26
Ampthill *Bedf* Th 46
* *Andover*, Hants S 65
* *Appleby*, Westm S 266
Appledore, *Kent* S 67
* *Arundel*, Sussex, W S 55
S Asaph, *Flint* S 211
Ashborn, *Darby* S 139
* *Ashburton*, Devon T 190
Ashby de la Zouch, *Leic* S 114
Ashford, *Kent* T 57
Askrig, *York* Th 241
Atherstone, *Warw* T 95
Attleborough, *Norf* Th 94
Auburn, *Wilts* T 73
Auckland, Bish *Durh* Th 250
Axeester, *Warw* T 102
St Austle, *Cornw* F 236
Axbridge, *Som* Th 121
Axminster, *Devon* S 146
* *Aylsham*, Bucks S 40
Aylesham, *Norf* S 121

Bakewell, *Derby* M 151
Bala, *Merion* S 193
Baldock, *Hert* Th 37
Bampton, *Oxf* W 69
Brampton, *Devon* S 167
* *Banbury*, Oxf Th 75
Bangor, *Carn* W 248

Barking, *Essex* S 9
Berkway, *Her* S 35
Barnard Castle, *Durh* W 247
Barnet, *Hert* M 12
Barnesley, *York* W 178
* *Barnstable*, Devon F 193
Barton, *Linc* M 166
Basingstoke, *Hants* W 46
Batel, *Suff* Th 57
* *BATH*, Som W S 107
Bawtry, *York* S 153
Beaconsfield, *Bucks*, Th 23
* *Beaumaris*, Anglef W 242
Beccles, *Suff* S 108
Bedal, *York* T 219
* *Bedford*, Bedf T S 51
* *Bedwin*, Wilts T 71
Bedford, *Northumb* Th 320
Bellingham, *Northumb* 295
Bemster, *Dorset* Th 140
Bere Regis, *Dorf* W 115
* *Beeralston*, Devon 212
Birkhamstead, *Hertf* S 26
Berkley, *Glou* W 113
* *Berwick*, Northumb S 336
Betley, *Staff* T 157
* *Beverley*, York W S 182
* *Bewdley*, Worc S 128
Bicester, *Oxf* F 57
Biddenden, *Devon* T 202
Biggleswade, *Bedf* T 46
Bildeston, *Suff* W 67
Billericay, *Essex* T 23
Billingham, *Northumb* T S 299
Bilston, or Bliss, *Leic* F 97
Binbrook, *Linc* W 149
Bingham, *Nott* Th 18
Birmingham, *Warw* Th S 6
* *Bishops Castle*, Shrop F 152
Bishop's Stortford, *Hertf* Th 29
Bisley *Glou* Th 97
Bidford, *Warw* F 100
Blackbourn, *Lanc* M 203
Blandford, *Dorset* S 106
* *Bletchingley*, Surry, 31
Blyth, *Nott* Th 143
* *Bodmin*, Cornw S 232
Bolingbroke, *Linc* T 154
Bolsover, *Darby* F 147

Bolton, *Lanc* M 195
Bootle, *Cumb* W 277
Borne, or Bourn *Linc* S 97
* *Boroughbridge*, York S 203
Boss-castle, *Cornw* Th 230
* *Bossiney*, Cornw 233
* *Boston*, Linc W S 119
Bolworth, *Leic* W 105
Bow, *Devon* Th 189
* *Brackley*, Northamp W 64
Bradfield, *Essex* Th 47
Bradford, *Wilts* M 95
Bradford, *York* Th 202
Bradnich, *Devon* S 167
Braintree, *Essex* W 40
* *Bramber*, Sussex, S 47
Brampton, *Cumb* T 311
Brecon, *Suss* T 178
* *Brecknock*, Breck W F 162
* *Bridgenorth*, Shrop S 139
* *Bridgewater*, Som Th S 142
* *Bridport*, Dorse S 138
Brightelmstone, *Suss* Th 60
* *BRISTOL*, Som W S 115
Bromley, *Kent* T 10
Bromley, *Staff* M 129
Bromyard, *Hertf* T 125
Bromsgrove, *Worc* T 115
Prough, *Westm* Th 258
Bruton, *Som* S 110
Buckenham, *Norf* S 96
* *Buckingham*, Bucks, S 58
Buddestace *Suff* Th 87
Builth, *Breck* M 166
Bungay, *Suff* Th 107
Buntingford, *Hertf* M 31
Burford, *Oxf* S 71
Burgh, *Linc* Th 138
Burlington, *York* S 208
Burnham, *Norf* M 110
Burnley, *Lanc* S 207
Burton Lather, *Linc* T 160
Burton on Trent, *Staff* Th 123
Burton, *Westm* F 245
Bury, *Lanc* Th 100
* *Bury St Edmund's*, Suff W 74

Caerphilly, *Glam* Th 154
Caerleon, *Monm* Th 148

Caermarthen, Caerm W S 208
Callington, *Cornw* W 215
Caerws, *Flint* T 026
* *Calne*, Wilts T 88
* *CAMBRIDGE*, Cam T S 52
* *Camelford*, Cornw F 228
Campden, *Glou* W 89
* *CANTERBURY*, Kent W S 56
* *Cardiff*, Glam W S 156
* *Cardigan*, Card T S 225
* *CARLISLE*, Cumb S 299
* *Caernarvon*, Carn S 248
Carmel, *Lanc* M 260
Castle Cary, *Somerf* T 117
* *Castle Rising*, Norf 102
Caufton, *Norf* T 114
Caston, *Linc* M 157
Cawood, *York* W 186
Caxton, *Camb* T 49
Cerne, *Dorset* W 123
Chapel in Frith, *Darby* Th 163
Chard, *Som* M 141
Chatham, *Kent* S 31
Cheadle, *Staff* S 144
Chelmsford, *Essex* F 29
Cheltenham, *Glou* Th 94
Chepstow, *Monm* S 133
Chertsey, *Sur* W 21
Chesham, *Bucks* W 29
* *CHESTER*, Ches W S 182
Chesterfield, *Darby* S 149
* *Chichester*, Suss W S 65
Chumleigh, *Devon* Th 190
* *Chippenham*, Wilts Th 93
Chipping-Norton, *Oxf* W 74
* *Chipping Wycomb*, Bucks, F 33
* *Christ Church*, Hants, M 102
Chudleigh, *Devon* S 182
Church Stretton, *Shrop* Th 153
* *Cirencester*, Glouc M F 89
Clare, *Suff* T 56
Clay, *Norf* S 115
Chorley, *Lanc* T 203
Cleobury, *Shrop* Th 136
Cliffe, *Northamp* T 84
* *Clitheroe*, Lanc S 215
* *Cockermouth*, Cumb M 299
Coggshall, *Essex* S 44
* *Colchester*, Essex S 51

Coln-

Colnbrook, Berks W 17
Coleshill, Warw W 103
Colford, Glou T 14
Colne, Lanc W 215
Columb, S Cornw Th 249
Columpton, Devon S 164
Congleton, Chef S 161
Corby, L W 90
Corffe Castle, Dorset F 170
COVENTRY, Warw 1 91
Coubridge, Glou T 168
Cranborn, Dorset Th 94
Cranbrook, Kent S 49
Crawford, Kent T 14
Crediton, Devon S 176
Crickhowel, Breck Th 149
Crickdale, Wilts S 83
Cromer, Norf S 1.7
Crookhorn, Som S 132
Crowland, Linc S 94
Crowle, Linc S 165
Croydon, Surry S 10
Cuckfield, Suff S 39
Cullinton, Devon Th 135

Dalton, Lan S 211
Darlington, Durh W 238
Dartford, Kent S 15
Dartmouth, Devon F 203
Daventry, Northamp W 72
St Davids, Pemb W 256
Deal, Kent Th 72
Dean Mitcel, Glou M 116
Debenham, Suff F 83
Deddington, Oxf S 62
Dedl m, Ffex T 58
Deeping, Linc Th 90
Dereham, East, Norf F 100
Denbigh, Denb W 210
Derby, Derbysh F 126
Devizes, Wilts Th 88
Dinasmouthy, Mer se F 192
Do, Norf F 94
Dodbroke, Devon W 218
Dolgelly, Merion T 202
Doncaster, York S 160
Downing on, Linc. S 117
Dorchester, Dorset S 120
Doking, Surry Th 23
Dover, Kent W S 72
Downham, Norf S 86
Dowrton, or Dunkton, Wilts. F 83
Drayton, Shrop M 153
Droitwich, Worc F 118
Dronfield, Derby Th 154
Dudley, Worc S 120
Dulverton, Som S 69
Dunmow, Effex S 40
Dunnington, Lan S 99
Dunstable, Bedf W 14
Dunster, Som T 163
Debenham, Suff S 99
DURHAM, Durh S 256
Dursley, Glou Th 107
East Grinsfield, Suff Th 30

East Looe, Cornw S 214
Fedlethall, Staf T 142
Edenstone, Lanc S 205
Edgware, Midd Th 8
Egremont, Camb S 298
Elham, Kent M 66
Ellesmere, Shrop T 172
Eltham, Kent M 7
Ely, Camb S 68
Enfield, Midd S 10
Epping, Effex F 6
Epsom, Surry Daily, 1
Efingwood, York F 210
Evesho, Dorset T 128
Evesham, Worc M 95
Ewell, Surry Th 13
EXETER, Devon W F 172
Eye, Suff S 90

Fairford, Glou Th 81
Fakenham, Norf Fl. 120
Falmouth, Cornw Th 263
Farcham, Hamp W 73
Farnham, Surry Th 38
Faringdon, Berks T 70
Fenny Stratford, Bucks M 45
Feversham, Kent W S 47
Fifkard, Pemb F 242
Flint, Flint 196
Folkingham, Linc Th 107
Folkiston, Kent T 73
Fordingbridge, Hamp S 91
Foulsham, Norf T 100
Fowey, or Foy, Cornw S 240
Framlingam, Suff S 87
Frodesham, Chef W 183
Foddingham, York Th 197
Froome, Som W 108

Gainsborough, Linc T 150
Garslang, Lanc Th 247
Gatton, Surry, 19
S Germen, Cornw F 223
Gisborough, York M 246
Gisbourne, York M 219
Glansford-bridge, Linc Th 156
Glasonbury, Som T 132
GLOUCETER, Glou W S 00
Godalming, Surry S 34
Gosport, Hamp S 78
Goudhurst, Kent W 43
Grampound, Cornw S 243
Grantham, Linc S 110
Gravesend, Kent W S 22
Grayes, Effex Th 25
Grimsby Great, Linc W 168
Guilford, Surry S 30

Hadley, Suff M 63
Halesworth, Suff T 101
Halifax, York S 202
Halston, Leic Th 93
Halstead, Essex F 47
Harborough, Leic T 83
Harlech, Merion S 220

Hackston, Norf W 112
Harling, Norf T 88
Harlow, Essex S 23
Harland, Devon S 218
Hartlepool, Durh S 259
Harwich, Essex T 93
Haslemere, Surry T 43
Haslington, Lanc W 195
Halyfield, Suffex W S 64
Hatfield, Effex S 30
Hatfield, Herf Th 19
Hatherly, Devon I 200
Hedon, Chef S 185
Havant, Hamp S 66
Haverfordwest, Pemb F S 246
Havent, Suff W 55
Hawkshead, Lanc M 272
Hay, Brec S 152
Haywood Great, Staff S 130
Hyton, York Fn 181
Helmsley, York S 221
Helston, Cornw M 270
Hensel Hempsted, Herts Th 20
Henley, Oxf W I S 35
Henley, Warw T 102
HEREFORD, Herf S 130
Hertford, Herts S 21
Hexham, Northumb F 286
Heytesbury, Wilts 93
Higham Ferrers, Northamp S 71
Highworth, Wilts W 77
Hindon, Wilts Th 96
Hingham, Norf S 98
Hinckley, Leic M 102
Hitching, Herf T 34
Hoddesdon, Herf Th 17
Holbeach, Linc Th 115
Home, Carl S 310
Holt, Norf S 100
Holywell, Flint T 211
Honiton, Devon S 155
Hornby, Lanc M 158
Horncastle, Linc S 142
Horndon, Effex S 0
Hornsey, York M 188
Horsham, Suffex, S 37
Hoathworthy, Devon S 25
Hounflow, Midd Fl 0
Hovingham, York S 214
Howden, York S 179
Hull, York T S 173
Hungerford, Wilts W 65
Hunmanby, York T 90
Hurtington, Hunt S 59
Huthersfield, York T 195
Hythe, Kent S 69

Ilchester, Somerset W 128
Ilfracomb, Devon S 186
Ilminster, Som S 142
Illey, Berks W 59
Ipswich, Suff W F S 69
Ireby, Camb Tn 301
St Ives, Cornw W, S 274

St Ive, Hunt M 64
Ivinglea, Bucks 1 32
Ixworth, Suff 1 79

Kellington, Cornw W 215
Kendall, W m S 257
Kelwick, Cumb S 287
Kettering, Northamp S 77
Kenisham, Som Th 59
Kidderminster, Worc Th 125
Killolly, Cornw I 16
Kilkhauron, Pemb W 248
Louisin, Som S 00
Kimbolton, Hunt I 63
Kincton, Warw I 88
Kingsbridg, Devon S 217
Kingskar, Hunt I 55
Kingston, Som S 12
Kington, Heref W 151
Kirkby Lonsdale, Westm Th 253
Kirkby Moorside, York W 272
Kirkby Stephen, Westm M 239
Kirkton, Lanc C 221
Kirkoswald, Camb Th 91
Kirkton Lindsey, Linc S 150
Knaresborough, York W 199
Krighton, Radnor F 157
Knutsford, Chef S 183
Kirkbythe, Cornw W 233
Kyneton, Herf W 151

Lambourn, Berks I 68
Lancaster, Lanc S 285
Launceston, Cornw S 214
LANDAFF, Glamor M 138
Langport, Som S 123
Lanrust, Denb T 50
Lavenham, Suff T 63
Lavington, Wilts W 59
Ledale, Chef I 70
Ledbury, Herf I 116
Leek, York T S 19
Leek, Staff W 154
Leicester, Leic S 98
Leighton Bezard, Bedf F 41
Lenham, Kent I 45
Leominster, Heref I 137
Lestharn, Cornw S 221
Lostwithiel, Suff W 111
Lostwithiel, Cornw I 229
Lewes, Suffex, S 50
Libney, Glouc W 124
Lime, Dorset I 137
Lincoln, Linc T 113
Linton, Camb Th 115
Litchfield, Staff T F 119
Liverpool, Lanc S 195
Llanellhy, Carm F 28
Llandlover, Carm F 195
Llanarch, Card T 233
Llangadock, Carm Th 287
Llanpeter, Card F 197
Llanvindovery, Carm S 181
Llangham, Carm W S 233
Llanyalos, Mont S 177

Llan-

Llantrissent, *Glam* F 161
Llanveiling, *Mont* 1 175
Loddon, *Norf* F 116
**London, *Midd* every Day except Sunday
Longtown, *Cumb* Th 313
Loughborough, *Leic* Th 109
Louth, *Linc* W S 155
*Ludlow, *Shrop* M 139
**Ledgershall, *Wilts* 75
Luton, *Bedf* M 3
Lutterworth, *Leic* Th 87
Lydd, *Kent* Th 70
*Lymington, *Hamp* S 97
**Lynn Regis, or *King*'. Lynn, *Norf* T S 98
Lifton, *Devon* S 208

Macclesfield, *Ches* M 170
Machynleth, *Montg* M 195
Maiden Bradley, *Wilts* M 105
Maidenhead, *Berks* W 26
**Maidstone, *Kent*, Th 36
**Maldon, *Essex*, S 37
Maling, *Kent*, S 29
**Malmsbu, *Wilts* S 95
Malpas, *Ches* M 166
**Malton, *York* S 215
Manchester, *Lanc* S 182
Manningtree, *Essex*, T 60
Mansfield, *Nott* Th 140
Marsh, *Camb* F 80
Market Deeping, *Linc* 90
Market Rasin, *Linc* Th 150
Market Jew, *Cornw* T 286
*Marlborough, *Wilts* S 75
**Marlow, *Bucks*, S 31
Marshfield, *Glou* T 104
Masham, *Essex*, S 21
**St Mawes, *Cornw* 268
**Melcomb Regis, *Dorset* T F 130
Melton Mowbray, *Leic* T 108
Melford, Long, *Suff* T 59
Mendlesham, *Suff* F 82
Mere, *Wilts* T 104
Methwold, *Norf* T 86
*St Michael, *Cornw* 247
Middleham, *York* T 253
Middlewich, *Ches* T 166
**Midhurst, *Sussex*, Th 52
**Milton Port, *Som* 115
Mildenhall, *Suff* F 69
Milton, *Kent*, S 42
Milton-Abbey, *Dorset* T 113
Minching Hampton, *Glou* T 90
*Minehead, *Som* W 166
Michel Dean, *Glou* M 116
Modbury, *Devon* Th 207
*Monmouth, *Monm* S 129
*Montgomery, *Mont* T 138
Mount-Sorel, *Leic* M 105
Merston Hampsted, *Devon* S 18
*Morpeth, *Northumb* W 287
Mould, *Flint* S 200
Nantwich, *Ches* S 161
Narberth, *Pemb* W 230

Neath, *Glam* S 172
Needham, *Suff* W 73
St Neots, *Hunt* Th 58
Netherstowey, *Som* T 130
**Newark, *Nott* W 124
Newburgh, *Angl* T 254
Newbury, *Berks* Th 56
**Newcastle, No thumb T S 272
**Newcastle-under-Lyne, *Stafford* M 149
Newcastle, *Caerm* T 216
Newent, *Glou* T 114
New Inn, *Caerm* S 146
Newmarket, *Camb* Th 60
Newnham, *Glou* F 116
**Newport, *Hamp* W S 97
**Newport, *Cornw* S 214
Newport, *Monm* S 141
Newport, *Pemb* S 235
Newport, *Shrop* S 110
Newport Pagnel, *Bucks* S 52
Newton Bushel, *Devon* W 187
*Newton, *Lanc* S 188
Newtown, *Mont* S 166
Neyland, *Suff* T 57
*Nor Laneston, *Cornw* W 223
*Northampton, *Northamp* S 66
North Curry, *Som* T S 139
Northleach, *Glou* W 80
No Jrwich, *Ches* F 172
**Norwich, *Norf* W F S 109
**Nottingham, *Nott* W S 123
Nuneaton, *Warw* S 98

Oakingham, *Berks* T 32
Odiam, *Hamp* S 41
Oakham, *Rutl* S 96
*Oakhampton, *Devon* S 193
Ongar, *Essex*, S 21
*Orford, *Suff* M 88
Ormskirk, *Lanc* T 205
Orton, *Westm* W 276
Olwester, *Shrop* W 171
Otley, *York* T 208
Ottery, St Mary, *Devon* T 160
Ouney, *Bucks* M 57
Oundle, *Northamp* S 76
**OXFORD, *Oxf* W S 54

Padstow, *Cornw* S 243
Painswick, *Glou* T 100
Patrington, *York* S 191
Pemoridge, *Heref* T 146
*Pembroke, *Pemb* S 238
Penkridge, *Staf* T 123
Penrith, *Cumb* T 283
Penrice, *Glou* Th 219
**Penryn *Cornw* W T S 261
Penzance, *Cornw* Th 289
Pen ford, *Som* T 117
Pershore, *Worc* T 102
**Peterborough, *Northamp* S 81
*Petersfield, *Hamp* S 55
Petworth, *Suff* S 49
Philips Norton *Som* Th 102
Pickering, *York* M 124

Pillerton, *Warw* 87
**Plymouth, *Devon* M T 217
*Plympton, *Devon* S 209
Pocklington, *York* S 196
*Pontefract, *York* S 175
*Pontypool, *Monm* S 147
**Poole, *Dorset* M 106
**Portsmouth, *Hamp* Th S 73
Potten, *Bedf* S 49
Poulton, *Lanc* M 229
Prescot, *Lanc* T 195
Presteign, *Radnor* S 150
*Preston, *Lanc* W F S 213
Pulhely, *Caern* W 240

**Queenborough, *Kent*, M Th 46

*Radnor, *New*, Rad Th 157
Ramsey, *Hunt* S 68
Ravenglass, *Cumb* S 282
Raleigh, *Essex*, S 34
*Reading, *Berks*. S 39
Reepham, *Norf* S 109
**Retford, *East*, Nott S 145
Riaddergowy, *Radnor* W 174
**Richmond, *York*. S. 231
Rickmansworth, *Herts* S 19
Ringwood, *Hamp*. W 94
Ripley, *York* F 103
*Rippon, *York* Th 209
Risbrough, *Bucks*. S 37
Rochdale, *Lanc* T 196
**ROCHESTER, *Kent*, F 30
Rockingham, *Northamp* Th 84
Ross, *Heref* Th 119
Rotherham, *York* M 163
Rothwell, *Northamp* M 79
Royston, *Herts* W 38
Rugby, *Essex* S 85
Rudgeley, *Staf* T 126
Rumford, *Essex*, T W 12
*Rumney, *New*, Kent, Th 72
Rumsey, *Hamp* S 76
Ruthin, *Denb*. M 205
*Rye, *Suff*. W S 64
*Ryegate, *Surry*, T 21

Saffron Walden, *Essex*, S 43
*SALISBURY, *Wilts* T S 82
**Saltash, *Cornw* S 220
Sanfleet, *Linc* S 163
Sandbach, *Ches* Th 161
**Sandwich, *Kent*, W S 67
*Sarum, Old, *Wilts* 83
Saxmundham, *Suff* Th 80
**Scarborough, *York* Th 237
*Seaford, *Sussex* 61
Seeching, *Norf* T 93
Sedgfield, *Durh* T 261
Selby, *York* M 182
Settle, *York* T 239
Sevenoaks, *Kent*, S 23
**Shaftesbury, *Dorset* S 103
Sheffield, *York* T 160
Shefnal, *Shrop* T 135
Shelford, *Bear* F 40

Shepton Mallet, *Som* F 117
Sherborn, *Dorset* Th S 119
Slerburn, *York* S 151
Shipston, *Wor* F 63
*Shardon, *New*, Sussex, S 57
**Shrewsbury, *Shop* W F S 154
Skipton, *York* S 224
Sleaford, *Linc* M 116
Smarden, *Kent*, T 55
Snathe, *York* T 174
Snetham, *Norf* T 111
Soceb ry, *Glou* Th 112
Soham, *Camb*. S 70
Somerton, *Som* T 123
Southam, *Warw* M 83
**SOUTHAMPTON, *Hamp* T. Th S 75
South Molton, *Devon* S 182
South Petherton, *Som* T 136
Southwell, *Nott* S 140
Southwold, *Suff* Th 103
Spalding, *Linc* T 104
Speen, *Berks* M 57
Spilsby, *Linc* M 136
**Stafford, *Staff* S 135
Staines, *Midd* F 17
Stalbridge, *Dorset* T 111
**Stamford, *Linc* M T 89
Standon, *Herts* F 27
Stanhope, *Durh* T 266
Stanley, *Cov* S 104
Stanton, *Linc* M 135
Stevenage, *Herts* W 31
*Steyning, *Sussex*, W 51
**Stockbridge, *Hamp* T 67
Stockport, *Ches* F 175
Stockton, *Durh* W 248
Stokesly, *York* S 238
Stone, *Staff* T 140
Stoney Stratford, *Bucks* T 52
Sow, *Glou* Th 81
Stow Market, *Suff* Th 75
Stowey, *Som* T 150
Stratford-upon-Avon, *Warw* Th 94
Stretton, *Corn* T 222
Stretton Church, *Shrop* Th 133
Stroud, *Kent*, F 29
Stroud, *Glou* F 101
Sturminster, *Dorset* Th 111
**Sudbury, *Suffolk*, S 56
Sunderland, *Durh* T 269
Sutton Colefield, *Warw* M 106
Swaffham, *Norf* S 94
Swinsea, *Glam* W S 197
Swindon, *Wilts* M 83

Tadcaster, *York* Th 189
Tame, *Oxf* T 46
*Tamworth, *Staff* S 113
Tarring, *Suff* S 56
Tatershall, *Linc* T 134
*Tavistock, *Devon* S 205
*Taunton, *Som* W S 145
Tenbury, *Worc* T 130
Tenby, *Pemb* W S 247
Tenterden, *Kent*, F 58
Tetbury, *Glou* W 99

C **Teuksbury**

[10]

Tewkſbury, Glou W S 103
Thaxted, Eſſex, F 42
Thetford, Norf S 79
Thorn, York W 166
Thornbury, Glou S 120
Thrapſton, Northamp T. 75
Thuſk, York M 220
Tickhill, York F 155
Tideſwell, Derby W 158
Tiverton, Devon T 166
Topſham, Devon S 175
Torrington, Devon S 196
Totneſs, Devon, S 135
Towceſte, Northamp T 60
Tregarron, Carl Th 102
Tregony, Cornw S 256
Tring, Hertf T 31
Trewbridge, Wilts S 98
Truro, Cornw W S 251
Tuddington, Beaf Th. 39
Tunbridge, Kent, I 35
Tutbury, Staf T 128
Tuxford, Nott M 138

Ulverſton, Lanc M 263
Uppingham, Rutl W 92
Upton, Worc Th 109
Uſke, Monm M 141

Uttoxeter, Staff W 134
Uxbridge, Midd. Th 15

Wainfleet, Linc S 135
Wakefield, York Th T 188
Wallingford, Berks J 1. 46
Walſall, Staff T 16
Waltham, Norf Th 123
Walſingham, Norf F 118
Waltham Abbey, Eſſex, T 10
Waltham, Hamp F 67
Waltham, Lec Th 113
Walham, Little, Eſſex, 33
Wantage, Berks S 59
Warebridge, Cornw S 241
Ware, Hertf T 21
Wareham, Dorſet S 115
Warminſter, Wilts S 97
Warrington, Lanc W 183
Warwick, Warw S 93
Watchet, Som S 158
Watford, Herf T 15
Watlington, Oxf S 45
Watton, Norf W 00
Welch Pool, Mont M 165
Weldon, Northamp, W 36
Wellingborough, Northamp W. 68
Wellington, Som Th 152
WELLS, Som. W. S. 122

Wem, Shrop, Th 166
Wendover, Bucks, Th 35
Wenlock, Shrop M 143
Weobly, Herf T 142
Weſtbury, Wilts T 101
Wiſtone, Cornw 232
Wetterham, Kent, W 21
Wetherby, York Th 191
Weymouth, Dorſet T F 130
Whitby, York S 244
Whitchurt, Hamp. T 58
Whitchurch, Shrop T 161
Whitehaven, Cumb T 312
Wickwar, Glou. M 112
Wigan, Lanc M T 195
Wighton, York W 101
Wigton, Cumb T 306
Wilton, Wilts W 85
Wimbourn, Dorſet F 108
Wincanton, Som W 112
Winchcomb, Glou S 93
Winchelſea, Suſſex, S 67
WINCHESTER, Hamp W S 63
Windham, Norf F 100
Windſor, Berks S 21
Winflow, Bucks T 50
Winſter, Derby, S 146
Workworth, Derby T 138
Wiſbeach, Camb, S. 89

Wiſton Pemb S 236
Witham, Eſſex, T 37
Witney, Oxf Th 64
Wivelſcomb Som T 154
Woburn, Bedf T 42
Wookam, Surry, T 26
Woodbridge, Suff W 76
Woodſtock, Oxf T 62
Wooler, Northumb Th 317
Wolverhampton, Staf W 124
Woolwich, Kent, T 10
WORCESTER, Worc W I S 111
Workſop, Nott W. 152
Wotton-under-Edge, Glou T 108
Wotton-Baſſet, Wilts F 190
Wrexham, Denb M Th 187
Wrington, Som T 130
Wrotham, Kent, T 24
Wotted, Norf S 129
Wycomb, Bucks T 49
Wye, Kent Th 57

Yarmouth, Hamp F 101
Yarmouth, Norf S 123
Yarum, York Th 237
Yaxley, Hunt. T 77
Yeovil, Som T. 123
YORK, York T Th S. 197

A LIST OF THE
Principal Post and Sub-Post-Towns, with their Receiving Houses,
In ENGLAND and WALES,

With the Price of Postage, and the Time of Arrival from, and Departure to, London.

N.B. The Sub-Post-Towns are indented, the Receiving Houses are in *Italic*.—m implies Morning, or between the Hours of Twelve at Night, to Twelve o'Clock at Noon, and af implies Afternoon, or from Twelve o'Clock at Noon to Twelve o'Clock at Night, 2d D implies Second Day, N D next Day, and S N same Night of the Arrival of the Post from London.

	Arrive	Time of Arrival	Time of Departure	Postage
ABERCONWAY, Carnarvonshire	2d D	10m	2af	6
Abergavenny, Monmouthshire	2d D	12n	4m	5
Abergeley, Denbighshire	2d D	8m	1af	6
Aberistwith, Cardiganshire	2d D	9af	5m	6
Trosdy, Whyad				
Abingdon, Berks	N D	7m	7af	4
Kingston Inn, Pensey Twys				
Acle, Norfolk	N D	11f	2af	5
St Albans, Hertfordshire	S N	11af	11m	3
Aldborough, Suffolk	N D	6af	12m	5
Alnwick, Northumberland	2d D	4af	4m	6
North Charlton, Felton				
Alresford, Hants	N D	4m	11af	4
Alton, Hants	N D	3m	1m	4
West Meon, Warnford, Droxford, Hambledon				
Amesbury, Wiltshire	N D	10m	3af	4
Amersham, Bucks	N D	8m	7af	4
Ampthill, Bedfordshire	N D	5m	7af	5
Andover, Hants	N D	5m	9m	4
Annan	2d D	5af	5m	7
Appleby, Westmoreland	2d D	10m	11m	6
Arundel, Sussex	N D	12m	3af	4
Littlehampton, Angmering				
St Asaph, Flintshire	2d D	7m	5af	6
Ashborn, Derbyshire	N D	4af	8m	5
Ashburton, Devonshire	2d D	6m	0af	6
Ivybridge, Brent, Buckfastleigh				
Ashford, Kent	N D	11m	3af	4
Atherstone, Warwickshire	N D	12m	1af	5
Attleborough, Norfolk	N D	9m	6af	5
Auckland Bishop, Durham	2d D	9m	11af	6
West Auckland				
Aulcester, Warwickshire	N D	11m	3af	5
St Austle, Cornwall	2d D	8af	9af	6
Penguigle, Grampond, Probus, St Blazey, and the Tollbar to Liskeard				
Axminster, Devonshire	N D	6af	8m	5
Colliton, Stafford, Beer, Seaton				
Aylesbury, Bucks	N D	4m	8af	4
Bagshot, Surry	S N	11af	3m	4
Bakewell, Derbyshire	N D	8af	4m	6
Matlock				
Bala, Merionethshire	2d D	2af	3m	6
Banbury, Oxfordshire	N D	11m	4af	4
Bangor, Carnarvonshire	2d D	1af	11m	6
Barmouth, Merionethshire	3d D	6m	9m	6
Barnard Castle, Durham	2d D	6m	2af	6
Staindrop				
Barnet, Hertfordshire	S. N.	10af	5m	2

	Arrive	Time of Arrival	Time of Departure	Postage
Barnsley, Yorkshire	2d D	1m	2m	6
Barnstaple, Devonshire	2d D.	10m	5af	6
Ilfracomb				
Basingstoke, Hants	N D	3m	12af	4
Battle, Sussex	N D	9m	4af	4
Catsfield-green, Norfolk-flocks, Dereham Street				
Bath, Somersetshire	N D	10m	5af	5
Bawtry, Yorkshire	N D.	6m	6m	6
Beaconsfield, Bucks	N D	12af	4m	3
Beaumaris, Anglesea	2d D	5af	1m	6
Beccles, Suffolk	N D	3af	11m	5
Bedal, Yorkshire	2d D	7m	2af	6
Middleham, Leyburn, Wensley, Asking Houses				
Bedford, Bedfordshire	N D	5m	6af	4
Bedwin, Wiltshire	N D	7m	5af	4
Belford, Northumberland	2d. D	7af	2m.	6
Benington, Oxford	N D	9m.	3m	4
Berkhamstead, Herts	N D	2m.	11af	4
Berkeley, Glocestershire	N D	5af	9m	5
Berwick, Northumberland	2d D	9af	12af	6
Coldstream				
Beverley, Yorkshire	2d D	6m	5af	6
Driffield				
Bewdley, Worcestershire	N D	7af	4m	5
Bicester, Oxford	N D	8m	6af	4
Biddeford, Devonshire	2d D	8m	4af	6
Biddender, Kent	N D	9m	4af	4
Bigglesworth, Bedfordshire	N D	6n.	6af	4
Billericay, Essex	N D	6m	6af	4
Bingley, Yorkshire	2d D	8m	2af	6
Birmingham, Warwickshire	N D	1af	3af	5
Sutton Cofield, Dudley, Bilston, Meriden, Castle-Bromwich, West Bromwich, Walsall, Willenhall				
Bishop's Castle, Shropshire	2d D	9m	4af	6
Clun				
Bishop's Stortford, Herts	S N	12af	3m	
Stansted, Quendon, Newport				
Blackburn, Lancashire	2d D.	9m	2af	6
Blandford, Dorsetshire	N D	11m	3af	5
Milborne St Andrew, Piddletown				
Bletchingley, Surry	N D	12m	1m	3
Bozeat, Northamptonshire	N D	1	1af	5
Bodmin, Cornwall	2d. D	3af	11m	6
Bolton, Lancashire	2d D	3m.	9af	6
Bourne, Lincolnshire	N D	10m.	10af	5
Boroughbridge, Yorkshire	N D	12af	8m	6
Boston, Lincolnshire	N D	3af	8m	5
Bolingbroke, Alfred, Spilsby				
Boxford, Suffolk	N D	12af	5af	4
				Brackley,

[12]

Place	Arrival	Depart	Post
Brackley, Northamptonshire	N D	9m	2af	4
Bradford, Yorkshire	2d D	6m	5af	6
Bradford, Wiltshire	N D	10m	5af	5
Braintree, Essex	N D	3m	8af	4
Brandon, Suffolk	N D	7m	8af	4
Hubborough, Munasfeld, Methwold				
Brecknock, Becknockshire	2d D	3m	12af	6
Brentwood, Essex	S N	11af	5m	3
Bradestow, Devonshire	—	—	—	6
Bridgenorth, Shropshire	N D	7af	8m	5
Bridgewater, Somersetshire	N D	5af	10m	5
Bridlington, Yorkshire	2d D	9m	1af	6
Bridport, Dorsetshire	N D	4af	11m	5
Charmouth, Chedick, Monkton's Lake, The Hut, Traveller's Rest, Winterborne				
Brightemstone, Sussex	N D	8m	7af	4
Bristol, Somersetshire	N D	11m	4af	5
Chepstow, Newport, Keynsham				
Broadway, Glocestershire	N D	10m	6af	5
Bromley, Kent	S N	10af	4m	2
Bromyard, Herefordshire	N D	7a	8m	5
Bromsgrove, Worcestershire	N D	7f	7m	5
Brough, Westmoreland	2d D	9m	1af	6
Kirkby Stephen				
Bruton, Somersetshire	N D	4af	8f	4
Buckingham, Bucks	N D	7m	6af	4
Builth, Brecknockshire	2d D	8m	2af	6
Bungay, Suffolk	N D	1m	3f	5
Burford, Oxfordshire	N D	7m	8af	4
Stow in the Wold				
Burnham, Norfolk	N D	5af	8m	5
Burnley, Lancashire	2d D	2af	8m	6
Burton upon Trent, Staffordshire	N D	5f	1af	5
Bury St Edmund's, Suffolk	N D	7m	7f	4
Buxton, Derbyshire	N D	9a	12m	6
Carmarthen, Carmarthenshire	2d D	12m	2af	6
Langadock, Llanelly, Kinvelly				
Calne, Wiltshire	N D	8m	8af	5
Cambridge, Cambridgeshire	N D	7m	8af	4
Camelford, Cornwall	2d D	4af	9m	6
Campden, Glocestershire	N D	12m	4af	5
Canterbury, Kent	N D	5m	9af	4
Cardiff, Glamorganshire	N D	9af	4f	6
Cowbridge, Bridge End, Pyle, Margam				
Cardigan, Cardiganshire	2d D	2af	5m	6
Carlisle, Cumberland	2d D	2af	6m	6
Brampton, Weston				
Carmarthen, Carnarvonshire	2d D	3af	8m	6
Castle Ashby, Bucks	—	—	—	4
Castle Cary, Somersetshire	N D	3af	5m	4
Castleton, Isle of Man	—	—	—	8
Caxton	N D	3m	9af	4
Arrington				
Chapel in Frith, Derbyshire	2d D	6m	10af	6
Chard	N D	5af	8m	5
Chard House, Oxfordshire	N D	7m	8af	4
Chatteris, Cambridgeshire	N D	8m	4af	4
Chilham, Kent	N D	6m	9af	4
Chelmsford, Essex	S N	12af	3m	4
Danbury, Bradwell				
Cheltenham, Glocestershire	N D	11m	4af	5
Chesham, Bucks	N D			4
Chester, Cheshire	2d D	1m	12af	6
Parkgate, Neston				

Place	Arrival	Depart	Post
Chesterfield, Derbyshire	N D	8af	6m	5
Chichester, Sussex	N D	11m	4af	4
Chumleigh, Devonshire	2d D	6n	9af	6
Chipping Norton, Oxfordshire	N D	7m	8af	4
Chippenham, Wiltshire	N D	9m	9m	5
Marshfield	N D	10m	4af	5
Chorley, Lancashire	2d D	7m	7af	6
Crafton, Layland				
Christchurch, Herts	N D	12m	3m	5
Cirencester, Glocestershire	N D	11m	4af	5
Clare, Suffolk	N D	11m	1f	4
Haverhill, Barbourn-end, Yeldon, Sible Hedingham				
Clay, Norfolk	N D	4af	10m	5
Cobham, Surry	S N	11af	4m	3
Cockermouth, Cumberland	2d D	11af	11af	6
Colchester, Essex	N D	3n	12af	4
Dedham, Stratford St Mary				
Colebrook, Bucks	S N	11af	4m	3
Coleshill, Warwickshire	N D	12m	2af	5
Colne, Lancashire	2d D	12m	9m	6
Colsterworth, Lincolnshire	N D	10m	2af	5
St Columb, Cornwall				
Columpton, Devonshire	N D	1af	6m	6
Congleton, Cheshire	N D	9af	5af	6
Corfe Castle, Dorsetshire	N D	4af	9m	5
Corsham, Hampshire	N D	5m	8af	4
Coventry, Warwickshire	N D	9m	4af	5
Cranbourn, Dorsetshire	N D	12m	1af	5
Cranbrook, Kent	N D	6m	5f	4
Crediton, Devonshire	2d D	3m	11af	6
Crewkerne, Somersetshire	N D	4af	10m	5
South Petherton				
Crossf hills, Yorkshire	2d D	10m	1m	6
Cross Hands, Suffolk	N D	9m	2af	4
Croydon, Surry	S N	9a	5m	3
Carshalton, Waddon, Sutton				
Darking, Surry	S N	1m	9af	3
Burs Green, Betchworth				
Darlington, Durham	2d D	7m	3af	6
Pearce Bridge, Gainford, Saberg, Largnewton, Standhop				
Dartford, Kent	S N	10af	3m	2
Dartmouth, Devonshire	2d D	10m	5if	6
Brixham				
Daventry, Northamptonshire	N D	7m	7f	4
Dunchurch				
Deal, Kent	N D	9m	5af	4
Dedington, Oxfordshire	N D	12n	12m	4
Dereham East, Norfolk	N D	11m	4af	5
Watton				
Denbigh, Denbighshire	2d D	9m	3af	6
Derby, Derbyshire	N D	3af	10m	5
Matlock	N D	6m	6af	6
Devizes, Wiltshire	N D	8m	7f	5
Diss, Norfolk	N D	11m	5af	5
Botesdale				
Dolgelly, Merionethshire	2d D	7af	11m	6
Doncaster, Yorkshire	N D	d	5m	6
Hatfield				
Dorchester, Dorsetshire	N D	2af	12m	5
Upway				
Dover, Kent	N D	7m	6af	4
Downham, Norfolk	N D	11m	4af	5
Harling, Aylsham, Long Stratton				

Drayton

[13]

	Arrival		Dep	Post
Drayton, Shropshire	N D	10af	5af	6
Dunmow, Essex	N D	10m	1af	4
Dunstable, Bedfordshire	N D	1m	2af	2
Dunkirk, Glocestershire	N D	2m	2af	5
Durham, Durham	2d D	10m	12af	6
Shipdam, Hetham, Gaist, Houghton le Spring, and Chester le Street				
Dursley, Glocestershire	N D	4af	10m	5
Easingwold, Yorkshire	2d D	2m	8af	5
East Grinstead, Sussex	N D	2m	12af	4
Uckfield, West Hoadley, Ardingley, Cuckfield, Lindfield, Hosted Cowes, Crawley, Hartfield and Maresfield				
East Bourne, Sussex	N D	10m	3af	4
East Looe, Cornwall	2d D	7m	2af	6
Edgeware, Middlesex	S N	10af	10af	2
Stanmore				
Ellesmere, Shropshire	2d D	5m	4af	6
Ely, Cambridgeshire	N D	2m	1m	4
Mitton Tallow, Streatham				
Enston, Oxfordshire	N D	6m	9af	5
Epping, Essex	S N	10af	10af	2
Epsom, Surry	S N	11af	12m	2
Esher, Surry	S N	10af	4m	3
Evesham, Worcestershire	N D	10m	5af	5
Exeter, Devonshire	N D	10af	5af	6
Ottery, Bradley, Sutton				
Eye, Suffolk	N D	11m	4af	5
Scole Inn				
Fairford, Glocestershire	N D	2m	5af	5
Fakenham, Norfolk	N D	1af	2af	5
Little Walsingham				
Falkenham, Lincoln	N D.	12m	1af	5
Falmouth, Cornwall	2d D	8af	6m	6
Fareham, Hants	N D	8m	5af	4
Titchfield				
Farnham, Surry	N D	2m	3m	4
Farringdon, Berkshire	N D	7af	6af	4
Fenny Stratford, Buckinghamshire	N D	3m	1m	4
Ferrybridge, Yorkshire	N D	8af	3m	6
Sherborne, Kippax, Wentbridge, Robin Hood's Well				
Feversham, Kent	N D	3m.	10af	4
Findon, Sussex	N D	1m	10m	4
Five Lanes, Cornwall	2d D	—	—	6
Folkestone, Kent	N D	10m	4af	4
Foots Cray, Kent	S N	11af	9af	2
St Mary's Cray, Orpington				
Fordingbridge, Hants	N D	9m	3af	5
Fowey, Cornwall	2d D.	7af	9af	6
Frodsham, Chester	2d D	2m	7af	6
Flogmill, Glocestershire	N D	11m	5af	5
Froome, Somersetshire	N D	11m	3af	5
Gargrave, Yorkshire	2d D	12m	9m.	6
Gainsborough, Lincoln	N D	7af	4m	5
Alton, Briggs, Barton				
Garstang, Lancashire	2d D	8m	3af	6
Gateshead, Durham	2d D	12m	10m	6
St Germains, Cornwall	2d D.	4m	6m	6
Gerrards Cross, Bucks	S N	11af	5m	3
Glastonbury, Somersetshire	N D	11af	1af	5
Glocester, Glocestershire	N D	11af	3af	6
Newnham, Mitchell Dean, Newent				
Godalming, Surry	N D	1m	2m	4

	Arrival		Dep	Post
Godstone, Surry	S N	12af	3m	3
Bletchingley				
Gosport, Hants	N D	7m	6af	4
Goudhurst, Kent	N D	8m	6af	4
Grantham, Lincolnshire	N D	10m	7af	5
Gravesend, Kent	S N	12af	3m	3
Greta Bridge, Yorkshire	2d D	5m	3af	6
Bowes				
Graves, Essex	S N	9af	6m.	3
Grimsby Great, Lincolnshire	N D	9m	1af	6
Guilford, Surry	S N	12af	2m	3
Gunplu, Carnarvonshire	2d D	5m	9m	6
Hales Owen, Shropshire	N D	1af	3af	5
Halifax, Yorkshire	2d D	7m	3af	6
Heptonstall, Elland, Ripponden, Lightcliff, Hightown, Dewsbury				
Halstead, Essex	N D	6m	6af	4
Ecrisline, Hedingham, Sible and Castle, Yeldham, Stock, Bythorn-end, Haverill, Ridgewell				
Halston, Norfolk	N D	1m	4af	6
Harlow, Essex	S N	11af	4m	2
Hartfordbridge, Hants	N D	1m	1m	4
Harwich, Essex	N D	8m	7af	4
Colfe Ferry, Walton, Curton, Petriston, Landguard Fort				
Haslemere, Surry	N D	5m	10af	4
Hilling, Norfolk	N D	9m	6af	5
Hastings, Sussex	N D	10m	3af	4
Hatfield, Herts	S N	11af	1m	3
Havant, Hants	N D	7m	5af	4
Haverford West, Pembrokeshire	2d D	9af	8m	6
Hawkhurst, Sussex	N D	8m	6af	4
Sandhurst				
Hay, Brecknockshire	N D	12af	4m	6
Bredwardine				
Heimsley, Yorkshire	2d D	10m	3af	6
Kirkey Moorside				
Helstone, Cornwall	2d D	1m	2m	6
Heme Hempsted, Herts	N D	1m	2m	4
Gaddesden, Ivingho, Wing				
Henley, Oxfordshire	N D	1m	3m	4
Hensfield, Sussex	N D	11m.	12m	4
Henley, Warwickshire	N D	1m	5af	5
Hereford, Herefordshire	N D	7af	8m	5
Hereston end, Birch, Collow, Goodrich, Weston Cross, Fanley				
Hertford, Hertfordshire	N D	8m	8m	2
Heytesbury, Wiltshire	N D	12m	2af	5
High Ferrers, Northamptonshire	N D	11m	1af	4
Highworth, Wiltshire	N D	2m	4af	5
Swindon, Wotton Basset, Binsworth, Cricklade, Malmsbury				
Hindon, Wiltshire	N D.	8m	12m	5
Hinckley, Leicestershire	N D	11m	2af	5
Market Bosworth, Nuneaton				
Hitching, Hertfordshire	N D	3m	8af	4
Baldock				
Holt, Norfolk	N D	4af	1m	5
Holkham, Norfolk	N D	—	—	5
Holyhead, Anglesea	2d D	7af	5m	6
Holywell, Flintshire	2d D	3m	10af	6
Honiton, Devonshire	N D	7af	7m	6
Wimpule, Sidbiana, Broad Hembury Ottery				
Horncastle, Lincolnshire	N D.	8af	1af	5
			Horsham	

D

[14]

Place	Arrival	Dep	Post
Horfham, Suffex	N D	3m	7af 4
Hounflow, Middlesex	S N	10af	5m 2
Houghton, Norfolk	N D	12m	4af 6
Howden, Yorkshire	N D	11af	4af 6
Hubberstone, Pembrokeshire	2d D	6nf	6
Hull, Yorkshire	2d D	8m	3nf 6
Hungerford, Wiltshire	N D	5m	11af 6
Huntingdon, Huntingdonshire	N D	5m	7a 4
Bugden, Ramfey			
Huddersfield, Yorkshire	2d D	9m	7af 6
Hurft Green	N D	6m	6af 4
Robertsbridge			
Hythe, Kent	N D.	10m	2af 4
Jevington, Suffex	N D	10m	10af 4
Ilchester, Somersetshire	N D	—	— 5
Ilminster, Somersetshire	N D	5af	8m 6
Ingatestone, Essex	S N	11m	4nf 3
Ipswich, Suffolk	N D	6m	10af 4
Stratton, Woodbridge, Melton, Wickham, Framlingham, Hadleigh			
Isleworth, Middlesex	S. N	11ar	3a, 2
Richmond, Petersham, Ham, Thames Ditton, Hampton Wick, Twickenham, Teddington, Hampton, East and West Moulsey, Walton, Weybridge, Witton, Hanworth, Sunbury, Littleton, Shepperton			
St Ives, Cornwall	2d D	—	— 4
Isle of Wight, Hampshire	N D	9m	3af 5
St. Ives, Huntingdonshire	N D	6m	5af 5
Keighley, Yorkshire	2d D	8m.	1af 6
Kellington or Callington Cornwall	2d D	7m	8af 6
Kelvedon, Essex	N D	1m	1m 4
Copgshall			
Kendal, Westmoreland	2d D	1af	10m 6
Keswick, Cumberland	2d D	10af	3m 6
Kettering, Northamptonshire	N D	10m	1af 4
Kidderminster, Worcestershire	N D	6af	5m 5
Keldwick, Yorkshire	2d D	11m	12m 6
Kimbolton, Huntingdonshire	N D.	8m.	3af 4
Bythorn, Great Cotworth			
Kineton, Warwickshire	N D	12m	2af 5
Kingston, Surry	S N	10af	3m 2
Kirkby Lonsdale, Westmoreland	2d D	6af	3m 6
Cowan Bridge, Topham Suntly, Ingleton, Clapham			
Knarefborough, Yorkshire	2d D	7m	5af 6
Harrowgate, Ripley			
Knutsford, Cheshire	N. D	11af	3m 6
Altringham			
Lamberhurst, Kent	N D	4m	8af 4
Lancaster, Lancashire	2d D.	9m	2af 6
Launceston, Cornwall	2d D	10m.	3af 6
Langley, Herts	S N	12af	2m 3
Langport, Somersetshire	N D	5af	9m 5
Lawton, Staffordshire	N D	7af	6m 5
Leatherhead, Surry	N D	1m.	1af 3
Lechlade, Gloucestershire	N D.	8m	6af 4
Ledbury, Herefordshire	N D	4af	8m 5
Leeds, Yorkshire	2d D.	2m.	11af 6
Adwalton			
Leek, Staffordshire	N D.	7af	6m 6
Leicester, Leicestershire	N D.	11m.	3af 5
Leighton Buzzard, Bedfordshire	N D	9m.	1af 5
Leeming, Yorkshire	2d D	3m	6af 6
Leominster, Herefordshire	N. D.	12af	4m. 5

Place	Arrival	Dep	Post
Liskard, Cornwall	2d D	4m	5m 6
Lowestoffe, Suffolk	N D	5af	9m 5
Lostwithiel, Cornwall	2d D	—	— 6
Lewes, Suffex	N D	6m	8af 4
East Hoathly, Werdon, Hailsham			
Lime, Dorsetshire	N D	5af	8m. 5
Lincoln, Lincolnshire	N D	5af	10af 5
Wragby			
Linton, Cambridgeshire	N D.	8m	7af 4
Bourne Bridge, West Wratting, Great Thurlow			
Litchfield, Staffordshire	N. D	1af	11m. 5
Canwell, Blackbrook, Longdon, Rudgeley, Sutton, Wolseley, Penkridge, Abbots Bromley, Wichnor Bridge			
Liverpool, Lancashire	2d D	4m	11af 6
Llanuchymead, Anglesea	2d D.	8af	5af 6
Llanymdovry, Cardiganshire	2d D	7m.	7af 6
Llangadock Cayo			
Llandillo, Montgomeryshire	2d D	6af	7m 6
Lampeter, Cardiganshire	2d D	2af	3af 6
Clautyfwrn, Rhyddorn, Pennylont, Ar-Garden, Eberresen, Pernbullan, Pant y Abes, Alpar Gate, Crimcey, Llanaith, New Quay, Yftrad, Pantly, New Bridge End, Aberayan, Talysarn, Rhrulas, Duffri n, Fraulywhiad, Llannsted, Chancery, Penybuse, Pumpsaint, Brynhope, Yftradmeynick, Kilganll			
Longstone, Cornwall	2d D	—	— 6
Looe, Cornwall	2d D	7af	12m 6
Loughborough, Leicestershire	N D	12m	1af 5
Afhby de la Zouch, Mount Sorrel, Kegworth			
Louth, Lincolnshire	N D	12af	10m 5
Ludlow, Shropshire	N D	9af.	8m 5
Luton, Bedfordshire	S N	10af.	9a 4
Barton in the Clay, Margaret Street, Redbourne, Harpenden			
Lutterworth, Leicestershire	N D	9m	3af 4
Lyndhurst, Hampshire	N D	10m	5af 4
Brokenhurst			
Lymington, Hampshire	N D	11m	4af 4
Lynn Regis, Norfolk	N D	12m	4af 4
Macclesfield, Cheshire	N D.	8af	4m 6
Machynleth, Montgomeryshire	2d D	6af	10af 6
Tafarn, Dolardin, Llanfair, Llanerfil, Can Office, Malluyd, Cemmes			
Maidenhead, Berkshire	N D.	1m	3m 3
Twyford			
Maidstone, Kent	N D	7m	8af 4
Malden, Essex	N D	8m	7af 4
Malton, Yorkshire	2d D	4m.	7af 6
Manchester, Lancashire	N. D	11af	2m 6
Afhton under Lyne, Bury			
Manningtree, Essex	N D	5m	10af 4
Mansfield, Nottinghamshire	N D	5af	8m 5
Marsh, Cambridge	N D	9m.	3af 5
Margate, Kent	N D	11m.	3af 4
St Peters			
Market Harborough, Leicestershire	N D	9m	7af 9
Glem, Kebworth			
Market Raisin, Lincolnshire	N D	6af	7af 6
Caiflor			
Market Jew, Cornwall	3d D.	2m	7af 6
Marlborough, Wiltshire	N D.	6m	10af 4
Beckhampton			

St. Mawes,

[15]

	Arrival	Dep	Post
St Mawes, Cornwall	2d D	10m.	2af	6
Melkfham, Wiltshire	N D	9m.	6af	5
Melton Mowbray, Leicestershire	N D	5af	6m	5
Mere, Wiltshire	N D	1af	8m	5
Mevagissey, Cornwall	2d D	10af	8af	6
Middlewich, Cheshire	2d D	8m	4af	6
Holmes Chapel				
Midhurst, Sussex	N D	7m	7af	4
Compton, Harting, Flfstead, Westbourne, Emfworth, Westmarden, Singleton, Lavant				
Hampton, Glocestershire	N D	12m	2af	5
Minehead, Somersetshire	N D	4af	2m	6
Dunster, Tarr, Yardmills, Ashbrar, Handy-Crofs				
Missenden, Buckinghamshire	N D	10m.	5af	4
Monmouth, Monmouthshire	N D	8af	8m	5
Montgomery, Montgomeryshire	2d D	7m	2af	6
Morpeth, Northumberland	2d D	3af	6m.	6
Morton in the Marsh, Glocestershire	N D	8m	7af	5
Mould, Flintshire	2d D	5m.	6af	6
Namptwich, Cheshire	N D	9af	10af	6
Tarperlay	N D.	11af	3m	6
Narbeth, Pembrokeshire	2d D.	4af	9m	6
Laugharne	2d D			6
Neath, Glamorganshire	2d D	3m.	10af	3
Needham Market, Suffolk	N D	8m	5af	4
St Neot's, Huntingdonshire	N D	6m	4af	4
Slaughton Highway				
Nettlebed, Oxfordshire	N D	1m.	2m	4
Shillingford, Dorchester, Watlington				
Newark, Nottinghamshire	N D	1m	10m	5
Southwall, Carlton upon Trent, Collingham				
Newbury, Berkshire	N D	9m	10af	4
Newcastle, Northumberland	2d D	1af	10m	6
Hexham				
Newcastle under Line, Staffordshire	N D	7af	7m	5
Newhaven, Sussex	N D	8m	7af	4
Newmarket, Cambridgeshire	N D	4m	11af	5
Newport, Isle of Wight, Hampshire	N D	12m	2a	5
Newport, Shropshire	N D	9af	6m	5
Newport Pagnel, Buckinghamshire	N D	3m.	12af	4
New, on, Lincolnshire	N D	3af	6m	4
Newton, Montgomeryshire	2d D	9n	12m	6
Neyland, Suffolk	N D	10m	6af	4
Northallerton, Yorkshire	2d D	5m	5af	6
Guysborough	2d D	9m	11m	6
Northampton, Northamptonshire	N D	6m	7af	4
Lamport, Highgate House, Welford				
Northlech, Glocestershire	N D	9m	6af	5
Northorpe, Flintshire	2d D.	3m	10af	6
Hawarden				
North Shields, Northumberland	2d D	2af	6m	6
Northwich, Cheshire	2d D	5m	6af	6
Norwich, Norfolk	N D	11m	4af	5
Aylesham, Cromer, Long Stratton				
Nothiam, Hampshire				4
Nottingham, Nottinghamshire	N D	3af	11m	5
Odiam, Hampshire	N D.	7m	5af	4
Southborough				
Oakham, Rutlandshire	N D	3af	8m	5
Oakhampton, Devonshire	2d D	7m	7af	5
Ollerton, Nottinghamshire				5
Ongar, Essex	S. N	10af	10af	3
Stanford Rivers, Pissingford Bridge, Abridge				
Orford, Suffolk	N D	7m.	2af.	5

	Arrival	Dept	Post
Ormskirk, Lancashire	2d D	6m	7af	6
Oswestry, Shropshire	2d D	2m	4af	6
Monford Bridge, Nescliffe, Felton, Chirk, Plysrauydd, Llangollen, Brynkilma, Corwen				
Oulney, Buckinghamshire	N D	8m	5af	4
Emberton, Clifton, Newton Torvey, Brafield, Lavendon, Carlton, Harrold, Weston, Ravenston				
Oundle, Northamptonshire	N D	9m	2af	5
Barnwell Castle, Thorpe Turnpike				
Overton, Hampshire	N D	4m	11af	4
Oxford, Oxfordshire	N D	4m	11af	4
Padiham, Yorkshire	2d D	2af	9af	6
Painswick, Glocestershire	N D	4a	2af	6
Pembroke, Pembrokeshire	2d D	7af	6m	6
Pennybont, Radnorshire	2d D	11m	11m	6
Penrith, Cumberland	2d D	11m	9m.	6
Penryn, Cornwall	2d D	8af	6m	6
Penzance, Cornwall	2d D	3m	6af	6
Pershore, Worcestershire	N D	1m.	4af	5
Peterborough, Northamptonshire	N D	8m	4af	4
Thorney, Croyland				
Petersfield, Hampshire	N D	4m	10af	4
Petworth, Sussex	N D	2m	1m	4
Fittleborough, Pulborough, Wisborough Green, Billinghurst				
Pewsey, Wiltshire	N D	10m	5af	5
Plymouth, Devonshire	2d D	10m	5af	6
Plympton, Devonshire	2d D	9m	5af	6
Pontefract, Yorkshire	2d D	5m	6af	6
Poole, Dorsetshire	N D	1m.	4af	5
Portsmouth, Hampshire	N D	6m	8af	4
Corshars				
Prescot, Lancashire	2d D	1m	12af	6
Presteign, Radnorshire	2d D	8af	6m	6
Preston, Lancashire	2d D.	6m	6af	6
Pulhely, Carmarthenshire	2d D	9af	6af	6
Queenborough, Kent	N D	7m	7af	4
Sheerness				
New Radnor, Radnorshire	2d D	9m	3af	6
Raleigh, Essex	N D	8m	8af	3
Ramsbury, Wiltshire	N D	7m	6af	4
Ramsgate, Kent	N D	10m	4af	4
Rawcliff, Yorkshire	N D	10af	8af	6
Snaith				
Reading, Berkshire	N D	6m	10af	4
Theal, Jack's Booth, Beckenham				
East Retford, Nottinghamshire	N D	4af	7m	5
Rhayader, Breconshire	2d D	2af.	3af	6
Ridergowy, Radnorshire				6
Richmond, Yorkshire	2d D	9m	2af	6
Reeth, Gilling, Aldborough, Kirkby Hill, Middleton Tyas				
Ride, Isle of Wight	N D	2af	10m	5
Ringwood, Hampshire	N D	10m	6af	5
Ripley, Surry	S N	1af	3m	3
Rippon, Yorkshire	2d D	8m.	6af	6
Pately Bridge				
Rochdale, Lancashire	2d D	10m	2af	6
Haslington, Bacop				
Rochester, Kent	S N	11m	1af	3
Rochford, Essex	N D	10m	3af	4
Prittlewell, Wakering				
Rockingham, Northampton	N D	1af	10m.	5

New

		Arrival		Dep	Post
New Romney, Kent	—	N D	2af	12m	5
Iven, Brookland					
Ross, Herefordshire	—	N D	9af	11m	5
Roxlam, Suffolk	—	N D	1a	3af	5
Royston, Hertfordshire	—	N D	1m	11af	4
Arrington, Buntingford, Puckeridge, Wadsham					
Rugby, Warwickshire	—	N D	9m	3af	4
Dunchurch					
Rumford, Essex	—	S N	10af	4m	2
Rumsey, Hampshire	—	N D	10m	6af	4
Rushyford, Durham	—	2d D	8m	1af	6
Sedgefield, Tarryhill					
Ruthin, Denbigh	—	2d D	8m	4af	6
Rye, Sussex	—	N D	9m	3af	4
Ryegate, Surry	—	N D	8m	8af	4
Saffron Walden, Essex	—	N D	3m	2m	4
Sandford, Saxton					
Salisbury, Wiltshire	—	N D	7m	62af	5
Wilton, Downton					
Sattersgate, Yorkshire	—	2d D	3af	3af	6
Sandwich, Cheshire	—	2d D	9m	10m	6
Sandwich, Kent	—	N D	9m	5af	4
St Peter's					
Sawbridgeworth, Hertfordshire	—	S N	12af	4m	3
Saxmundham, Suffolk	—	N D	10n.	3af	5
Tesford, Framlingham, Debenham, Hangford Southwold					
Scarborough, Yorkshire	—	2d D	8m	2af	6
Seaford, Sussex	—	N D	9n	4f	4
Alfriston					
Sedly, Yorkshire	—	2d D	7m	4af	6
Settle, Yorkshire	—	2d D	1af	6m	6
Bentam, Clapham, Ingleton, Totham, Suvry, Gow n Bridge					
Sevenoaks, Kent	—	S N	12af	1m	3
Shoreham, Brasted, Westerham, Wrotham					
Shaftesbury, Dorsetshire	—	N D	11m	3af	5
Sheffield, Yorkshire	—	N D	9af	4m	6
Rotherham					
Shemal, Shropshire	—	N D	7f	10m	5
Wincock, Basesley, Madeley Wood					
Shepton Mallet, Somersetshire	—	N D	4af	11m	5
Evercreech					
Sherborn, Dorsetshire	—	N D	9af	1af	5
Shapston, Worcestershire	—	N D	8m	8af	5
New Shoreham, Sussex	—	N D	8m	8m	4
Shrewsbury, Shropshire	—	N D	9af	7m	6
Wem					
Sidmouth, Devonshire	—	2d D	8m	—	6
Silsoe, Bedfordshire	—	N D	3m	8af	4
Sittingbourn, Kent	—	N D	3m	11f	4
Skipton, Yorkshire	—	2d D	11m	10af	6
Conestar, Hessfield, Long Preston					
Sleaford, Lincolnshire	—	N D	2af	4af	5
Sodbury, Glocestershire	—	N D	3af	11m	5
Somerton, Somersetshire	—	N D	5af	9m	5
Southam, Warwickshire	—	N D	9m	5af	6
Southampton, Hampshire	—	N D.	7m	8af	4
Readbridge, Totten, Hythe, Beuley					
Southall, Middlesex	—	S N	10af	6m	2
Hayes, Drayton, Harmondsworth, Harlington, Harrow, Pinner, Rickmansworth					
South Shields, Durham	—	2d D	2af	6m	6
Spalding, Lincolnshire	—	N D	12m	11m	5

		Arrival		Dep	Post
Sprout, Gorleston, Sittleton					
Stafford, Staffordshire	—	N D	5af	8m	5
Eccleshall					
Staines, Middlesex	—	S N	10af	5m	3
Egham, Chertsey					
Stamford, Lincolnshire	—	N D	8m	3af	5
Stevenage, Hertfordshire	—	N D	3m	2af	4
Steyning, Sussex	—	N D	2u	3af	4
Stilton, Huntingdonshire	—	N D	6m	5af	4
Stockbridge, Hampshire	—	N D	4af	4af	4
Stockport, Cheshire	—	N D	11af	3m	6
Stockton, Durham	—	2d D	9m	10m	6
Stoke, Cheshire	—	2d D	10m	6am	6
Stoke, Norfolk	—	N D	10m	7 f	5
Wortham, Stradset, Stebbe, Methwold					
Stone, Staffordshire	—	N D.	5af	8m	5
Haywood, Woseley, Rugeley, Trentham, Sandon, Cheadle, Weston					
Stone Crouch, Kent	—	N D	5m	7af	4
Tunstall, Wadhurst					
Stoneham, Suffolk	—	N D	8m	8af	4
Stony Stratford, Buckinghamshire	—	N D	2m	11af	4
Storington, Sussex	—	N D	2af	7m	4
Stow-market, Suffolk	—	N D	9m	4af	5
Coddingham, Clayton					
Stratford upon Avon, Warwickshire	—	N D	9m	5af	5
Wellborne					
Stourbridge, Worcestershire	—	N D	5af	6m	5
Stroud, Glocestershire	—	N D	1af	1af	5
Sudbury, Suffolk	—	N D	7m	4af	1
Bures, Milford, Lavenham					
Sunderland, Durham	—	2d D	1af	6m	6
Swaffham, Norfolk	—	N D	7m	5 f	5
Castle Acre					
Swansea, Glamorganshire	—	2d D	4m	8af	6
Tadcaster, Yorkshire	—	N D	10f	11m	9
Abberford, Bramham, Thorp-Arch, Sherbon					
Tame, Oxfordshire	—	N D	8m	6af	4
Tamworth, Staffordshire	—	N D	2 f	12n.	5
Tavistock, Devonshire	—	2d D	11m	3af	6
Taunton, Somersetshire	—	N D	5af	9m	6
Tenbury, Worcestershire	—	N D	8af	10m	5
Teaby, Pembrokeshire	—	2d D	4af	6m	6
Tenterden, Kent	—	N D	9m	3af	4
Tetbury, Glocestershire	—	N D	1m	2af	5
Tetworth, Oxfordshire	—	N D	2m	1m	4
Tewkbury, Glocestershire	—	N D	1af	2af	5
Thetford, Norfolk	—	N D	7m	3af	5
Thorn, Yorkshire	—	N D	8af	8af	6
Thornbury, Glocestershire	—	N D	11m	1af	5
Thrapston, Northamptonshire	—	N D	11m	1af	5
Thirsk, Yorkshire	—	2d D	4m	7af	6
Thwaite, Suffolk	—	N D			5
Tidewell, Derbyshire	—	N D	9af	2m	5
Tiverton, Devonshire	—	2d D	8m	6af	5
Topsham, Devonshire	—	2d D.	2af	4m	6
Totnes, Devonshire	—	2d D.	7m	7m	6
Kingsbridge					
Towcester, Northamptonshire	—	N D	6m	10af	4
Tregory, Cornwall	—	2d D	7m	3af	6
Tring, Hertfordshire	—	N D	3m.	10af	4
Prince Risborough					
Trowbridge, Wiltshire	—	N D	10m	5af	5
Truro, Cornwall	—	2d D	6af	8m	6

Tunbridge,

[17]

Town		Arrival	Depart	Post
Tunbridge, Kent	—	N D	2m	10af	4
Woodgate, Lamberhurst, Groubourst, Tunbridge Wells	N D	4m	10af	4
Tuxford, Nottinghamshire	—	N D	3af	8m	5
Uppingham, Rutland	—	N D	11af	9m	5
Usk, Monmouthshire	—	2d D	11m	12m	5
Caerleon					
Utoxeter, Staffordshire	—	N D	7af	6m	5
Abbots Bromley					
Uxbridge, Middlesex	—	S N	10af	4m	2
Wakefield, Yorkshire	—	2d D	2m	12af	6
Deersbury					
Wallingford, Berkshire	—	N D	8m	4af	4
Walsingham, Norfolk	—	N D	11m	11m	5
Waltham Cross, Essex	—	S N	10at	4m	3
Enfield, Fortyhill, Northam, Hoddesdon, Woorley, Cheshunt Street, Clockgate, Culver Street, Waltham Abbey					
Waltham, Hants	—	N D	10m	4af	4
Walton, Norfolk	—				
Wantage, Berkshire	—	N D	10m	6af	4
Market Isley, Lambourne					
Ware, Hertfordshire	—	S N	11af	2m	3
Buntingford, Puckridge, Wells Hill					
Wareham, Dorsetshire	—	N D	3af	10m	5
Warminster, Wiltshire	—	N D	12m	3a	5
Warrington, Lancashire	—	2d D	2n	11m	6
Prescot, Newton, Asheton					
Warwick, Warwickshire	—	N D	12m	3af	5
Watford, Hertfordshire	—	S N	11af	3m	3
Watton, Norfolk	—	N D	10m	5af	5
Welch pool, Montgomeryshire	2d D	4m	5af	6
Wellingborough, Northamptonshire	N D	8m	4af	4
Wellington, Somersetshire	—	N D	7af	8m	6
Wivelscome, Milverton					
Wells, Somersetshire	—	N D	1af	1af	5
Axbridge					
Well, Norfolk	—	N D	4af	10m	5
Welwin, Hertfordshire	—	N D	1m	11af	4
Wendover, Buckinghamshire	N D	8m	4af	4
Westbury, Wiltshire	—	N D	11m	4af	5
Wetherby, Yorkshire	—	N D	10af	9af	6
Spafforth, Plumpton, Harwood, Pool, Arthington, Otley					
Weymouth, Dorsetshire	—	N D	2af	12af	5
Wheatley, Oxfordshire	—	N D	12m	3m	4
Whitby, Yorkshire	—	2d D	9m	11r	6
Robin Hood's Bay, Staithes, Lyth, Sand-end					

Town		Arrival	Depart	Post
Whitchurch, Hants	—	N D	3m	10af	4
Whitchurch, Shropshire	—	2d D	3n	0af	6
Whitehaven, Cumberland	—	3d D	3n	8af	6
Whitehaven, Isle of Man	—				
Whittlesea, Cambridgeshire	—	N D	8af	12m	4
Wickwar, Glocestershire	—	N D	11n	2af	5
Wigan, Lancashire	—	2d D	4m	10af	6
Seamouth					
Wimborn, Dorsetshire	—	N D	11m	2af	5
Wincanton, Somersetshire	—	N D	2n	6m	5
Winchester, Hampshire	—	N D	6m	10af	4
Windham, Norfolk	—	N D	11m	5af	5
Windsor, Berkshire	—	N D	8m	8af	3
Eaton					
Wingham, Kent	—	N D	7m	9af	4
Winslow, Buckinghamshire	—	N D	7m	9af	4
Wirkworth, Derbyshire	—	N D	5tt	6at	5
Wisbeach, Cambridgeshire	—	N D	11m	1af	5
Long Sutton					
Witham, Essex	—	N D	1n	2m	4
Witney, Oxfordshire	—	N D	6m	9af	4
Isimpton					
Wokingham, Berkshire	—	N D	8m	4af	4
Woolover, Bedfordshire	—	N D	2m	11af	4
Woodstock, Oxfordshire	—	N D	6m	10af	4
Chailour					
Woolehampton, Staffordshire	—	N D	4af	12m	5
Worcester, Worcestershire	—	N D	2m	3af	5
Droitwich					
Wore, Staffordshire	—	N D	7af	5m	5
Workington, Cumberland	—	3d D	5m	9af	6
Worksop, Nottinghamshire	—	N D	7af	5m	5
Welbeck, Newton, Cuckney, Cuckney Mill, Olleston, Gupson, Edmondslow					
Wotton, Norfolk	—				
Wotton under Edge, Glocestershire	—	N D	2af	11m	5
Wickesar, —			12m	2af	5
Wrexham, Denbigh	—	2d D	5m	4af	9
Pulford, Marford Hill					
Wycomb, High, Buckinghamshire	S N	12af	3m	3
Great Marlow, West Wycomb					
Yarmouth, Norfolk	—	N D	4af	12m	5
Burgh, Gorliston					
Yarm, Yorkshire	—	2d D	9m	12m	6
Yeovil, Somersetshire	—	N D	3af	12m	5
York, Yorkshire	—	N D	1af	12m	6

The above Table, it is presumed, will prove both acceptable and useful, and at once point out the great Importance of the present Mode of conducting the Mails, by which it is conveyed in one Half of the time it used to be, to most parts of the Kingdom, and in one Third, and even in one Fourth to many of the Cross Posts, and these Posts are all made Daily, instead of Three times a Week, to 320 Towns, likewise the same additional convenience is given to 201 Towns on the General Posts—this, together with its affording a like expeditious and safe conveyance to Passengers, with a Guard, to most parts of the Kingdom, is a convenience which no other country in Europe can boast of.—The Departure of the Mails *for* London from any place where a Cross Post is established, will generally shew the Arrival of the Cross Post at such place, those Arrivals being mostly so timed, as to enable the Post Masters to select from the contents of the Cross Mails such Letters as are to be forwarded directly to London.

LIST OF SUBSCRIBERS.

A

HIS Grace the Duke of Argyle
Right Hon Viscountess St Asaph
Right Hon Earl of Aylesbury
Right Hon Earl of Albemarle
A Court, William Pierce Ashe, esq Heytesbury
Adams, ——, esq Upper Harley-street
Adams, Mr Bread street
Alderson, Rev Mr M A Eckington
Alexander, William, esq Halifax
Alexander, M South Lambeth
Allen, Geo Edw esq Charlotte-street, Bloomsbury
Anderson, Mr Lyme-street
Anderson, Mr Upper Tufsatia
Andrews, Rev Mr Leicester
Ansell, Mr Whitehall
Arden, Sir Richard Pepper
Arden, ——, esq
Arnot Mr Buckingham-street
Ashe, Rev Mr Robert, Bling, Hants
Askew, Mr Ludgate hill
Astell, William Thornton, esq Clapham
Athawes, Sir ... esq St Martin's-lane, Cannon street
Atkinson, ——, esq Pall Mall
Atkinson, Mr Leeds
Atwaters Mr John, Fordingbridge
Atwood, Mr King street, Covent Garden
Auriol, ——, esq Stratford Place
Aust, G. esq Whitehall

B

Right Hon, Lord Viscount Barrington
Right Hon Lord Breadalbane
Baber, E esq Park street
Bailey, Mr Sunderland
Bailey, Mr Hope
Bakewell, Mr
Baker, M Salisbury-square
Baker, Mr Bolwell-court
Baldwin, Joseph, esq Serjeants Inn
Baldwin, Mr
Ballard, Mr W A Bratton, Wilts
Ball, Mr Ludgate hill
Bank, Sir Joseph, Soho-square
Banks, J C esq Nunnington
Bannet, Mr Thomas, Upper Thames street
Barclay, Mr Haymarket
Bainard, Henry Boldero, esq South Cave
Bainard, Mr Charles, Berkley-square
Barnes Rev Mr M D Devizes
Barker, Rev Mr M A Chesterfield
Barker, Rev Mr student of Christ Church, Oxon.
Baker, Richard, esq Tavistock-street
Binam, Mr G C Christ Church, Oxon
Bargus, Rev Mr Winchester
Baron, Mr Nathaniel, Codsey Wilts
Barrett, William, esq Palace Yard
Barret, Mr
Barlow, ——, esq Essex-street
Barlow, ——, esq Clement's Inn
Barnard, John, esq Bandford
Basilico, Mr Whitehall
Pavesicke, Mr Windsor
Bayley, Thomas, esq F R S Hope Derbyshire
Bayley, James, esq Bishopstow, Wilts
Bayliffe, George Searle, esq Corsham, Wilts
Bayne, ——, esq Inner Temple
Bearcroft, ——, esq Temple
Beaufort Rev Dr M R T. A Dublin
Beaison, Mr Rotherham
Beckett, John, esq Leeds
Beddome, Mr Nailsworth
Becke, Rev Mr fellow of Oriel College, Oxon
Bellamy, Mr Thomas, Standground, Hants
Bell, Mr James
Belcher, Miss Great Ormond street
Bennett, Rev Mr Piccadilly
Bennett, Thomas, esq Cobham Row
Benyon, Richard, esq Grosvenor square
Benwell, Rev Mr Trinity College, Oxon
Benson, Mr Wadham College, Oxon
Benson, Mr Leeds
Bentham, Rev Thomas, M A student of Christ Church, Oxon
Berna d, Scroope, esq Pludyer-street
Bertram, Mr Hull
Battison Jonas, esq Holme Pierpoint, Notts
Bicknell, Mr Staples Inn
Bidwell, Thomas, esq Whitehall
Bifre, Rev Mr Ham, Surry
Billingsley, John, esq Ashwick
Billinge, Mr Caterton street
Bilsborrow, Mr William, Manchester
Billington Mr Poland-street
Bingham, Mr Robert
Birns, Mr John, Leeds
Birch, Thomas, esq New Bond street
Bircce, Joseph Seymour, esq Bury Hill, Notts
Birchett, Nicholas, esq Leeds
Bishop, Mr Duke-street, St James's
Black, William, esq Temple
Black, Mr Epping
Blackett, John, esq
Blackett, Mr Newcastle
Blakeway, ——, esq Lincoln's Inn
Blake, John, esq Temple
Bland, Mr Racquet court
Boddy Mr John
Bold, Thomas, M A Brazen Nose College, Oxon
Bolton, ——, esq South Cave
Bonnor, Charles, esq Broad street
Bond, Rev Mr fellow of Wadham College, Oxon
Bond, Mr Lambeth
Bootle, Edward Wilbraham, esq Christ Chur Oxon
Borough, Mr Henley upon Thames
Bosanquet, Henry, esq Lincoln's Inn
Bottomly, Mr High Holborn
Bource, Richard, esq Charlotte street
Bouchet, Rev Mr Epsom
Bourne, Mr Thomas, Kingston, Surry
Bourne, Joseph esq Bolton
Bowles, Mr Charles, Shaftesbury
Bowman, John, esq Beverley
Bowther, Rev Mr Bath
Bradyke, Wilton, esq Bruton-street
Bland, Charles, esq Lincoln's Inn
Brand, Rev Mr Seymour Place
Bracher, Joh, esq Fonthill, Wilts
Bramby, Martin, esq Gainsborough

Bradley, Mr Joseph, Chesterfield
Bray, Mr G Russel street, Bloomsbury
Bridgeman, Mr Grocers Hall
Broadley, Peter, esq High-street, Borough
Broadley, Mr Charles, Hull
Broderick, Hon Mr
Brooke, Mr T Heath
Brooke, Rev Mr fellow of Oriel College, Oxon.
Brooke, Mr Frederick, Dorchester
Brooke, Mr John, Bridgewater-square
Brooks, Mr Thomas, Curtain, Moorfields
Broomhead, John, esq Hailes street, Cavendish square.
Broughton, Bryan, esq
Broughton, esq G C Christ Church, Oxon
Broughton, Rev Mr Everton
Browne, Charles, esq Lincoln's Inn
Browne, Mr Thomas, Hatton, Wilts
Browne, Mr William, Ch Pelsor, Wilts
Brown, William, esq Bedford Row
Brown, M William, Leeds
Brown, Mr Joseph, Bolton, Lancashire
Brown, M Christopher, Charles-street, Hatton-str.
Brown, Mr Essex-street
Brown, Mr B Canterbury
Brown, Mr Strand
Bruges, Mr Thomas, Melksham
Bryer, Mr Strand
Bryan, Mr Reygate
Buckland, Rev Mr fellow of Corpus Christi Coll. Ox.
Buckell, Rev Dr Weymouth street
Ball, Mr Bath
Bunbury, Mathew, esq
Bunn, ——, esq Clement's Inn
Bunn, Thomas, esq Froome
Burgess, Mr William, Westbury
Burrows, Mr Charlotte street
Burton, Robert, esq Lincoln's Inn
Burton, ——, esq Grosvenor Place
Burton, R LL D
Burke, Mr M A
Burland, T B esq Dorset
Busfield, J A. esq Myrtle Grove, Bingley
Butler, Mr Edward, Warminster
Butt, Mr John, Warminster
Butt, Mr Robert, Warminster
Buxton, Mr Bath

C

Right Hon Countess of Courtoun
Right Hon Earl of Cork
Right Hon Lord Dudworth
Right Hon Lord Caryfort
Right Hon Lord J Cavendish
Right Hon Lord F Cavendish
Calverley, John, esq Leeds
Cavely, Mr Hartingdon, Cheshire
Calcutt, Mr Charles
Campbell, Mathew, esq Uckfield, Sussex
Campbell, Mr George Br't, Portman-square
Campbell, M esq Charlton, Kent
Carew Reynal Pole, esq Charles str Berkley square
Cutwright W K esq Christ Church, Oxon
Carver, Rev Mr M A Chesterfield
Carr, William, esq
Carr Mr Thomas, Newcastle
Carr, Mr Dunnington

Carrington,

LIST OF SUBSCRIBERS TO

Carrington, Rev Mr Buford, Wilts
Carter, Mr D ke Street
Chadwick, ——, esq
Chauntr ll, T esq Highbury Place
Chaumette, Francis de la, esq Spital Square
Challie, John, esq Bedford Square
Chambre, ——, esq Gray's Inn
Chaplin, Mr Aylesbury
Chancey, ——, esq Castle Street
Chamber, Mr Siothelf, Derby
Cheere, Charles, esq Gower-street
Chesson, William, esq New College
Church ll Mr Abingdon street
Church, ——, esq Sackville-street
Clarke, Thomas, esq Kirkby Hardwick, Notts
Clarke, I P esq Witney, Oxon
Clark, Mr Robert, Castle Cary
Clark, Mr Bank Buildings
Clapham Sr Trinity College, Cambridge
Clay, Mr Thomas, Liverpool
Clayton, Rev N D D Nottingham
Clayton, Miss, Carr Hall, Colne
Cleverley, Mr Lisle-street, Leicester-fields
Clitheroe, ——, esq Lincoln's Inn
Clowes, Samuel, esq Manchester
Clutton, Rev John, M A Kinnersley, Hereford
Clutton, Rev Mr Birmingham
Cobb, Rev Dr fellow of St John's College, Oxon
Cockerell, Mr Joseph, Upton, Essex
Cockle, Mr John, Carpmantrade, Wilts
Colebrooke, Sir George, bart
Collett, Richard, esq Chancery-lane
Collier, Rev Mr Trinity College, Cambridge
Colman, William, esq Hatton Garden
Collins, Mr Pasgrave Place
Collins, Mr John, Devizes
Collins, Mr John, Trowbridge
Constable, Maraduke, esq Wassand
Constable, William, esq Burton Constable
Constable, Mrs Barkley, Yorkshire
Conrad, George, esq Berkeley Square
Coney, William, esq fellow of Oriel College
Couch, Mr Newport Pagnel
Cooke, George, esq Streetthorpe, Yorkshire
Cowper, Mr Corsley, Wilts
Coombes, Mr Caredols-street
Cooper, Rev Mr Bix, Oxon
Cooper, Rev Mr Braston, Wilts
Cooper, General, Charles street, Berkeley square
Cooper, R Brantby, Newhouse, Gloucester
Cooper, Mr Featherstone Buildings
Costa, Joshua Mendez da, esq Serjeant's Inn
Cotton, Mr Henry, Harley-street
Cotten, Thomas, esq Haigh, Yorkshire
Cotten, Stapleton, esq
Cotham, Mr A Watley, Lancashire
Coulthard, Miss John street, King's Road
Coulthurst, John, esq
Couchman, Mr Warwick
Cox, Charles, esq
Coxe, Capt Charles, Stone Eaton
Cracheroede, Rev Mr Queen's Square
Craig, Mr Scotland Yard
Crane, Charles, esq Badge Row
Crane, Mr Token House Yard
Crathorne, Thomas, esq York
Crook, Mr George, Liverpool
Crook, Mr Thomas, Tytherton, Wilts
Compton, Samuel, esq Derby
Crompton, Mr John, Derby
Crompton, Mr Gilbert, Derby
Crompton, Peter, M D Derby
Cross, M Great street, Soho
Crutwell, Mr Bath
Cunnington, Mr William, Heytesbury
Curtis, Mr Oxford
Curtis, Mr Canterbury

D

Right Hon Earl Darnley
Da Costa, J M esq Serjeants Inn
Dalley, I esq Kingsland
Dalton, Nathaniel, esq Shankshouse
Dalton, R esq
Dampier, Rev Mr West Meon, Hants
Daumier, ——, esq Clifford street
Darsey, Mr John, Blandford
Daniel, esq C C Pembroke College, Oxon
Daniel, Mr Yeovil
Dan el, Mr John, Poultry
Darell, Major
Darbyshire, Mr Manchester
Darbyshire, Mr James, Bolton
Dashwood, Sir Henry, Lower Grosvenor street
Davenport, T esq Bishopsgate street
Davenport, ——, esq Charles street, St James's
Davidson, John, esq Newcastle
Davidson, Mr Leeds
Davidson, Mr Walthamstow
Davidson, Mr James, Walthamstow
Davis, Mr Thomas, Longleat
Davy, Rev C M B fellow of Caius College, Cambridge
Dawes, Edwin, esq Angel-court, Throgmorton street
Day, Mr William, York-street
Deane, Charles, esq Warmley
Delafosse, Rev Mr Richmond, Surry
Delegh, Mr Lucgate hill
Denison, Robert, esq Kilnwick Percy
Denman, D Old Burlington-street
Dennison, Mr Featherstone Buildings
Deserett, Mr Fenchurch street
Dickenson, Thomas, esq Bedworth Close
Dickenson, Mr Edward, Drayton Manor, Stafford
Dickens, Mr Joseph, Higher Park, Stafford
Dickens, Mr Crown street
Duke, Capt. Upper Seymour street
Dilworth, T esq Leeds
Dixon, Jeremiah, esq. Leeds
Dixon, Mr R East Retford, Notts
Dixon, Rev Mr
Dodwell, Rev Henry, Harlaxton, Lincolnshire
Dodwell, Robert, esq Doctors Commons
Dodwell, T esq
Dominicus, Mr Mark lane
Dormer, Mr Bury-street, St James's
Dorrien, Thomas, esq Portman-square
Dorrington, Capt Hull
Dover, Rev Mr Chichester
Douce, William H esq Fenchurch street
Douce, Mr Francis, Gray's Inn
Douglass, ——, esq
Douglass, Capt Leigh, Somerset-street
Dowland, Mr James, Mansfield, Woodhouse, Notts
Downes, Rev Mr Witham, Essex
Downes, ——, esq Christ Church College
Downing, Mr P A Dudley
Draper, William, esq Worton Deddington, Oxon
Draper, Capt
Drax, Edward, esq
Druce, Mr Chancery-lane
Drummond, John, esq
Drummond, A esq Spring Gardens
Drummond, Rev H Spring Gardens
Drummond, Rev George Hay, Doncaster
Dunnage, F esq Philpot-lane
Dunsford, Mr George, Tiverton
Durrsford, Mr Martin Tiverton
Du Pan S Gourgas, esq Leeds, Yorkshire
Dury, Colonel
Dyson, Thomas, esq Halifax

E

Right Hon. Earl of Effingham
Eastborn, Mr Aldgate
Eton, Mr A B Trinity College
Libertill, ——, esq Buford House, Surry
Eudew, s, Mr T
Eddowes, Mr William
Edge, Mr student of Christ Church, Oxon
Efred, Harry, esq Standerwick, Somerset
Edmonds, Mr Chancery-lane
Eortidge, Edmead, esq Chippenham
Edward, John, esq Chilcot House
Edwards, Mr Carlton Place
Egerton, Mr Gray's Inn
Egerton, Mr Bentinck street, Soho
D'Linsfendl, Count, Reibersdorf, Upper Lusatia
Elder, Mr
Ellis, Mr Emanuel College
Ellis, Charles, esq Dean-street, Soho
Elms, John, esq
Emmatt, Mr Elizabeth, Longleat
England, Mr J Dorchester
Ensoy, Mr Rockingham Row
Entwissle, John, esq Leeds
Eisdale, ——, jun esq Duke-street, Westminster
Eteners, Mr R Cadman, Fenchurch street
Evans, Mr J
Evans, Mr
Everett, John, esq Heytesbury
Everett, W esq Heytesbury
Everett, Mr W Mornington, Wilts
Everett, ——, esq Greenwich
Ewart, James, esq Portland street
Ewer, ——, esq
Lyle, Vincent, esq
Lyce, Col Upper Grosvenor street

F

Farshaw, Mrs Chiplake, Oxon
Farith, Mr Magdalen College, Oxon
Farrer, Oliver, esq Bedford-square
Farrer, James, esq Chancery-lane
Fawcett, Gen Sir W George street, Westminster
Fawkes, Mr Upper Thames street
Fellows, Mr New Inn
Fellows, Mr John
Fellows, Mr Finchley
Tellow, Richard esq Snettesham, Norfolk
Fenton, Mr Ann, Car House
Ferrand, Benjamin, esq St Ives, Bingley
Field, Mr Corn hill
Fikes, Mr Abel, Dizes
Finch, William, esq Grosvenor square
Finch, Rev Henry Greatham, Rutland
Fisher, Rev R A M fell of Caius Coll Cambridge
Fisher, Rev John, fellow of Caius College, Cambridge
Fisher, Mr Richard, New alle
Fitzgerald, James, esq
Fletcher, Mr Joseph, Liverpool
Fletcher, Mr Chadsworth
Fletcher, Mr Whitwell, Derbyshire
Fole t, Mr G Temple
Fennereau, Martin, esq Hereford-street
Fonte, Mr Justice, D an street, Soho
Food, ——, esq Baliol College, Oxon
Ford, Rev Dr Milton Mowbray
Ford, Mr Temple
Ford, Mr Henley upon Thames
Fortescue, Mr
Foster, Mr Felneck
Foster, William, esq Fetter-lane
Fountell, Rev James, M A Dalton la Dale, Durham
Fothergill, Rev T M A fell of Queen's Coll Oxon
Franington, James, esq fell com St John's Coll Oxon
Frankland, Sir Thomas
Franklin, Mr Freeman street
Fraser, R esq Pimlico

Fraser,

THE ENGLISH ATLAS.

Fraser, William, esq Whitehall
Frost, John, esq Spring Gardens
Froud, M Richard, Brixton Deverell, Wilts
Frewen, Charles, esq Cluer, Berks
Fry, M Peter, Axbridge
Fry, M S John's square
Fryer, Mr Aldermanbury
Fynes, Rev C D D Cromwell, Notts

G

Right Hon Lord Viscount Galway
Gagg, Rev M Axbridge
Gall, Mr Joan, Sert, Wilts
Garfield, Mr
Garfield, Mr Bristol
Gazeley, Mr Gray's Inn
Geddes, Dr Cliptone-street
Gee, Mr Wimborn Minster
George, Mr George, Froome
Gibbs, Vickery, esq Bloomsbury Square
Gibbons, Rev Mr New Cavendish street
Gibson, ——, esq Loomuit Hill, Kent
Gibson, Mr
Glover, Mr A Ryegate, Surry
Glynn, Anthony, esq New College, Oxon
Goddard, Rev Mr Wood Hay, Hants
Goddard, John, esq Woodford, Essex
Goddard, Rev Mr Winchester College
Goddard, Mr Beaufort Buildings
Goddard, Mr Oxford-street
Goleborn, —— esq
Goll, Mr Leeds
Gould, Rev Mr South Brent, Somerset
Goodings, Thoms, LL D Leeds
Goodenough, Major, Abingdon-street
Gordon, Rev Mr Air-street, Piccadilly
Gote, Mr T Liverpool
Gosnell, Mr Rolls Building
Gough, Richard, esq Enfield
Gower, M C New Inn
Gray, Charles Gordon, esq Warminster
Gray, Mr Lancaster
Greig, Mr Thomas, Coleshull, Herts
Greeton, Rev Mr Hitcham
Greene, Chapman, esq Emanuel College
Greene, Rev Henry, R Ileston, Leicester
Green, Major Gen Sir William
Greenhill, Robert, esq Lincoln's Inn
Greenland, ——, esq Newman street
Greenup, William, esq Dersey Hay, Yorkshire
Gregory, Rev Mr Lugar, Notts
Gregory, ——, esq Charlotte street
Gregory, Mr Leadenhall street
Gregory, Rev Mr Minor Canon, Canterbury
Grenville, Hon Mr Folks, Upton
Greville, Hon Mr King's Mews
Grey, Mr
Grice, Rev Charles le, Bury, Suffolk
Griffith, Mr New Bond-street
Griffiths, ——, esq
Grimston, Henry, esq Wiltow
Grinfield, Col Old Burlington-street
Grinfield, Rev T Bath
Grove, William, esq Lichfield
Grundy, Mr James, Liverpool
Guorgas Mr Leeds

H.

Right Hon. Lady Howe
Hacker, Andrew, esq Great Margaret-street
Haddon, Rev Mr Leeds
Haigh, Rev Mr Newcastle
Hale, Rev Mr St Paul's Church Yard
Hall ——, esq full com of Trinity Coll Cambridge
Hall, John, M D
Hall, Mr Park-street
Hallam, Capt Park street

Hamilton Hon Mr Holles street
Hamilton, Rev Dr Leicester square
Hamilton, Rev Dr Lemon street, Goodman's Fields
Hamilton, Ms dito
Hamilton, Mr Lincoln's Inn Fields
Hamilton, Mr Bolton Row
Hamilton, Mr Bedford Row
Hammersley, ——, esq Pall Mall
Hammersley, Mr Temple
Hammond, Mr Charlotte street
Hanham, Sir William, bart
Hankey, Joseph Chaplin, esq Charles-st Maryborn
Hanmer, Sir Thomas
Hanmer, William, esq
Hardisty, Mr Great Marlborough street
Harewood, Rev Mr Sowerby
Hargrave, Francis, esq Boswell Court
Hargreaves, John, esq Fall Edge, Lancashire
Harrison, R A esq Hull
Harrison, Rev H G Thorpe Morieux, Suffolk
Harrison, ——, esq Temple
Harrington, Rev Dr Buxton
Harman, Mr Artillory, Gravesend
Harman, Mr Princes-street
Hartley, Col Bedford square
Hartley, ——, esq dito
Hart, Anthony, esq Temple
Harvey, Mr Robert, Blithfield
Haslang Count
Haverfield, Mr Kew Green
Havell, Rev Mr Knaresborough
Hawes, John, esq Mansell-street
Hawkins Rev Mr Barebone Hall, Worcestershire
Hawley, Mr Wortley
Hawkesworth, Walter, esq fell com of Trinity Coll.
Hayter, Francis Thomas, esq
Haycons, Messrs Plymouth
Hazard, Mr Bath
Headeach, Mr Fleet street
Hearne, Mr Macclesfield-street
Heath, Rev Mr Eton College
Heberden, Mr A B fell of St John's Coll Cambridge
Heron, Rev Mr Warrington, Lancashire
Heron, Mr High-street, Southwark
Heslop, Mr
Hetherington, T esq Black Friars Road
Hey, Rev Dr Stony Stratford
Heywood, Mr Nottingham
Hibbert, F esq Upper Grosvenor street
Hibbert, Mrs
Higden, William, esq
Hill, Walter, esq Gray's Inn
Hill, Mr
Hinchman, Mr New Burlington-street
Hincliffe, Mr Lincoln's Inn Felds
Hinckes, P T esq Tetterhall, Stafford
Hinckes, Rev Mr New Palace Yard
Hinckes, ——, esq Manchester
Hippsley, Mr Wimpole-street
Hoare, Charles, esq Fleet street
Hoare, Henry, esq ditto
Hobhouse, Mr T Temple
Hodgson, Henry, esq Reading
Hodgson, Mr Leeds
Hoghton, Henry, esq fellow com of St John's Coll.
Hole, Mr A B Trinity College, Cambridge
Holt, John, esq Lawnle
Holwell, ——, esq fell. comm of Exeter Col. Oxon
Holyoake, Francis, esq. Tottenhall, Stafford
Holland, Rev John, Bolton
Holton, I esq Critleton, Wilts
Holroyd, T esq
Hornby, William, esq Upper Harley street
Horner, Thomas, esq Mells Park, Somerset
Horner, Thomas Strangeways, esq. ditto

Hoskins, Mr A Burton upon Trent
Howard, ——, esq Heath, Yorkshire
Howard, ——, esq Argyle-street
Howe, Hon Mrs Grafton-street
Hudson, Rev Mr Tipperholme, Notts
Huddesford, Rev Mr
Hughes, Mr Putney
Hughes, Rev Thomas, Dorchester
Hughes, Mr A B Trinity College, Cambridge
Hughes, Mr
Hugnes, Rev Mr Burton Joice, Notts
Hughes, Mr John, Warminster
Hugonin, Major
Huish, Mark, esq Notts
Hulse, Edward, esq Portman-square
Humble, R esq Middleton
Hunn, Mr Richard, Bristol
Hunter, Dr York
Huntingford, Rev George James, Warminster
Hurlock, Mr St Paul's Church Yard
Hutton, Rev Mr M A Magdalen College, Oxon
Hutton, Mr
Hyde, Mr Halifax

I

Right Hon Lady Viscountess Irwin
Jacob, Rev Edward, Shillingstone, Dorset
Jacob, Mr Nackington, Kent
Jackson, Cyril, D D dean of Christ Church
Jackson, Mr Clerkenwell Close
Jackson, Rev Mr Lincoln's Inn
Jacques, Thomas, esq Leeds
Jagger, Mr Marybone-street
James, Mr Terrace, Walworth
Jameson, ——, esq Maidstone
Ibbotson, Mr Ludgate-hill
Ideson, Luke, esq Poland street
Jeckell, John, esq Temple
Jekyll, Joseph, esq Spetisbury, Dorset
Jemmett, Mr Canterbury
Jennings, Mr Cheswell street
Jennings, Mr Coleman street Buildings
Jenkins, John, esq Whitehall
Jerningham, Sir William
Jerrard, Mr Essex street
Jessyman, Mr York
Jessop, Mr Southampton street
Illife, Mr
Ingnam, Rev Mr Stump's Cross
Johnson, Dr Beverly
Johnson, Isaac, esq Gray's Inn
Johnson, ——, esq Gray's Inn
Johnson, Mr General Post Office
Johnson, Thomas, esq Holbeck
John, Rev Mr St Dogmersfield
John, Sir Harry Stubart Dogmersfield, Hants
John, Sir Andrew St Westenham Hall, Norfolk
Jones, Rev John, Blandford
Jones, William, esq Wellington
Ireland, Mr Staple Inn
Irving, Lieutenant Col
Jupe, Mr Liskeard

K

Kaye, Richard, LL D dean of Lincoln
Kedington, Rev R Rongham Hall, Suffolk
Kelson, Samuel, esq Midsummer Norton
Kempson, Rev Mr Sardon, Stafford
Kemble, Francis, esq Swithin's lane
Kent, Nathaniel, esq. Fulham
Kershaw, James, esq Shawhill, Yorkshire
Kirshaw, Rev Mr, Leeds
Kyfall, Rev Mr Langmund
Keyworth, Miss
Kilburn Mr Richard, S John's street
Kinnard, Mr Holborn
King, Mr William, Richmond, Yorkshire

Kirby

LIST OF SUBSCRIBERS TO

Kirby, Lieut. of the 4th Dragoons
Kirby, Rev. M. Barham, Suffolk
Knight, Thomas, esq Goosnersham Park, Kent
Knight, Mr James, Longcoat, Wilts
Knight, M C th Kent
Knowlesley, ———, esq Hull
Kerby, D Southampton-street
Kuttaer, Mr Eton

L

Right Rev Lord Bishop of Lincoln
Right Hon Lord Louvain
Right Hon Lord Lismore
Lacey, Mr Thomas, Froome
Lambert, ———, esq Temple
Lamb——, Mr St Martin's-lane
Lane, Richard, esq
Lane, ———, esq, Lincoln's Inn
Lane, Rev Mr fellow of Christ's College, Cambridge
Landon, Dr Warwick
Langton, Mr Hatton Garden
Langton, T esq Clifford-street
Langton, Mr Cheapside
Lawidge, Mr Samuel, Hampton Court
Lascelles, ———, esq
La Trobe, Rev Mr. Christian, War e Office Court
Lawrence Mr Sergeant, Temple
Leddard, Mr Samuel, Road Bridge, Somerset
Lee, Launcelor, esq fellow of New College
Lee, Henry, esq Oriel College
Lee, Rev Henry, fellow of New College
Lee, Mr Frith-street
Lee, Rev Mr
Leith, ———, esq fellow commoner of Christ Church College, Oxon
Lett, Rev Thomas Ditcheatt
Lerooks, ———, esq Somers Town
Lethrullier, ———, esq
Lexmagerty, Mr. Old Broad-street
Lilly, Mr Pancras lane
Lipcroft, Rev John
Liveus, Peter, esq Duke street, Portland Place
Lloyd, Thomas, esq Leeds
Lloyd, Miss, York
Lloyd, Gamaliel, esq Parson's Green
Lobley, ———, esq Bingley
Locke, Wadham, esq Devizes
Lodge, Edmund, esq Willow Hall, Yorkshire
Lodge, Richard, esq, Leeds
Lomax M Lower Grosvenor-street
Long Richard, esq Row'd Ashton, Wilts
Long Robert, esq East-street Red Lion Square
Long, Edward, esq Wimpole-street
Lounder, Mr North Street
Lowe, Jeremiah esq Oriel College
Lowndes, Mr Richard, Southampton Row
Lowth, Per Mr Winchester
Lucas, Rev Mr Shrewsbury
Lucas, Capt n, Leeds
Luckombe, M Johnson's Court, Fleet-street
Lumley, M Bell Yard
Lye, Mr George, Warminster
Lynn, Captain
Lyon, George, esq

M

Right Hon. Lord Macartney
Right Hon Lord Mulgrave
Mc george, William, esq Hamilton-Street
Mackworth, Sir Herbert, Cavendish square
Mukes, Richard, esq Bedford street
Ma ee, Mr
M ntton, ———, esq Essex street
M r, Henry, esq Lariegon
Mair, Mr James Gravesend
Major, M.
Manby, Mr, Knaresborough

Martin, James, esq Downing-street
Martin, Edwin, esq Priory, Berks
Martin Mr
Marshall, Mr Bath
Marsh, Rev Mr George, Blandford
Marsh, Mr William, Crook street
Mascall, Mr M c Court, Milk street
Masley, Rev Millington, Warminster
Muskelyn, Mr John Warminster
Mathias, Thomas, esq Scotland Yard
Matheys, Mr J Shand
Mavor, William, esq Woodstock, Oxon
Maude, Mr Trinity College
Maxwell, Cap Edward
Mears, Mr John, Froome
Meaux, Richard, esq Bloomsbury
Meech, Mr Thomas, Westbury
Meggit, Mr John, Wakefield
Millin, M Leeds
Mensa Mr Pasquel, Cadiz
Mercer, Gerg, esq Great Margaret-street
Merrill, Messrs T and J Cambridge
Messier, Mr R Winchester
Meyricke, ———, esq Parliament street
Michell, David Robert esq Dewlish, Dorset
Middleton, Sir Charles, Hertford street
Middleton, Sir William
Middleton, M. William, Troome
Mint, ———, esq Preston Hall Maidstone, Kent
Miller, ———, esq fellow comm of St John's College
Milner, Sir William, bart. Nun Appleton
Milnes, John, esq Wakefield
Milnes, James, esq Thorne House
Milne, ———, esq Calston, Bassett, Notts
Mills, Mr C South Audley-street
Mills, Mr ditto
Mitlingto, Mr Great George-street
Millington Langford, esq Caroline street
Mist, James, esq Gate street
Moodly Mr
Money, William, esq
Moore, Rev John, St Paul's Cathedral
Moore Mr Peter, Hadley
Moody, Mr Robert, Bath
Mordaunt, Sir John, bart Walton
Morewood, George, esq Alfreton Hall, Derby
Morewood, Rev Mr Highfield, Derby
Morgan, C esq Bata
Morgan, Rev B Devizes
Morgan, Edward, esq
Morgan, Mr
Moriston, ———, esq fellow of New College
Morton, ———, esq Leadenhall street

N

His Grace the Duke of Norfolk
His Grace the Duke of Northumberland
He Grace the Duchess of Northumberland
Nairne George, esq Bucklebury
Nairn, Capt Bury street, St James's
Naires, Edward, esq
Naires, ———, esq South Molton-street
Naicr, ———, esq Lincoln's Inn
Nadey, B esq
Naffau, Hon George, Clifford-street
Neate, Mr Thomas, Devizes
Needham, Mr Cork street
Nicholson Rev Mr Twickenham
Neville, Mr
Newby, William, esq Sharcoat, Yorkshire
Nuddick, ———, esq Ely Place, Holborn
Newdigate, Mr B tt Biggesford
Noncliff, Mr fellow of New College, Oxon
Newman Mr Prof, M ckham
Newman, M Julia, ditto
Newman, Mr Old Bond street
New on Mr James Antrobus, Stockport

Nichols, Mr John, Red Lion Passage, Fleet-street
Nicholls, M Pettin, rear Ron rd
Nicholson, Mr Mathew, Manchester
Nicholson, Mr jun Manchester
Nicholson, Mr Notts
Nind, Rev Mr Philp, Wargrave, Berks
Nith, Mr Great Queen-street
Neyss, Rev Mr, student of Christ Church, Oxon
Nutte, Mrs

O

Oates, S H, esq Leeds
Oades, Mr J sub, Leeds
Ogden, Edmund, esq Shafton
Ogilvie, Scroope, esq Sackville-street
Oglander, Rev Mr fellow of Winchester College
Olcishaw, Rev Mr fellow of Emanuel College
Oldfield, Dr Halifax
Oliphant, Robert, esq Lincoln's Inn
Oliver, Rev Mr
Onslow, Rev Dr canon of Christ Church, Oxon
Orchard, Peal, esq Chesterfield street
Orme, ———, esq Manchester
O Reilly, Mr Old Broad street
Orrell, Mr Temple
Osborn, John, esq New Norfolk street
Osbourne, Mr William, Hull
Overend, Mr Illsworth
Owen, Mr Temple

P.

Right Rev Lord Bishop of Peterborough
Right Hon Lord Powis
Right Hon Lord Parker
Right Hon Lady Pelworth
Pudles, Robert, esq
Page, John, esq Gough Square
Pagett, Rev Mr Croxton Vineyatt, Notts
Palmer, ———, esq Finsbury
Panton, Paul, esq Lincoln's Inn Fields
Panton, ———, esq Stone Buildings, Lincoln's Inn
Parry, John, esq Bernard's Inn
Parton, Sir William
Parker, Mr Milk-street
Parker, Mr Chancery Lane
Partridge, Capt Normanton, Wilts
Parkes, Mr Palgrave place
Parke, Rev Gilbert, Germains, Norfolk
Pase 1 Minor
Pashley, Rev Mr M A. Barlborough
Pasteur, ———, esq
Patton, Thomas, esq
Patton, Mr Butcher Row, Ratcliffe
Pettin, ———, esq
Pitton, Thomas esq Cheadle, Stafford
Peachee, ———, esq
Pearker, M St Paul's Church Yard
Pearso, Mr Leeds
Pecnall Augustus, esq Portman Square
Pennant, Thomas, esq Upper Brook street
Penwan, Rev Mr. St Germains
Peiryn, Mr Bacon
Perkins, M Canterbury
Pett, Rev Mr student of Christ Church, Oxon
Phoenix Fire Office, Directors of
Phillips, John L nh, esq Manchester
Phillips, Rev Mr Lancer
Phipps, Mr Southampton street
Philip, Mr Robert
Phelps, Capt Stanley Place, Chester
Phillips, Edward, esq Cudleck, Dorset
Philliot, Mr Henry, Bath
Phipps, Hon Mr Lincoln's Inn
Phipps, A esq Lincoln's Inn
Philipp, Mr
Pickering, Rev Mr Bishop Cleave
Pilkington, William, esq Manchester Buildings

P ne,

THE ENGLISH ATLAS.

Pine, Charles James, esq Old Palace Yard
Pitman, Mr Watling street
Pitman, Mr Aldersgate street
Pitter, Mr T Strand
Plaskett, M A B Queen's College
Plaske, Mr Clifford street
Plowes, M Leeds
Plumer, Mr Billeter Square
Poggenpohl, W Henry, esq Upper Marybone
Pole, Rev Mr Milton, Kent
Portman, H W esq Bryanstone, Dorset
Porny, Mr Windsor
Pott, Rev Mr Milton, Kent
Potenger, Mr Windsor
Potts, ——, esq
Powell, James, esq Inner Temple
Powell, Mr A B Merton College
Powlett, Pawlett, esq Somborn, Hants
Powys, Rt Mr Shrewsbury
Pratt, Joseph Steven, esq Devonshire street
Precious, Mr Coleman-street
Prime, John Marshall, esq Staveley, Derby
Prince, Mr George, Water street
Price, Mr B Salisbury Close
Post Office, General
Preston, ——, esq Bradford
Priestly, Joan esq Pond, near Halifax
Priestly, Joseph, esq White Window, near Halifax
Procter, M Major, Wolverhampton
Pryce, Mr Benjamin, Sarum
Pye, Henry A esq fellow of Merton College, Oxon
Pye, Henry James, esq Old Palace Yard
Pym, Rev Wollaston, Hatch Hall, Bedford
Pym, Francis, esq Hatch Hall

R

Right Hon Earl of Rochford
Right Hon Lord Rivers
Radcliffe, Rev Dr Manchester
Radcliff, Mr New Inn
Raine, Mr Furnival's Inn
Ram, Mr C Selwin, Oxford
Ramsden, R esq Carlton Hall, Notts
Ramsden, Thomas, esq Upper Brook street
Randolp, Rev Mr
Randolp, Rev Dr canon of Christ Church, Oxon
Randolp, Rev Mr Wimbledon, Surry
Rawson, Mr William, esq Halifax
Read, Mr Great James street, Bedford Row
Reaston, F B esq Temple
Reeves, ——, esq Thanet Place
Remlin, Mr Stephen
Rennell, Major, Suffolk-street
Renshaw, Mr Owthorpe Hall, Notts
Repington, Charles Edward, esq Armington, Waywk
Rhodes, Mr Leeds
Richardson, Mr Richard, Devizes
Richardson, Mrs Carver Elfketon, Yorkshire
Richardson, Mr York
Ridding, Mr Southampton
Ridding, Mr Winchester
Ridley, Nicholas, esq Gray's Inn
Ridout, Mr Jesus College
Roake, John, esq Lower Halliford, Middlesex
Robertson, Rev Abram, M A. Christ Church, Oxon
Roberts, ——, esq Brentford
Roberts, Rev Mr William, Eton College
Roberts, ——, esq King's Road
Robinson, Mr Francis, Lichfield
Robinson, ——, esq
Robinson, Mr Temple
Robinson, A esq Pall Mall
Robinson, Mr A Ramsey, Kensington
Robinson, Mr Silkworth, near Sunderland
Robinson, Mr Piccadilly
Rodbard, T esq Leeds

Rodes, C H esq Barlborough Hall, Derbyshire
Rogers, Rev John Metruen, Berkley
Rogers, Mr Edward, Liverpool
Rohde, Carsten, esq Wellclose Square
Rolleston, Stephen, esq
Rooke, Hayman, esq Woodhouse Place, Notts
Roope, Mr Bennett's College, Oxon
Ross, ——, esq Old Burlington-street
Ross, Mr sen Crown street
Routh, ——, esq Gray's Inn
Rowley, Owsley, esq Huntingdon
Royds, Richard, esq Halifax
Rudde, Mr Great Russell-street
Rudell, Mrs Bath
Russell, M Queen street, Westminster

S

His Grace the Duke of Somerset
Right Hon Earl of Stafford
Right Hon Earl of Stamford
Lord William Seymour
Salmon, Rev Mr fellow of St John's College
Salisbury, R A esq Chapel Town
Sandford, H esq Bath
Sarjeant, Mr Queen street, Lincoln's Inn Fields
Southier, Mr Northumberland House
Sawbridge, Rev Mr Christ Church, Oxon
Saxton, Charles, esq South Molton-street
Sayer, John, esq Bedford Row
Sayer, ——, esq Temple
Schaw, ——, esq Adelphi
Schaw, Mr Edward
Schofield, Rev Mr Birmingham
Scholfield, Mr. Trinity College, Cambridge
Schomberg, Rev Mr fellow of Magdalen Coll Oxon
Scott, William, esq Woodhall
Scurr, Mr Leeds
Searles, ——, esq Powis Place
Searle, Mr Kent Road
Sech r, John, esq Windsor
Sewell, ——, esq Terrace, Adelphi
Seymour, Mr Norfolk House
Shaw, Mr Alsford, Middlesex
Shaw, ——, esq
Shaw, Mr S Temple
Shaw, Mr J St Martin's lane
Sheephanks, Rev Mr Leeds
Sneldon, William, esq
Shepperson, Mr W Mansfield Woodhouse, Notts
Sneppard, William, esq Froome
Sheppard, Mr William, Froome
Sheppard, Mr John, ditto
Sneppard, Mr Basinghall-street
Shepherd, Mr Carey-street
Sherson, Mr Thomas, Bridge-street, Black Fryars
Shropshire, Mr William, Wrenbury, Cheshire
Sibley, ——, esq Hatton Garden
Silvester, ——, esq Chancery-lane
Simpson, T esq Babworth, Notts
Simpson, Mr Thomas, George street, Adelphi
Simpson, Rev Mr fellow of University College, Oxon
Simson, Mr George, St Paul's Church Yard
Simmons, Mr Butt House, Leicestershire
Singer, Mr Thomas, Corsley
Sivale, ——, esq
Skirne, ——, jun esq Bath
Skynner, Mr. Workjop, Notts
Smalley, ——, esq King's Arms Yard, Coleman st
Smed, Rev Mr Gilden, Notts
Smithson, Gill, esq Leeds
Smith, Sir John, bar Sydling, Dorset
Smith, Rev Mr Aldermanbury
Smith, Mr John, Trinity College
Smith, Mr Charlotte-street
Smith, M- Cowley-street
Smith, Mr. Beely, Derby

Smith, Rev Mr fellow of Pembroke College
Smith, Mr. Oriel College
Smith, Mr Wells Walk, Hampstead
Smith, Mr J sen A B Trinity College, Cambridge
Smith, Mr William, A B Trinity College, Cambridge
Smith, Mr Roope's College, Oxon
Smith, ——, esq Bath
Smith, Miss, Somersford, Wilts
Snivence, ——, esq Upper Marybone street
Soame, Mrs Henrietta-street, Cavendish Square
Sollers, Mr Blandford
Southgate, Rev Mr British Museum
Sowerby, John, esq Hatton street
Speldove, Mr Swithin's-lane
Spink, Mr Bedford-street, Covent Garden
Spring r, ——, esq Chancery-lane
Spurgeon, Rev T G Melton, Suffolk
Squire, Mr S Temple
Stainforth, George, esq Berkley Square
Stainforth, ——, esq Old Broad-street
Stansfield, Mr J
Stamford, Mr William
Stanton, Mr
Stanhope, ——, esq Temple
Stanger, ——, esq Gray's Inn
Stanger, Mr Cheapside
Seaman, Rev Mr
Stephenson, Mr
Stevenson, Mr Park-street, Westminster
Stevenson, Mr
Stevenson, Mr William, Cobham Hall, Kent
Stillman, Mr Thomas, Steeple Ashton
Stiles, Mr Robert Gravesend
Stiles, William, esq Tower
Stinton, Rev Dr rector of Exeter College, Oxon
Stokes, Mr William, Longiest
Stone, Thomas, esq Holcorn Court, Gray's Inn
Stofford Mr Halifax
Storey, John, esq No. 5
Stroud, Rev Mr Southill, Somerset
Stroud, Mr Somerset-street
Sunderland, Mr
Surtees, Rev Mr fellow of University College, Oxon
Sutton, Mr Francis, Devizes
Sutton, Rev Charles, Norwich
Sutton, ——, esq
Swainson, J T esq Dover Place
Swain, Ms Halifax
Swaffield, Mr Clement's Inn
Swale, F esq Gower-street, Bedford Square
Swertner, Rev John, Nevile's Court
Swinnerton, Rev Mr Hough, Cheshire
Symmonds, John, esq

T

Right Hon. Lady Townsend
Tappin, Mr Kew Bridge
Taylor, M F Austin Friars
Taylor, Andrew, esq Norton street
Taylor, Rev Mr Lincoln's Inn Fields
Taylor, Mr Austin Friars
Taylor, M B esq Wolverhampton
Taylor, John, esq Kirby House, Berks
Taylor, William, esq Panton-street
Taylor, Rev Thomas, Wotton, Surry
Taylor, Richard, esq Norton street
Taylor, Mr Chatham Place
Taylor, L R esq
Tempier, George, esq Shapwick, Somerset
Temple, G esq Mortlake
Templeton, Mr N B Trinity College, Cambridge
Tenant, Mr Leeds
Terley, Mr Leeds
Teschemacher, M R Nottingham
Thompson, Mr John, Croydon
Thompson, Dr Kensington
Thomas, David, esq Pay Office

Thomas,

LIST OF SUBSCRIBERS.

Thomas, Harry, esq Parliament street
Thorold, Sir John, bart
Thornton, Godfrey, esq Austin Friars
Thornbury, Rev Mr
Thoroton, Rev Mr Trinity College
Thring, Mr John, Warminster
Thynne, Hon Thomas, Longleat, Wilts
Tufton, ——, esq C C Christ Church, Oxon
Timms, Mr Whitcrall
Timbrell, Mr Thomas, jun Trowbridge
Todd, Mr York
Todd, Rev Henry, M A Wotton Basset, Wilts
Tomline, Marmaduke
Tomkins, William, esq Abingdon, Berks
Tomkins, Joseph, esq Abingdon, Berks
Tomkins, Mr Benjamin, Upper Thames street
Toplis, Mr Cuckney, Notts
Topham, John, esq Gray's Inn
Toulmin, Mr Hackney
Towles, Mr High-street, Borough
Townsend, Marmaduke, esq Ruby Grove, Lincoln
Townsend, Mr Chelsea
Townsend, Mr St George's, Borough
Townsend, Charles, esq. Old Burlington street
Tracey, Hon and Rev Dr All Souls College
Trant, Mr Leeds
Tremells, Mr Roger, Northumberland
Trevelyan, Sir John, bar Nettlecomb
Tripp, Henry, esq Temple
Trollope, Sir Thomas, Lincolnshire
Tryon, Mr Grosvenor street
Tuke, Mr Henry, York
Tuke, Mr John, ditto
Tunstall, Marmaduke, esq Wycliffe, Yorkshire
Turton, Thomas, esq Meanwood
Turner, Rev Mr Newcastle
Turner, ——, esq Sackville street
Tufon, Edward, esq Wells
Tyley, Mr Thomas, Wedmore
Tylee, Mr John, Devizes

U.

Valpy, Rev Richard, Reading
Vanderbergh, Mr Kensington Gore
Vere, ——, esq Bishopsgate-street
Vigor, Mr Robert, Bristol
Vincent, Mr A. B Trinity College, Cambridge
Vincent, ——, esq
Uppleby, Mrs.

W

Right Hon Lord Viscount Weymouth
Right Hon Viscountess Weymouth
Right Hon Lord Viscount Wentworth
Wade, Benjamin, esq New Grange
Wakefield, Mr William Steele, Andover
Walpole, ——, esq Sowerby Bridge, Yorkshire
Walker, Joseph, M D Leeds
Walker, William, esq Leeds
Walker, Joseph, esq Eastwood
Walker, ——, esq
Walker, ——, esq Temple Cloisters
Walker, E esq Serjeants Inn
Walker, Robert, esq Labour-in-vain Hill
Walcot, ——, esq Temple
Walter, Mr
Walters, Mr Thomas, Shadwell
Walton, Mr Bank of England
Walton, Mr. Girdlers Hall
Waller, T G, esq Winchester
Ware, Gregory, esq Shelford, Cambridgeshire
Walsh, John, esq. Chesterfield-street
Ward, Rev Mr Netherthorpe
Ward, ——, esq Gower street
Wardel, ——, esq St James's-street
Wathen, Mr James, Hereford
Watts, Mr Bath
Watts, Mr Scotland Yard
Watson, William, esq Bath
Watson, Mr Holland, Stockport
Watson, Mr T. Bank Buildings
Watson, Mr Park-lane
Webb, Mr Francis, Sarum
Webb, Mr Charles, Warminster
Webb, Mr Benjamin, Melksham
Webb, John, esq Doctors Commons
Webb, ——, esq. Milton, Wilts
Webster, Rev Mr Tibshelf, Derby
Webster, Mr Morley
Weby, ——, esq fellow of Emanuel College
Weld, Thomas, esq Lullworth Castle
Well, Mr William, Fleet-street
Western, Mr Gainsborough
Western, Maximilian, esq Cokethorpe, Oxon
Whalley, Mr Minories
Whitaker, Mr James, Froome
Whitaker, Miss
Witteing, Mr. Broad street, Ratcliff
Whitfield, Rev. Dr rector of Lothbury
White, S M D. Nottingham
White, Mr William, Wedmore
White, Mr J Garlick Hill
White, Mr Queen's street, Southwark
White, John, esq Weymouth-street
Wick, Nathaniel, esq Bath
Wickham, William, esq
Wickham, Mr James, Froome
Wicken, Mr John, jun.
Wiggs, Mr Wapping
Wight, Rev. Mr. Osborne, Ponsbury, Shropshire

Wigly, ——, esq Temple
Wight, Rev Osborn, Ponsbury
Wight, Rev Henry, Lichfield Cathedral
Wilkes, John, esq Princes Court
Wilkes, Joseph, esq Meltham, Leicester
Williamson, Mr Little Smith street
Williams, M. Thomas, Bratton
Wilson, Capt Farnham, Surry
Wilson, Robert, esq Froome
Wilson, Mr Leeds
Wilson, Rev Mr
Wilson, Thomas, esq Leeds
Wilson, Mr Vauxhall
Wilson, Mr
Wilson, Mr Hackney
Wilkinson, Edward, esq Leeds
Wilkinson, ——, esq fellow commoner of T n y Hall
Wilkinson, Abram, esq Dublin
Wilkinson, Mr. Leadenhall-street
Wilmot, Mr
Whishabam Rundle, esq Rode Hall, Cheshire
Windle, Mr Leeds
Windham, William, esq. Chandois street, Cavendish Square
Windham, Dr Corton, Dorset
Windus, Mr Arthur, War Office
Windus, Mr Bishopsgate-street
Winter, T B esq Froome
Wise, Mr Newgate street
Wolfe, ——, esq Temple
Wood, Rev Mr Leeds
Wood, Mr P Mansfield
Wood, ——, esq Hall in Close, Rippon, Yorkshire
Woodfall, Mr Dorset-street
Woodford, Ralph, esq New Norfolk-street
Woodward, ——, esq Chevenage
Woolcombe, Mr Oriel College
Wollin, Mr Fetter-lane
Worgan, Rev Mr Andover
Wotton, ——, esq Lower Brook street
Wright, Mr J
Wright, Mr Leadenhall-street
Wyatt, Mr Essex street
Wyatt, Mr Samuel, Burton upon Trent

Y

Yarde, Mr
Yates, John, esq Charter House Square
Yeatman, Rev John, fellow of Oriel College
Yorke, Philip, esq New Cavendish street
Yorke, Charles, esq Lincoln's Inn
Young, Rev Mr Watling-street
Young, Sir William, Stretton street

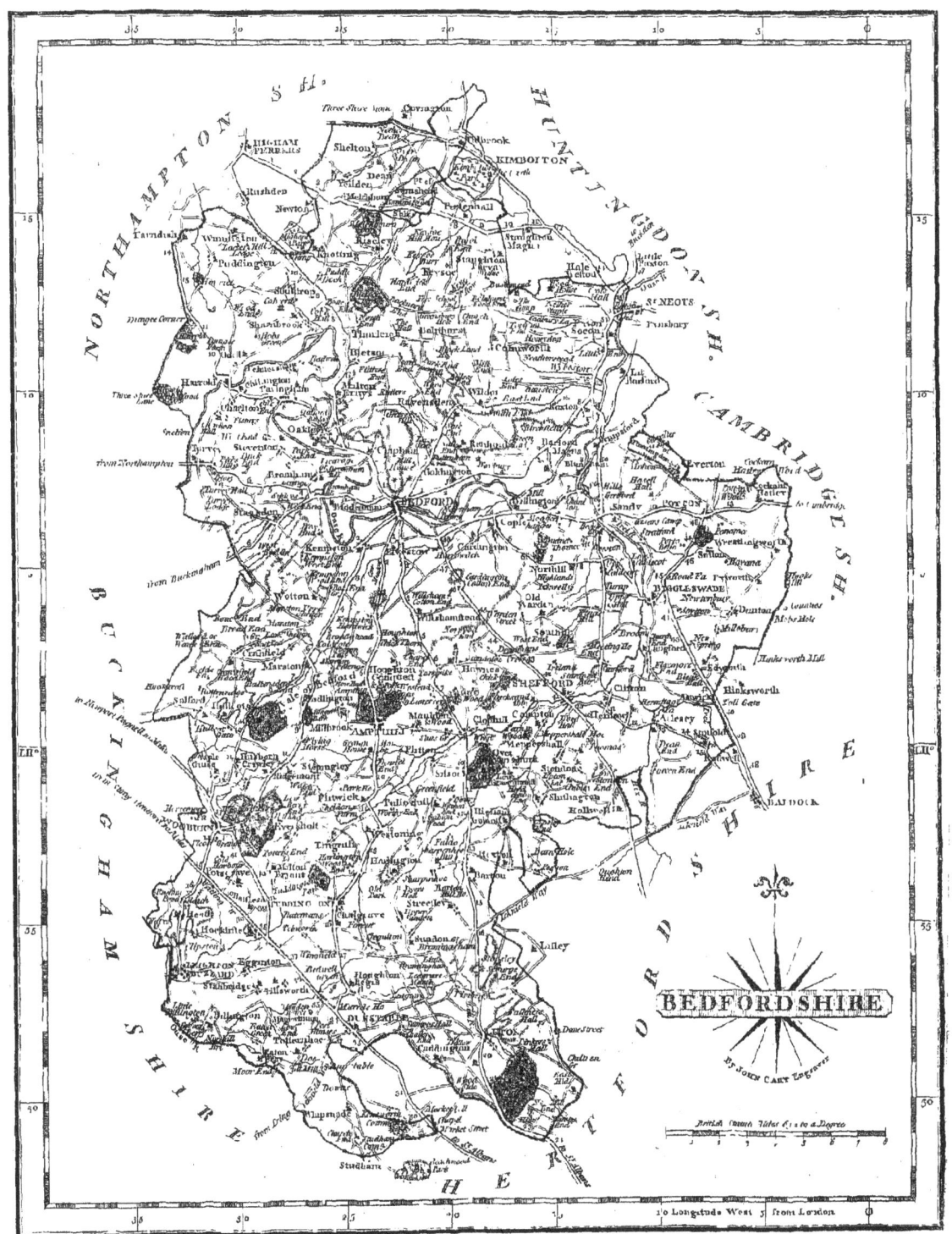

BEDFORDSHIRE

Is a small inland county, which, during the Saxon heptarchy, belonged to the kingdom of Mercia; it is now in the province of Canterbury, bishoprick of Lincoln, and the Norfolk circuit, being 35 miles from north to south, 20 miles broad from east to west, and 145 in circuit, containing an area of 480 square miles, or 307,200 square acres, divided into 9 hundreds, 124 parishes, with 10 market towns, viz Bedford, the county town, which sends 2 members to parliament, and gives the title of Duke to the Russel family, Ampthill; Biggleswade, Dunstable, Leighton Beaudesart, Luton, Potton, Shefford, Tuddington, and Woburn. Among the villages Turvey gives the title of Baron to the Mordaunt family, and Bromham the same title to the Trevor family. It sends 4 members to parliament, 2 for the county, and 2 as before mentioned, pays 7 parts of the land-tax, and provides 400 men to the national militia. Its rivers are the Ouse, navigable to Bedford, and divides the county into two parts, the Ivel, Lea, and other small streams. It produces abundance of corn, cattle, wood, barley, woad for dying, and rich pastures, its chief manufactures are malt, bone-lace, and straw goods. Its most noted places are Dane's Fields, remarkable for two pits 15 feet diameter. It is a pleasant county, diversified with fruitful plains and rising hills. The air is healthy, and the soil in general a deep clay. It produces fullers earth, an excellent ingredient for our woollen manufactures. There are many remains of Roman, Saxon, and Danish antiquities.

The most considerable Seats in this county are,

Ampthill Park, near Ampthill.
Barmead, near Hale Wefton
Battelfden, near Woburn
Beachwood Park, near Luton
Bletfoe Park, near Thurleigh
Bro'torough Park, near Ampthill
Chickfand Abbey, near Shefford
Clapham, near Bedford

Laton Bray House, near Dunstable
Eaton Socon House
Hafell Hall, near Potton
Hinwick, near Puddington
Hockliffe, near Tuddington.
Houghton Conqueft Park, near Ampthill
Luton Park, near Luton
Melchburne Park, near Rifeley

Oakley
Odell, near Harold
Sandy, near Potton,
Southill, near Shefford.
Sutton, near Potton
Tuddingham Park, near Tuddington
Woburn Park, near Woburn
Wreft Park, near Shefford.

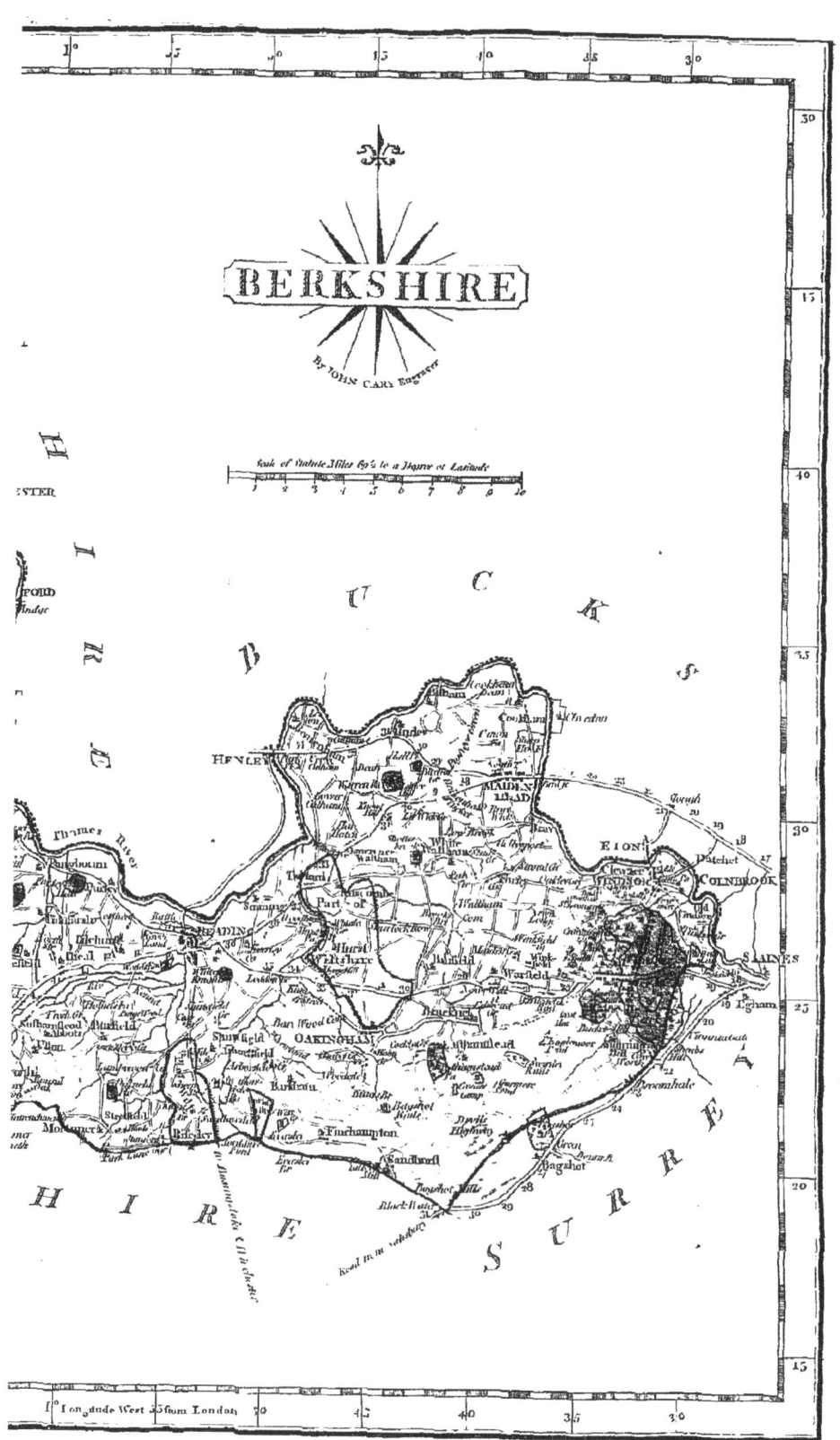

BERKSHIRE

Is an inland county, which gives the title of Earl to the Howard family, and sends 2 members to parliament. During the Saxon heptarchy it belonged to the West Saxons. It is now in the province of Canterbury, diocese of Salisbury, and circuit of Oxford; containing 467,500 square acres, or 730 square miles, being 40 miles long, 29 broad, and about 180 in circuit, divided into 20 hundreds, has 140 parishes, 62 vicarages, 12 market towns, viz. Windsor, which gives the title of Baron to the Hickman family, and sends 2 members to parliament, Abingdon, gives the title of Earl to the family of Bertie, and sends one member to parliament, Hungerford, gives the title of Baron to the Hastings family, Newbury, gives the title of Baron to the Cholmondeley family, Reading, sends 2 members to parliament, Wallingford, sends 2 members to parliament, besides East Ilsley, Lower Lambourne, Maidenhead, Ockingham, and Wantage. It has about 671 villages, among whom Mortimer gives the title of Earl to the family of Harley. This county sends 9 members to parliament, pays but 10 parts of the land tax, and supplies but 560 men to the national militia. Its principal river is the Thames, besides which, it has the Isis, the Kennet, the Loddon, the Ocke, and the Lambourne, the later, contrary to all others, is always the highest in summer, and shrinks as winter approaches. The most remarkable places in this county are the Royal Castle of Windsor, the fertile Vale of White Horse, and White Horse Hill, where the rude figure of a horse takes up near an acre of ground on the side of a green hill, said to have been made to commemorate the defeat of the Danes by Alfred, in 841, on Ashdown, now the seat of Lord Craven. The air of this county is healthy, even in the vales, which are remarkably pleasant. It is well stored with fine timber, particularly oak, elm, and beech, and produces great plenty of grain, and the rivers produce fine trouts and craw-fish. It has manufactures of woollen cloth, sail cloth, and malt.

The most considerable Seats in this county are,

Aldermarston Park, near Aldermarston
Ashampstead Park, near East Ilsley
Ashdown Park, near East Ilsley
Ashley Hill, near Henley
Bagshot Rails, and Bagshot Green, near Windsor
Basseldon Park, near Pangbourn
Beaumont Lodge, near Old Windsor
Bill Hill
Binfield
Coley, near Reading
Compton Park, near Ashbury
Cranbury Park, at Windsor
Dunston Park, near Newbury
Easthamstead, near Ockingham
Englefield House, near Englefield
Hawley, near Welford
Frogmore, near Windsor
The Grove, near Newbury
Hall Place, near Maidenhead

Hemstead Marshall Park, near Kintbury
Hurst Park, near Reading
New Lodge, near Windsor
Oakfield House, near Reading
Oakley, near Abingdon
Ozenwood, near Bullermere
Park Place, near Henley
Purley Hall, near Pangbourn
Radley Hall, near Sunningwell
Strately
Shottesbrooke, near Waltham
Sunninghill Park, near Windsor
Swallowfield Park, near Reading
Spurfholt House, near Wantage
Swinley Rails, near Bracknell
Tharcham, near Newbury
Uffingham
Welford, near Winterborn
White Knights, near Reading

White Waltham
Windsor Castle
Windsor Great Lodge
Wittenham Little, near Dorchester
Wooley, near Farnborough
Wodley, near Farringdon
Yattenden Park, near Pangbourn

The most remarkable and extensive Views in this County are from

Cumner Hurst, near Appleton
Cooper's Hill, near Windsor, St Leonard's Hill, near Windsor, Windsor Terrace, and Cranbourne Lodge,
The Road from Reading to Wallingford
White Horse Hill, near Woolston
The Road from Wantage to Sparfholt
The Hill between Maidenhead and Henley

BUCKINGHAMSHIRE

Is an inland county, which gives title of Earl to the Hobart family. During the Saxon heptarchy it belonged to the kingdom of Mercia, and is now included in the province of Canterbury, in the diocese of Lincoln, and in the Norfolk circuit. Its form is oblong, the greatest extent from North to South is 45 miles long, 25 broad, and 110 in circuit, containing 467,000 square acres, or 730 square miles, divided into 8 hundreds, having 185 parishes, and 15 market-towns, viz. Buckingham, the county town, which gives the title of Marquis to the Temple family, and sends 2 members to parliament, Aylesbury, which gives the title of Earl to the Brudenel family, and sends 2 members to parliament, Wycomb, which gives the title of Baron to the Petty family, and sends 2 members to parliament, Marlow, Wendover, and Amersham, each sends 2 members to parliament, Newport Pagnel, Winslow, Beaconsfield, Chesham, Stony Stratford, Colnbrook, Ivinghoe, Oulney, and Risborough, besides the considerable villages of Eton, Fenny Stratford, Burnham, Brickhill, Hanslope, Iver, &c. It sends 14 members to parliament, pays 12 parts of the land-tax, and provides 560 men to the national militia. Its rivers are the Thames, Ouse, Coln, Wickham, Amersham, Isis, Tame, and Loddon. The most noted places are the Chiltern Hills, Vale of Aylesbury, Bernwood Forest, and Woburn Heath. Its chief manufactures are bone lace, paper, and malt. It produces fine wool, beech wood, cattle, sheep, and is noted for its breed of rams, and woad for dying. The air is generally good, and the soil is mostly chalk or marle.

The most remarkable Seats in this county are,

Ashridge, near Ivinghoe.
Black Parks, near Langley.
Bulstrode, near Beaconsfield.
Cheynes, near Amersham.
Clifden House, near Hooker.
Chesham.
Denham Court, near Uxbridge.
Ditton Park, near Windsor.
Duddeshall Park, near Queynton.
Downey Court.
Lathorp.
Gregorys, near Beaconsfield.
Hall Barn, near Beaconsfield.

Latimer, near Chesham.
Langley, near Colnbrook.
New House, near Charlfont, St. Giles's.
Nettleden, near Great Gaddesden.
Oving, near Whitchurch.
Percy Lodge, near Colnbrook.
Shardloe, near Amersham.
Stanton, near Haversham.
Stoke Park, near Eaton.
Stow Park, near Buckingham.
Turfield Court, near Henley.
Lythorpe, near Thame.
Whitton Park, near Beaconsfield.

West and High Wycomb.
Wine Park, near Leighton Buzzard.
Wotton, near Brill.

The most remarkable Places for extensive Prospects are,

Taplow, on the Thames.
Root House and Bapsey Point.
Great Marlow.
Cawley Wood.
Harleyford, near Marlow.
Prince Risborough.
The Road from Hadsor to Great Marlow.

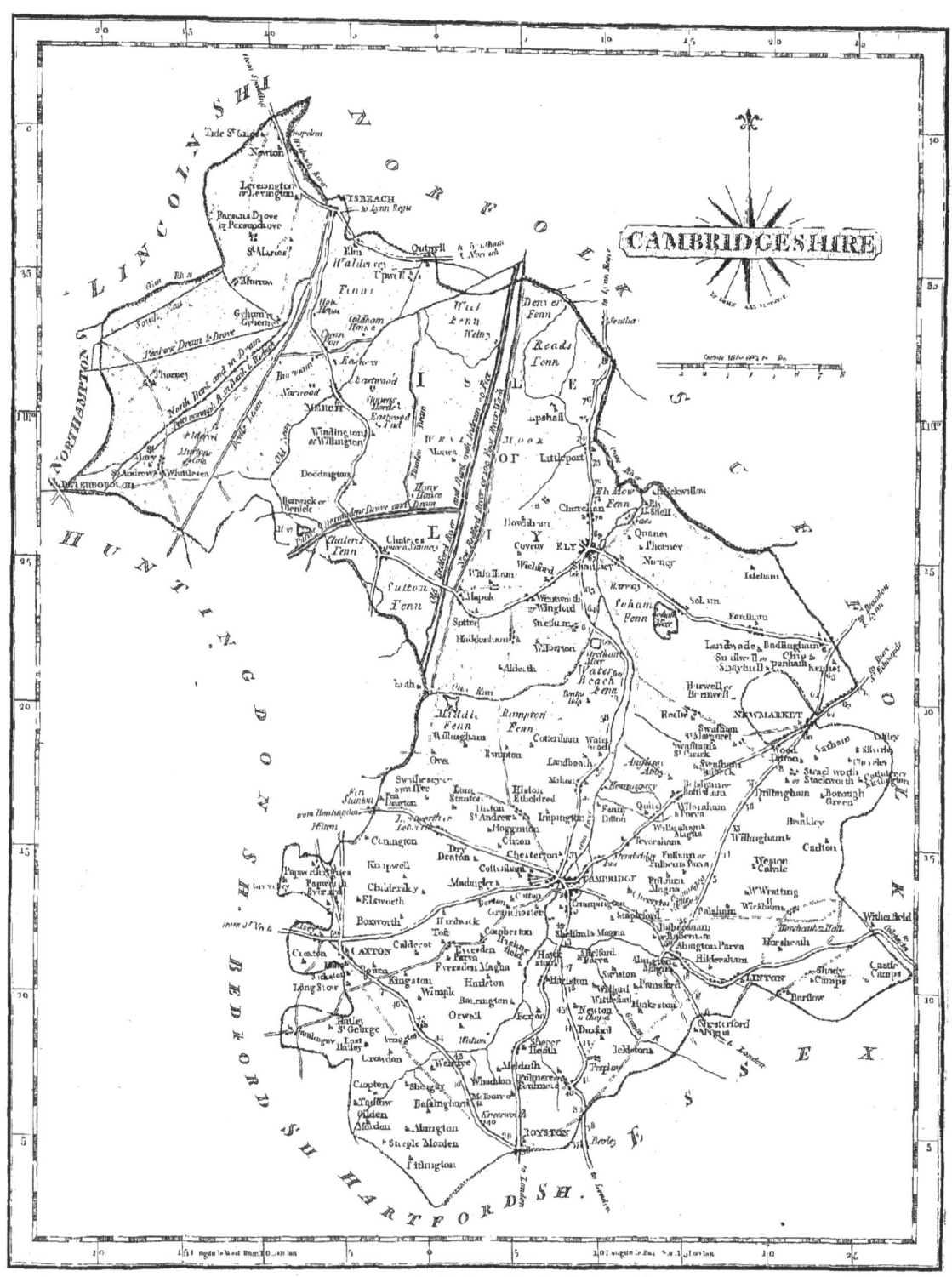

CAMBRIDGESHIRE

Is an inland county, which, during the heptarchy, belonged to the kingdom of the East Angles. It is now in the province of Canterbury, diocese of Ely, (except a small part in the diocese of Norwich,) and it is included in the Norfolk circuit. It is 44 miles long, 26 broad, and 160 in circumference, containing 670 square miles, or 428,800 acres, divided into 17 hundreds, 163 parishes, one city, viz. Ely, which is a bishoprick, whose bishop is a prince palatine within its district, and appoints a judge to try all criminal causes, one university, viz. Cambridge, the second in the kingdom, founded in 531, consisting of 12 colleges and 4 halls, and containing about 1500 students, and sends 2 members to parliament, the town contains 14 parish churches, sends 2 members to parliament, and gives the title of Duke to the Royal family, Royston, which gives the title of Viscount to the Yorke family, and enjoys a market, as does Linton, Wisbeach, Caxton, Mersh, Thorney, Soham, and Newmarket, remarkable for its horse-races, is part in this county. Among the villages Horseheath gives the title of Baron Mountford to the family of Bromley. The rivers are the Ouse, Cam, Welney, and Nene. The most remarkable places are, Balsham and Gogmagog Hills, Newmarket Heath, Soham and Streatham Meers, Royston Cave, the Devil's Ditch, Sturbridge Field, &c. The Isle of Ely is an inland spot, surrounded by the Ouse and other streams, and is the Northern division of the county, consisting of a spacious level, containing 300,000 acres of land, extending into the counties of Norfolk, Suffolk, Huntingdonshire, and Lincolnshire, divided by innumerable channels and drains. The whole level, of which this is a part, forms a rude kind of semicircle resembling a horse-shoe. In the Isle the air is damp, foul, and unwholesome, but in the south-east parts of this county it is more pure and salubrious. The soil also is very different; in the Isle of Ely it is fenny and very spongy, yet affords excellent pasture, in the Uplands it is fruitful in grain. Its chief products are cattle, saffron, game, poultry, and river fish, and they make great quantities of malt. It sends 6 members to parliament, viz. 2 for the county, and 4 as above shewn, pays 9 parts of the land-tax, and provides 480 men to the national militia.

The Gentlemens' Seats in this County are,

Abington, near Linton.
Babraham, near Linton.
Barrington, near Cambridge.
Bottisham, near Newmarket.
Bourne, near Cambridge.
Catridge, near Newmarket.
Catley, near Linton.
Cherrington, near Cambridge.
Cheveley, near Newmarket.
Chippenham, near Newmarket.
Connington, near Caxton.
Croxton, near Caxton.
Doddington, Isle of Ely.
Dullingham, near Newmarket.
Exning, near Newmarket.
Fordham Abbey, near Newmarket.

Fulburn, near Cambridge.
Gamlingay.
Gogmagog Hills, near Cambridge.
Hildersham, near Linton.
Hinkeston, near Linton.
Horseheath, near Linton.
Impington, near Linton.
Kneesworth, near Royston.
Long Stanton, near Cambridge.
Madingley, near Cambridge.
Milton, near Linton.
Newton, near Cambridge.
Qui Hall, near Cambridge.
Shady Camps, near Linton.
Sleford.
Snailwell, near Newmarket.

Soham, near Ely.
Swaffham, near Newmarket.
Trompington.
Whaddon, near Royston.
Wilbraham Temple.
Wimple, near Caxton.
Wisbeach Palace.
Wratting, near Linton.

The most considerable Views are from,

Gogmagog Hills, near Cambridge.
Cambridge Castle Hill.
Newmarket Heath.
Coton Church.

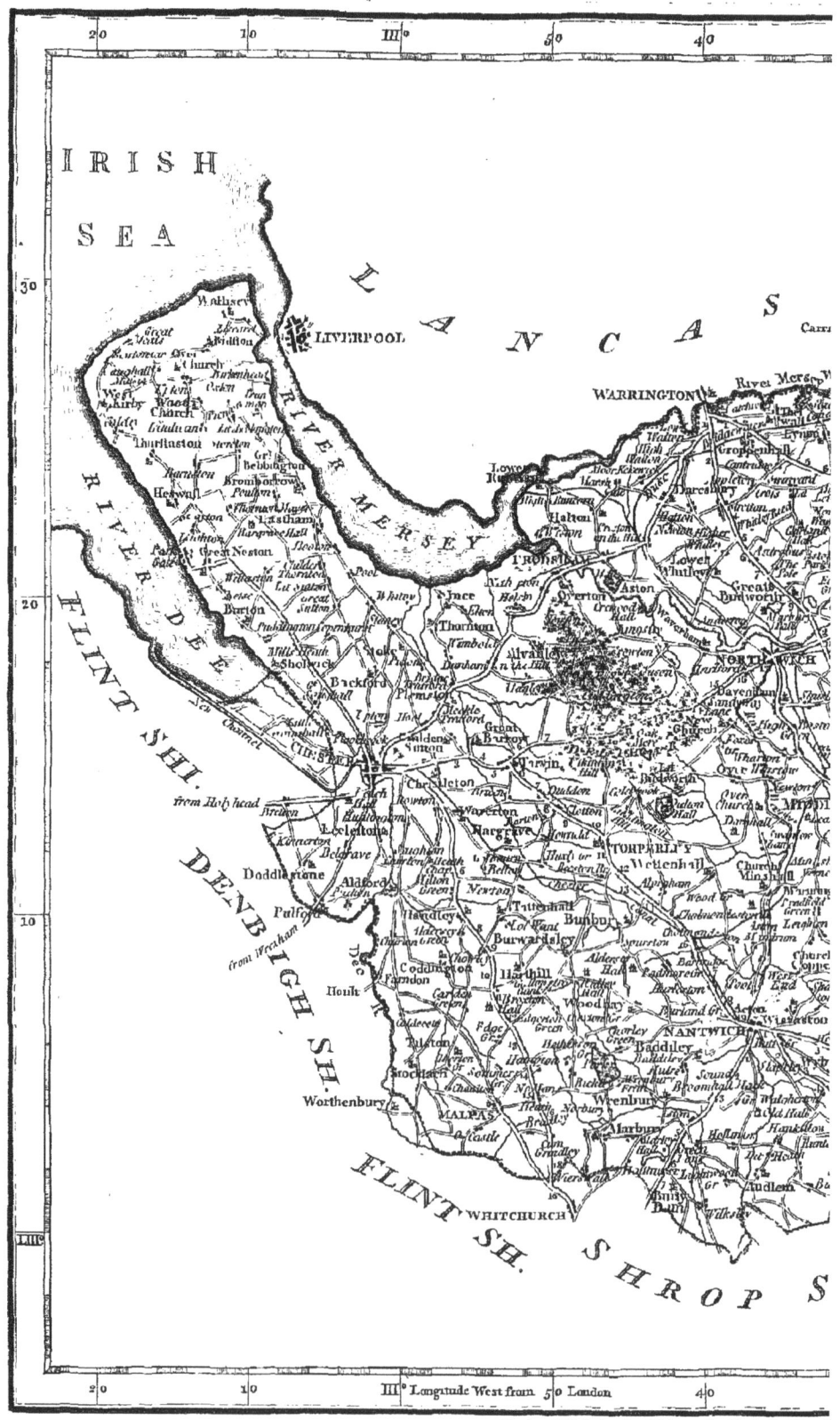

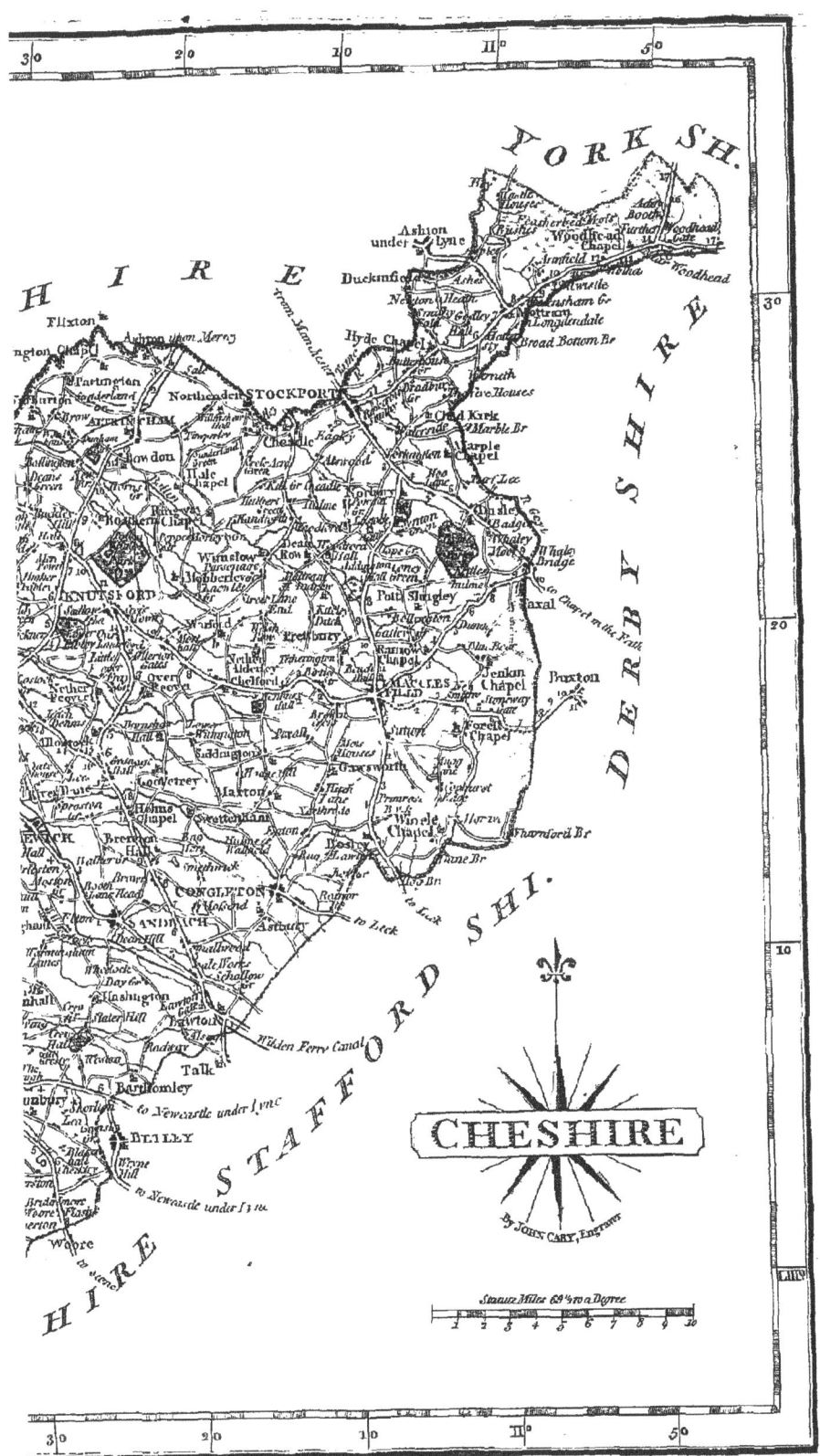

CHESHIRE

Is a maritime county; during the Saxon heptarchy it belonged to the kingdom of Mercia; and William the Conqueror made it a county palatine, and granted it peculiar privileges, viz. having its own judge for all criminal cases, a court of exchequer, &c. It is included in the province of York, and a diocese of its own name. It is 50 miles long from East to West, 33 broad from North to South, and 200 miles in circumference, containing 1050 square miles, or 672,000 acres, divided into 7 hundreds, 101 parishes; it contains one city, Chester, which is a bishop's fee, and gives the title of Earl to the Prince of Wales, as eldest son of the King of England, first conferred in 1247 by Henry III. and sends 2 members to parliament, with 11 market-towns, viz. Nantwich, which gives the title of Viscount to the family of Cholmondeley, Macclesfield, gives the title of Earl to the family of Parker, and Malpas, the title of Viscount to the family of Cholmondeley, also Middlewich, Northwich, Congleton, Altringham, Frodsham, Knotsford, Stockport, and Sandbach. Among the villages, Kinderton, gives the title of Baron to the family of Vernon, Cholmondeley, those of Earl and Baron to the noble family of that name, Dutton, that of Baron to the family of Hamilton, Eaton, that of Baron to the family of Grosvenor. The principal rivers in this county are the Mersey, Dee, Weelock, Croke, Dan, Fulbrook, Wever, Goyte, Bolling, and Ringay. It sends 4 members to parliament, 2 for the county, and 2 for Chester, as before mentioned, pays 7 parts of the land tax, and provides 560 men to the national militia. On the coast is the Isle of Hilbree, with Black Rock, Barbo, Dove, and Hoyle Sands, with Bugg Wharf, Middle and High Lake, also Warren Bay, with the Entrances of the Mersey and Dee Rivers, and a peninsula between both. It enjoys the most extensive and beneficial inland navigation in the kingdom, that of the Duke of Bridgewater, deserving particular attention. Among the other remarkables are Moncap, Frodsham, Alderney, and Shuding Hills, the forests of Delamere and Maxfield, with several lakes, meers, pools, heaths, and mosses. It produces excellent cheese, cattle, corn, iron, mill-stones, timber, an immense quantity of fine salt, alum, hops, &c. The soil rich and fertile.

The following are the most remarkable Seats,

Addington Hall, near Macclesfield;
Afton Hall, near Frodsham.
Capesthorne
Eaton Hall, near Chester
Cholmondeley, near Malpas,
Crewe Hall, near Sandbach
Cambermere Abby, near Busley Dam.
Davenport Hall.
Doddington Hall, near Nantwich.

Eaton
Henbury Hall, near Macclesfield.
Lower Tabley, near Knutsford
Lyme Park, near Disley
Marbury Hall, near Budworth.
Mere Hall, near Knutsford.
Motham St Andrew, near Stockport.
Oulton Hall, near Torporley
Poynton, near Stockport.

The most remarkable Situations for beautiful and extensive Views are,

Delamere Forest, N. E. of Chester
Goyte Vale
Disley Hill, in the Road from Buxton,
Manchester
Houlton Castle.

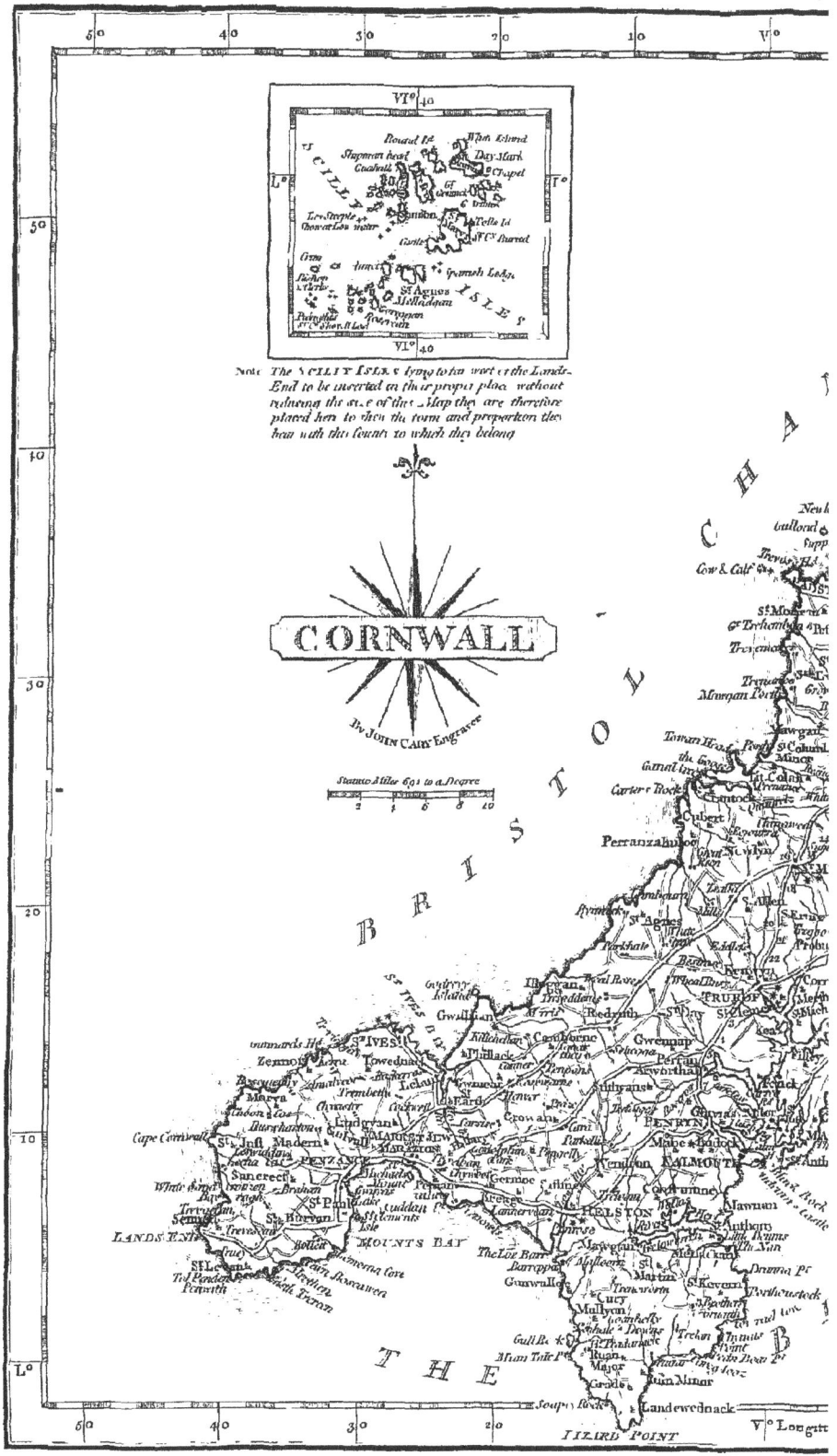

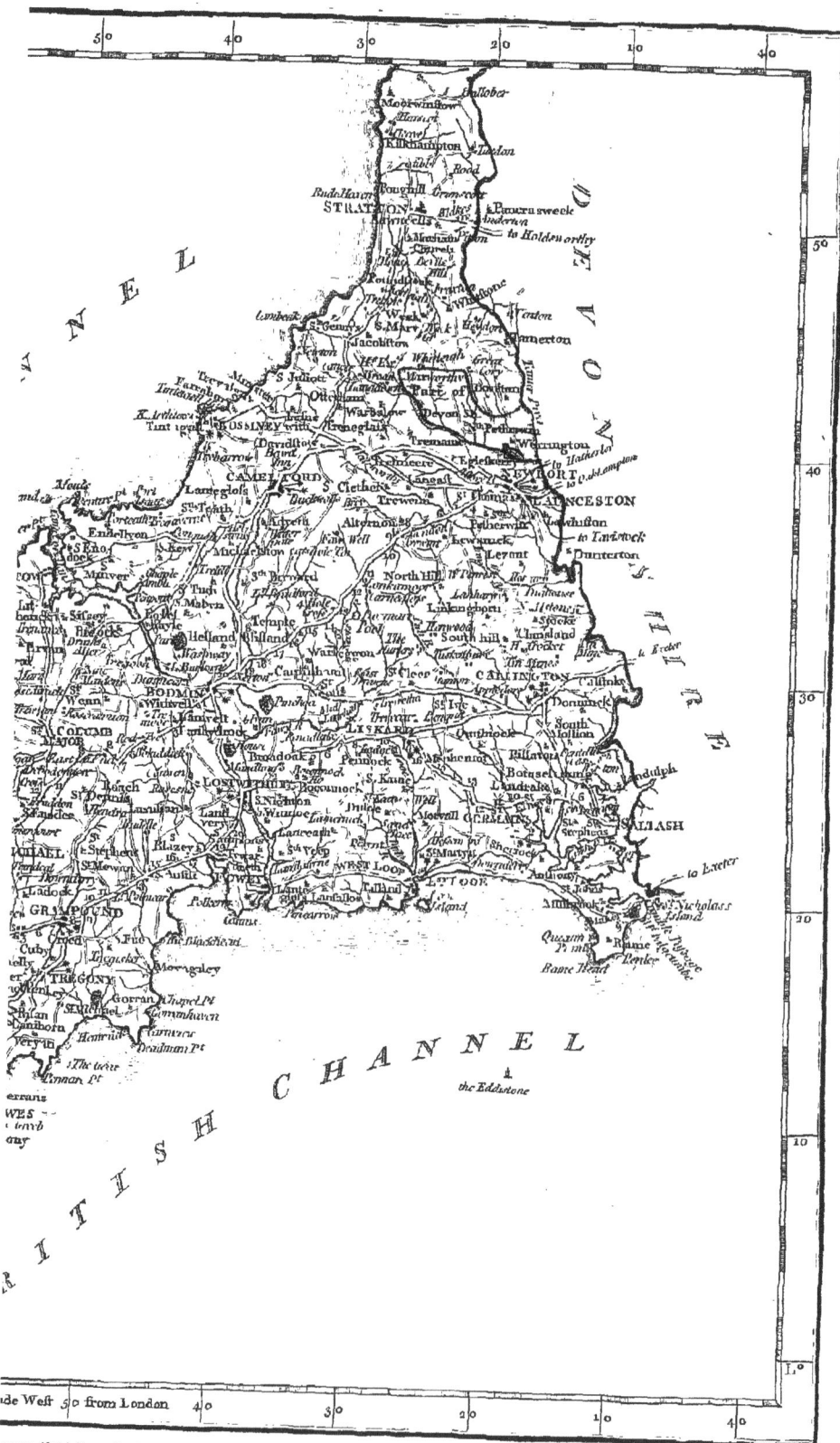

CORNWALL

Is a maritime county, the most western extremity of Great Britain, and gives the title of Duke to the eldest son of the King of England as soon as born. It was included in the county of Devon by Alfred in his division of the kingdom into counties, and belonged to the West Saxons during the heptarchy. It is now belonging to the province of Canterbury and diocese of Exeter, and is included in the Western circuit. The Prince appoints the sheriff for this county, which is 75 miles long from East to West, and 45 broad at its eastern end, but not above five miles broad at the Western extremity, and it is about 250 miles in circumference, containing 1450 square miles, or 928,000 acres at this time, though in the reign of Edward I according to a survey then made it contained 1,500,000 acres, a sufficient proof that large tracts of it have been swallowed up by the sea, as it is supposed the Island of Scilly also did formerly, though now separated from it by the sea, at the distance of 40 miles, and are 145 in number, of which St Mary's Island, though only 9 miles round, is the largest. This county is divided into 9 hundreds, 161 parishes, and 27 market towns, viz Launceston, the county town, which sends 2 members to parliament, Falmouth, which gives the title of Viscount to the family of Boscawen, Camelford, which gives the title of Baron to the family of Pitt, Helston, with Truro, Saltash, Bodmin, St Ives, Tregory, Fowey, St Germain, Penryn Callington, Botney, East and West Loo, Grampound, Leskard, Lostwithiel, St Mawes, St Michael, and Newport, each send 2 members to parliament, but the three last places have disused their markets, but the following enjoy that privilege, viz Padstow, St Columb, Penzance, and Market Jew. The village of Bocconoc gives the title of Baron to the family of Pitt, Port Elliot the same honour to the family of Craggs, and that of Boscawen to the family of the same name. Its numerous remarkable places are those of the Land's End, Lizard-point, Cape Cornwall, Deadman's-head, Rame-nead, Nate-point, Stopper-point, Trevoza-point, Gogmagog's-leap, Predannet-point, Pengwenon-point, Lamorney-point, Tallart-point, Gudreny Isle, Meneg Peninsula, the Scilly Islands, Pendennis and St Mawes Castles, Michael's Mount, Padstow Haven, St Ive's Bay, Mount's Bay, Falmouth Harbour, Trewardreth Bay, Fowey Haven, Beed's Haven, Duck Pool, Helfield Haven, Cary Bay, Gumdrath Bay, Predmouth Bay, Sythe Bay, Hamoze Bay, the Godolphin Hill, Hengston and Pendennis Hills, Roseland, Temple Moores, St. Austle, St. Muan, and Helston Downs, Loophoie Lake, and the Hurlers. Its principal rivers are the Tamer, Cober, Loo, Camel, Lydd, Fowey, Haile, and Liver. It produces the best tin in the world, with copper, lead, fine stone, blue slate, silver ore, mundick, crystal, moor stone, load stone, pasture, cattle, corn, poultry, game, fish of every kind, particularly herrings and pilchards. It sends 44 members to parliament, 2 for the county, and 42 as already shewn, which is more than any county in England, and within one as many as the whole kingdom of Scotland. It supplies 640 men to the national militia, and pays 8 parts of the land-tax. It abounds with Druidical monuments, and St Germains and Bodmin were bishopricks as early as 905. The coinage-towns for tin are Leskard, Lostwithiel, Truro, Helston and Penzance. The packets sail from Falmouth for Spain, Portugal, and the West Indies.

The most remarkable Seats in this County are,

Antony House, near East Anthony.
Bocconoc House, near Lostwithiel.
Boscawen Park.
Boswoigey, near St Columb.
Botham, near Helston.
Carclew, near Penryn.
Castle Horneck, near Penzance.
Carybayes, near Tregony.
Clowance, near Redruth.
Coldrinock, near Liskard.
Crockerton House near Callington.
Glyn, near Lostwithiel.
Godolphin Park, near St Hillary.
Gumnap, near Penryn.
Heyworthy, near Launceston.
Lanborn, near St. Columb.

Lany, near St Austle.
Menhilly, near Fowey.
Moivaul House, near St Loo.
Nimphydr House, St Columb.
Pencarrow, near Wadebridge.
Pengeap, near Redruth.
Penheal, near Launceston.
Penrose, near Helston.
Penwarn, near Mevagezey.
Pinealey Park, near Bodmin.
Port Elliot, near St Germains.
Polscow, near Penryn.
Stow, near Kilhampton.
Tehidy, near Redruth.
Tretohis, near Falmouth.
Tregotnan.

Trelawne, near Loo.
Tielowaren, near Helston.
Terence, near St Michaels.
Trevethoe, near Lelant.
Werrington, near Launceston.

The most considerable Towns are from,

Godolphin Hills, near Market Jew.
Hengston Hills.
Launceston Castle.
Madern Hills, near St Ives.
Pendennis and St Mawe's Castle.
St Michael's Mount.
Tintagel Castle.

CUMBERLAND

Is a maritime county, which gives the title of Duke to a branch of the Royal Family, and, during the Saxon heptarchy, belonged to the kingdom of the Northumbrians, though by some supposed to have belonged to the kingdom of Scotland, on the borders of which it is situated. It is now in the province of York, in the dioceses of Chester and Carlisle, and in the Northern circuit. It is 53 miles long, 45 miles broad, and 225 miles in circuit, containing 1,330 square miles, or 979,200 acres, divided into 5 wards, having 58 parishes, one city, Carlisle, which gives the title of Earl to the family of Howard, is a bishop's see, and sends 2 members to parliament, and 14 market-towns, viz. Cockermouth, which gives the title of Baron to the Wyndham family, and sends 2 members to parliament, Egremont, which gives the title of Earl to the same noble family, Penrith, Whitehaven, Keswick, Ravenglass, Alnecster, Holm, Brampton, Alston Moor, Ireby, Kirk-Oswald, Longtown, and Wigton; among the villages, Delaval gives the title of Baron to a family of that name, Greystock, the same honour to the family of Howard, Gillesland, the title of Baron to the same noble family. Its principal rivers are the Eden, Aln, Irt, Petteril, Caude, Derwent, Cocker, Duddon, Leven, Esk, Wiza, and Tyne. Remarkable places in this county are Morecambo Bay, Derwent Foot Haven, and Solway Frith, with Cheviot Hills, Hard Knot Hills, Mole Hill, Dents Hill, Skiddaw Mount, and Wrynose, the Fells, Penrith Fells, Newton Beacon, Derwent, Ulles, and Broad-water Lakes, as well as those of Bassingthwaite, Lowater, Waidale and Dalgarth Lakes, with a few other smaller ones; Geltsdale, Westward, Copeland, and Englewood Forests. This county is very mountainous, and has more Roman antiquities than any other in the kingdom, of which the Picts' Wall, which passes through this county, is no inconsiderable part, built by Adrian in 121, which crossed the whole island from sea to sea about 100 miles, was 8 feet broad, and 12 high, besides which there were 25 strong castles, and all the houses of the nobility and gentry were built castle-wise, to defend them from the incursions of the Scots and Picts; here also ended the Great Roman highway. This county produces black lead, copper, iron, coals, lapis calaminaris, game, fish, &c. and has manufactories of fustians, coarse woollens, linen, &c. It sends 6 members to parliament, viz. 2 for the county, and 4 others as above mentioned, pays one part of the land-tax, and provides 200 men to the national militia. There is a medical spring in Lanecroft.

The most remarkable Seats are,

Alleroy Hall, near Cockermouth
Brayton Hall, near Wigton
Camerton Hall, near Workington,
Clea Hall, near Wigton
Corby Castle, near Carlisle
Crookrake Hall, near Wigton.
Gawbarrow Park, near Penrith
Greystock, near Penrith
Hail Hall, near Egremont.
How Hall, near Ennerdale.
Hutton Park, near Penrith.
Irton, near Ravenglass
Isle, near Cockermouth
Moncastle Hall, near Ravenglass.
Naward Castle, near Brampton
Ulpha Park
Whitehall, near Hesketh.

The most remarkable Views are those from,

Keswick Lake, or Derwent Water, at the Foot of Skiddow
Ullefwater
Irton Hall.
The West Side of Dunmallert Hill
Borrodale, and the Top of Craig Castle.
Lawdown Waterfall and Grange.
Braithwaite Brewes
Beacon Hill, near Penrith
Warnal, near Rose Castle
Mole on Brampton
Bassingthwaite Water
From Ewsbridge.
Blackcomb, near Millum, has an extended view of 100 miles

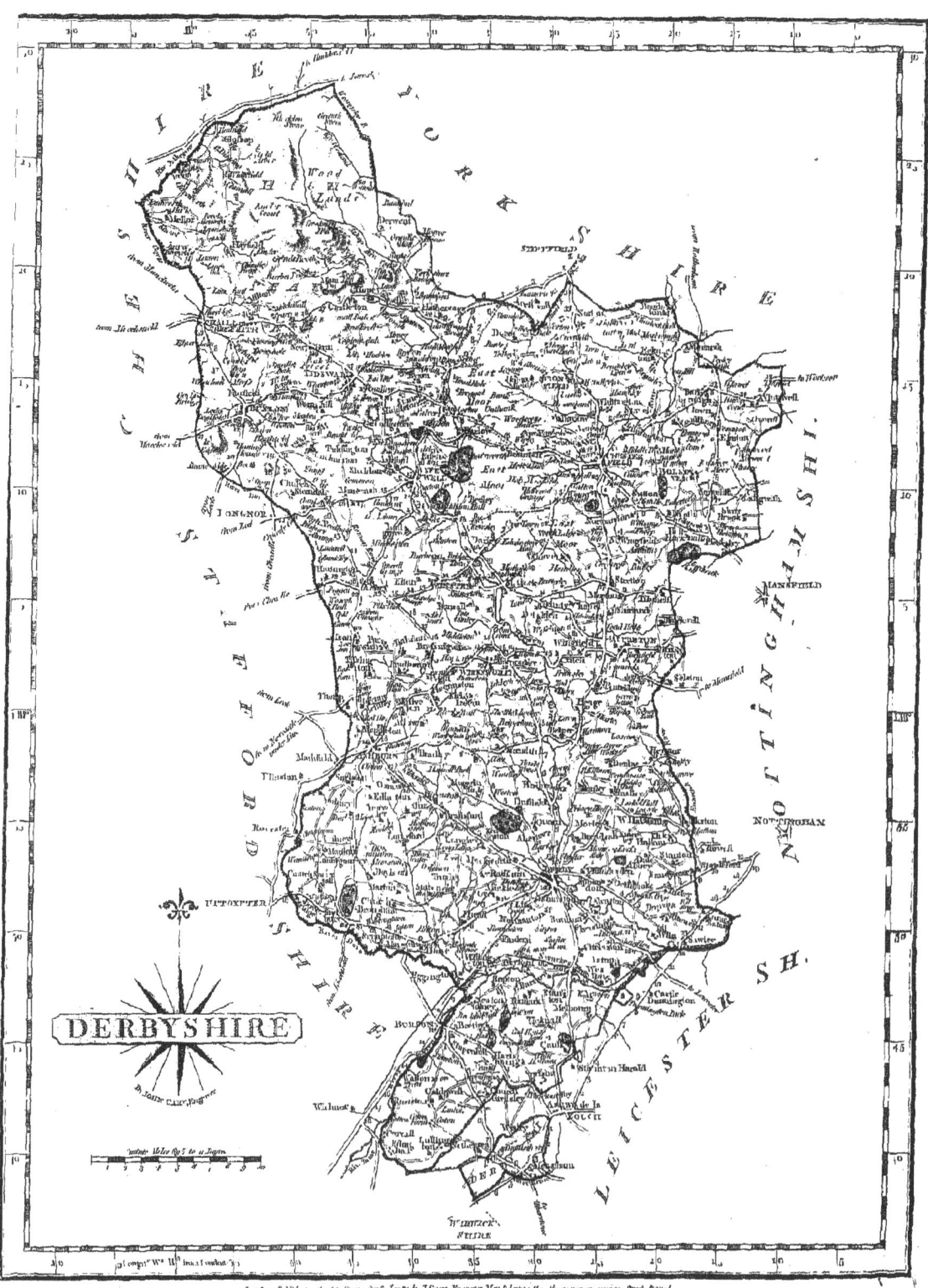

DERBYSHIRE

Is an inland county, whose general figure is nearly triangular, and, during the Saxon heptarchy, belonged to the kingdom of Mercia; is now in the province of Canterbury, the diocese of Litchfield and Coventry, and in the Midland circuit. It is 55 miles long, 34 broad, and 175 in circumference, containing 988 square miles, 632,320 square acres, and is divided into 6 hundreds, 106 parishes, and has 10 market towns, viz. Derby, the county town, which gives the title of Earl to the Stanley family, and sends 2 members to parliament; Chesterfield, which gives the title of Earl to the family of Stanhope, Wirksworth, Bakewell, Ashborne, Bolsover, Alfreton, Chapel in Frith, Dronfield, and Tidefwell: among the villages, Elvafton gives the title of Baron to the Stanhope family, Haddon, that of Baron to the family of Manners, Hartington, that of Marquis to the Cavendish family, Hardwicke, the title of Baron to the Cavendish family also, Stanley, that of Baron to the Murray family, and Scarsdale, that of Baron to the Curzon family. Its principal rivers are the Derwent, Trent, Wye, Lath, Crawlock, Dove, Compton, Rother, Ibber, and Nore. It sends 4 members to parliament, viz. 2 for the county, and 2 for Derby town, pays 6 parts of the land tax, and provides 560 men to the national militia. It produces great quantities of lead, antimony, mill-stones, grinding-stones, marble, alabaster, coarse crystal, azure spar, green and white vitriol, allum, pit coal, and iron. Its chief manufactories are hosiery in silk, cotton, thread, and worsted, China-ware, malt and beer, brown earthen ware, iron, and tobacco pipes, and at Cromford some capital cotton-mills. The western parts on the side of the Derwent, which divides the county into two parts, are barren, chiefly consisting of bleak hills, and its vallies feed great flocks of sheep, and other cattle. The soil of the east and south parts are fertile, and abound with Gentlemens' seats. It has several medicinal springs, viz. Buxton, Quarn, Matlock, &c. with several woods, many parks, and Peak forest. The Peak is the highest hill in England, under which is the cavern called the Devil's Arse, which has a horizontal entrance, 30 feet perpendicular, and at least twice as broad. Near Byrchover is a large rocking stone, 4 yards over, and 12 in circumference, easily moveable by a single person. At the bottom of several mountains are cavities called Swallows, because they receive streams of which there appears no vent. Mam Tor, near Castleton, under which are several lead mines, is a perpendicular height of 123 yards, which is continually crumbling away, and yet does not apparently diminish. Another remarkable, called one of the wonders of the Peak, is Elden-hole, a horrible chasm in the side of a mountain, which, with a line of 884 yards, could not be fathomed. At Tidefwell is a spring that ebbs and flows irregularly. Poole's Hole is a cave at the foot of a mountain called Coitmofs, with a small entrance, but of great extent within, abounding with petrifactions; and near it are two small brooks, whose water is hot and cold, united in one stream, so that you may put your finger in the hot and your thumb in the cold.

The most remarkable Seats are,

Bretby Hall, near Burton
Caulk, near Ashby de la Zouch
Chatsworth Park, near Bakewell
Drakelow, near Burton
Haddon Hall, near Bakewell
Hardwicke Hall, near Bolsover
Kedleston Park, near Derby
Loftou, near Burton
Sudbury Park, near Utoxeter
Sutton, near Bolsover
Warsop Park, near Mansfield
Wingworth Hall, near Chesterfield.

The following Places are remarkable for extensive Views

From the Devil's Arse in the Peak, near Castleton, and the Descent into Hopedale.
Pool's and Elden's Hole, W and N E of Castleton, and from Mam Tor
Matlock, near the Derwent, and from High Tor
Dove Dale, three miles N of Ashbourne
Monsal Dale, two miles N W of Bakewell
Eham, or Middleton Dale, E of Tidefwell.
Upper Dove Dale, five miles N of Ashbourne

Donnington Cliff on the Trent, five miles S E of Derby
Hopping Mill Ware on the Derwent, five miles S E of Derby
Chee Tor, on the Wye, near Buxton
Near Ashford in the Water, in the Road from Tidefwell to Bakewell
Windley Hill between Derby and Wirksworth.

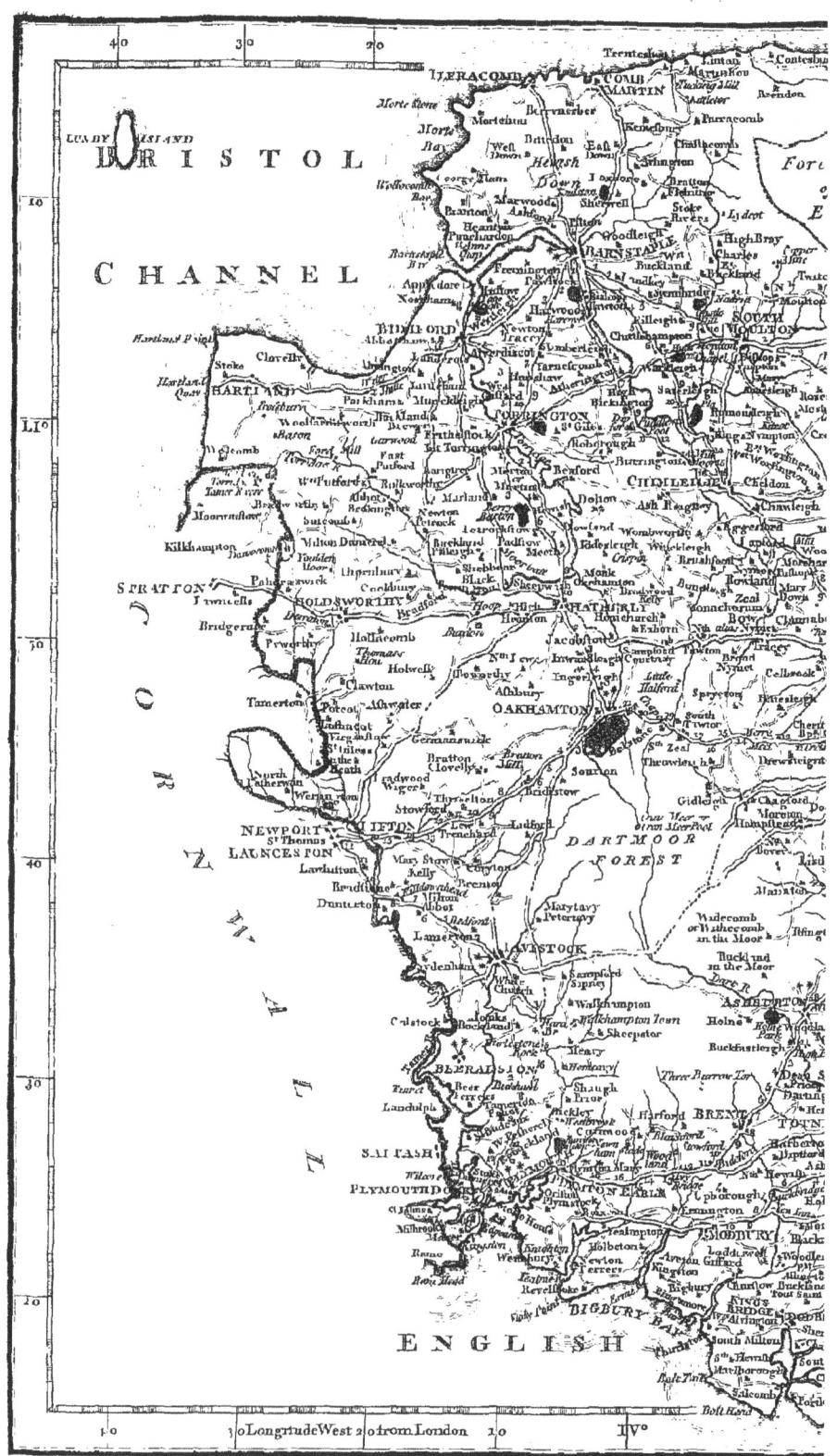

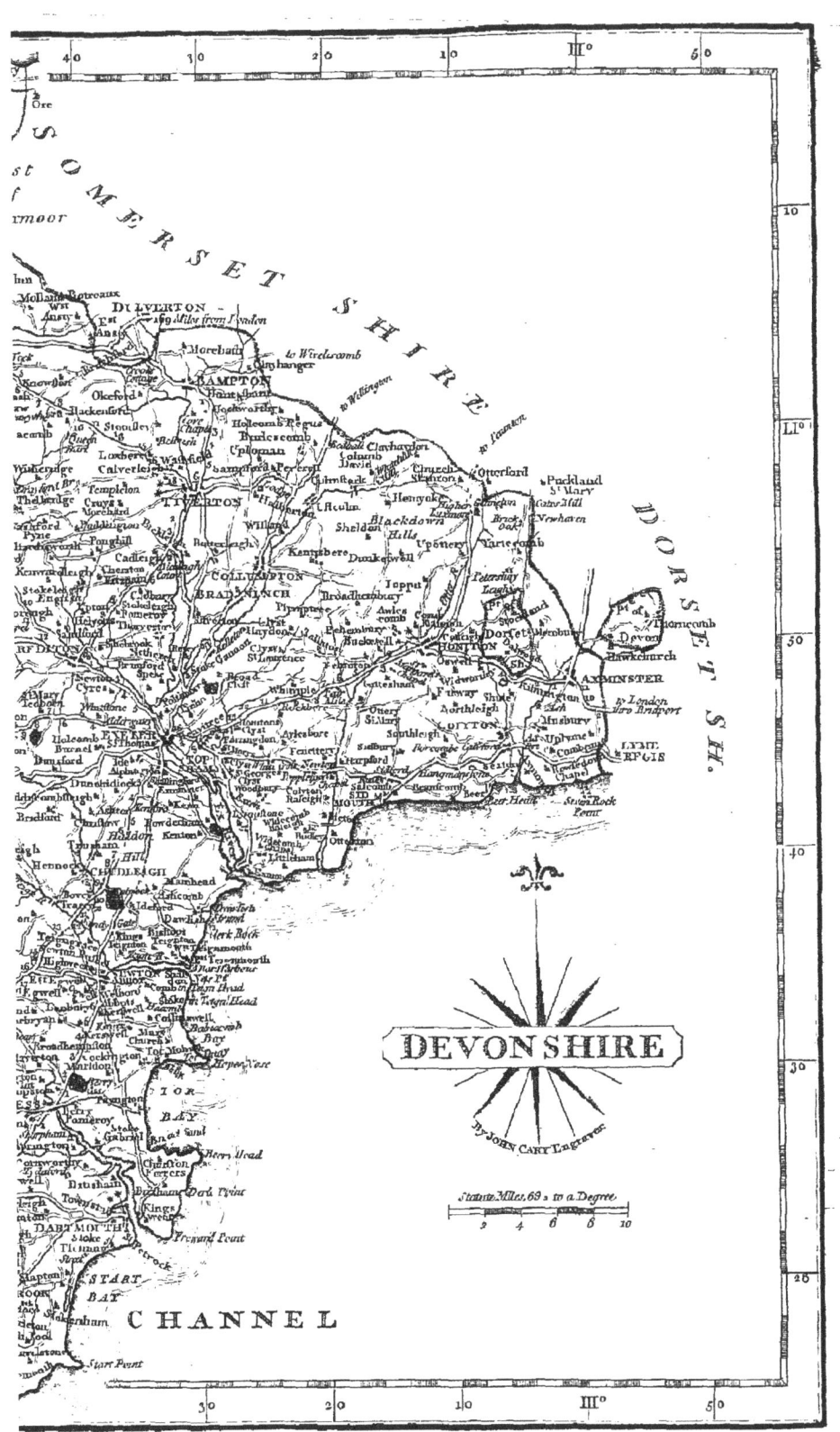

DEVONSHIRE

Is a maritime county, which sends 2 members to parliament, and gives the title of Duke to the family of Cavendish. During the Saxon heptarchy it belonged to the kingdom of the West Saxons; it is now in the province of Canterbury, diocese of Exeter, and is included in the Western circuit. It is 70 miles from North to South, 65 from East to West, and 280 miles in circumference, containing 2520 square miles, or 1,612,800 acres, divided into 33 hundreds, 394 parishes, one city, Exeter, which is a county of itself, is the see of a Bishop, sends 2 members to parliament, and gives the title of Earl to the Cecil family, and 37 market-towns, viz. Plymouth, one of the principal arsenals for the naval stores of the kingdom, which gives the title of Earl to the family of Windsor-Hickman, and sends 2 members to parliament, Tavistock, which sends 2 members to parliament, and gives the title of Marquis to the family of Russel, Dartmouth, sends also 2 members to parliament, and gives the title of Earl and Baron to the family of Legg, Ashburton, which sends 2 members to parliament, and gives the title of Baron to the family of Dunning, Barnstaple, Tiverton, Oakhampton, Honiton, Plympton, Totness, and Beeralston, each send 2 members to parliament, Torrington, gives the title of Viscount to the family of Byng; besides these there are the following market-towns, viz. Crediton, Biddeford, Topsham, Axminster, Bampton, Newton Abbot, Lyston, Bowe, Bradninch, Brent, Kingsbridge, Dodbrook, Chudleigh, which gives the title of Baron to the family of Clifford, Chumley, Columpton, Comb Martin, Culliton, Hartland, Hatherley, Holdsworthy, Ilfracomb, Modbury, Morton, Sidmouth, and Southmolton. The following villages are remarkable for giving the following titles, viz. Edgecumbe, which gives the title of Viscount to the family of the same name, and Boringdon, which gives the title of Baron to the family of Parker. Its rivers are the Time, Exe, Plym, Torridge, Taw, Yalm, Otter, Oke, Dart, Tavy, Aven, Erme, Culm, Teigne, Ax, and Loman. The most remarkable places are Lydford, Cataract, Start, Hartland, Combes, Beg, Brul, Store, and Otterton Points, Bolt Head, Burypoint, Bob's Nose, Lundy Island, Eddistone Rock and Light-House, Tor Bay, Dartmouth Haven, Salcomb Haven, Start Bay, Plymouth Sound, Barnstaple Bay, Portlidge Mouth, Hamoaze, Catwater, St. Nicholas Island, Sutton Pool, Exmore, Æther Rocks, Halden Hills, Crockern Tor, Brent Tor, Dartmore Forest, Morley, &c. It sends 26 members to parliament as already shewn, pays 21 parts of the land-tax, and provides 1600 men to the national militia. It produces copper, tin, lead, iron, timber, slate, marble, free-stone, moor-stone, load-stones, corn, apples, cyder, perry, fowls, game, fish in abundance, pill corn, wild madder, and woad. Its chief manufactures are the different kinds of woollen cloth to an enormous amount. Near Tor Bay is a remarkable well that ebbs and flows, never freezes, is very transparent, and sometimes bubbles up like a boiling pot. In Exeter Cathedral is the largest organ in the world, some of the pipes being 15 inches in diameter. There are mineral waters at Tavistock, Cleave, Lamerton, Brampton, and Leston. The air is sharp and healthy, and the soil hilly, woody, and barren, till rendered fruitful by manure brought from the sea-side.

The chief Seats in this county are,

- Abbey, near Hartford.
- Berry Barton, near Hatherley.
- Berry Pomeroy Castle, near Totness.
- Bickton, near Otterton.
- Blatchford, near Cornwood.
- Buckleigh Court, near Bradninch.
- Castle Hill, near Southmolton.
- Cleave, near Exeter.
- Cockington, near Tor Bay.
- Creedy, near Crediton.
- Downs, near Crediton.
- Eggesford, near Chumleigh.
- Elsott, near Honiton.
- Ford Abby, near Axminster.
- Ford, near Newton Abbot.
- Fursdon, near Silverton.
- Great Fulford, near Dunsford.
- Little Fulford, near Crediton.
- Guttisham, near St Mary Otery.
- Haccombe, near Torbay.
- Halden House, near Exeter.
- Heanton, near Hatherley.
- Heanton Court, near Heanton Punchardon.
- Hymoury Fort, near Honiton.
- Holn Park, near Ashburton.
- Kelleton, near Bradninch.
- Kitley, near Plymouth.
- Mamhead, near Haldown.
- Monks Buckland, near Tavistock.
- Mount Edgecumb, near Plymouth.
- Mount Radford, near Exeter.
- Netherton, near Honiton.
- New Court, near Topsham.
- New Place, near Chumleigh.
- Oaklampton Park, Oakhampton.
- Otterton, near Sidmouth.
- Peamore, near Exeter.
- Pickwell, near Barnstaple.
- Pilton, near Barnstaple.
- Poltimore, near Exeter.
- Powderham Castle, near Starcross.
- Pynes, near Exeter.
- Rockbeer House, near Honiton Clyst.
- Saltren, near Plymouth.
- Slute, near Honiton.
- Stevenstone, near Torrington.
- Tapeley, near Bidesford.
- Tawstock, near Barnstaple.
- Tiverton Castle.
- Wear, near Topsham.
- Werrington House, near Launceston.
- Whiteway, near Chudleigh.
- Zoulston, near Barnstaple.

The most extensive Views and Situations are,

- Æther Rocks on the Edge of Dunmore, near Illington.
- Halden Hill, near Exeter.
- Mamhead Obelisk.
- Bailey House, near Exeter.
- Thatcher Rock, in Torbay.
- Babicombe.
- Between Exeter and Tiverton.
- Knowles Hill, near Newton.
- A Tal Hill, near Ashburton.
- Milberdown, near Newton.
- Stoke Common.
- Oywell Hill, near Newton.
- Near Honiton.
- Eddstone Light House.
- Mount Edgecumbe.
- Castle Walls of Exeter.

DORSETSHIRE

Is a maritime county, which gives the title of Duke and Earl to the family of Sackville, and, during the Saxon heptarchy, belonged to the kingdom of the West Saxons. It is now in the province of Canterbury, diocese of Bristol, and in the Western Circuit. It is 58 miles long, 36 broad, and 200 miles in circumference, containing 1250 square miles, or 800,000 square acres, containing 5 districts, sub-divided into 60 liberties or hundreds, having 250 parishes, and 14 market-towns, viz. Dorchester, the county town, which sends 2 members to parliament, and was formerly a bishoprick, Shaftesbury, sends 2 members to parliament, and gives the title of Earl to the Cooper family, Lyme, sends 2 members to parliament, as does Pool, Bridport, and Wareham, 2 members each, Melcomb-Regis, incorporated with Weymouth, sends four, the latter place gives the title of Viscount to the family of Thynne; the market-towns, besides those before-mentioned, are Milton Abbas, which gives the title of Baron to the family of Damer, Beaminster, Winborne, Cerne, and Sherborne which gives the title of Baron to the Digby family, Corfe Castle, sends 2 members to parliament; and Cranborne, which gives the title of Viscount to the Cecil family, the village of Woodford gives the title of Baron to the family of Strangewrys-Fox, and the Isle of Portland gives the title of Duke and Earl to the family of Bentinck. The most considerable rivers are the Froom, Birt, Piddle, Stour, and Liddon. On the coast are Chesil Bank, Portland Road and Isle, Weymouth and Ringstead Bays, St Alban's Head, Durlston Head, and Swanage Bay, Handfast Point, and Studland Bay, Pool Harbour, Furze, Green and Round Isles, with Branksea, Sandsfoot, and Portland Castles. The most remarkable inland places are the Vale of Whitehart, Marshwood Vale, Whitehart, Gillingham, and Holt Forests, Cranborne Chace, Black Moor, Luckford Lake, and Fordington Moor. The chief product is abundance of sheep, cattle, fowls, and game of every kind, with plenty of river and sea-fish, freestone, marble, marle, timber, and hemp. The manufactures are linen and woollen goods, bone-lace, and tobacco-pipes. This was the county where the Saxons made their first settlement, and in it are upwards of thirty Roman and Saxon camps to be traced. It sends 20 members to parliament, viz. 2 for the county, and 18 as above shewn, pays 9 parts of the land-tax, and provides 640 men to the national militia. The air of this county is in general healthy, and the soil rich and fruitful, and has often been stiled the Garden of England. On the hills it is somewhat sharp, but mild and pleasant in the vallies. Here are extensive woods of very fine timber, especially in the Northern parts of the county.

The most considerable Gentlemens' Seats are,

Abbotsbury
Blandford
Bowridge, near Cranbourn
Came, near Dorchester
Charborough, near Winborn Minster.
Cranbourn
Eastbury House, near Blandford
Horton, near Winborn Minster.
Leweston, near Sherborne
Lytchett Matravers, near Wareham.
Maperton, near Beaminster

Melbury, near Lye shot
Merley, near Winborn Minster
Milbourn St Andrew, near Piddletown.
Milton Abbey, near Piddletown
More Critchill, near Winborn Minster.
Moreton near Piddletown
Parnham, near Beaminster
Sherborne Castle.
Stalbridge
Sydling St Nicholas, near Frampton.
Winborn St. Giles, near Cranbourn.

The most extensive Prospects are from,

A Hill 10 miles from Dorchester in the Road to Exeter
Charmouth Hill, near Lyme.
Chesil Bank
Corfe Castle, in the Isle of Purbeck.
Maumbury, near Dorchester
Portman's Cliff, near Dorchester
Quines, near the Old Church in the Isle of Portland
Ridgeway Hill, near Upway
Shutehill, near Pool
West Lulworth Cove and Dern Door.
Zoatman's Walk under the Rocks.

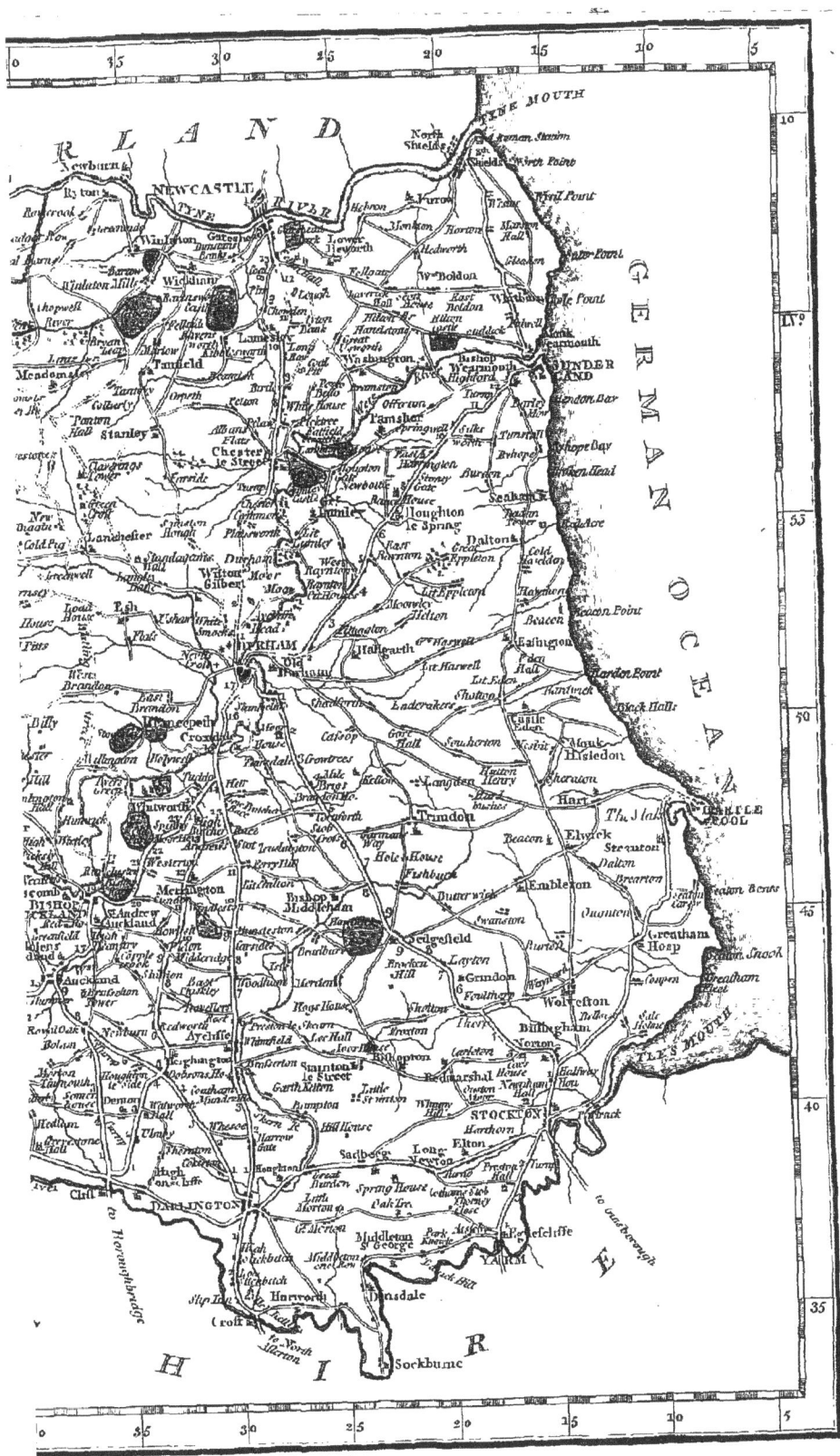

DURHAM

Is a maritime county, with the privileges of a principality, or county palatine, which, during the Saxon heptarchy, made part of the kingdom of the Northumbrians. It is in the diocese of its own name, the province of York, and is included in the Northern circuit. It is 40 miles from East to West, 35 broad from North to South, and 160 in circumference, containing 920 square miles, or 588,800 acres, divided into 4 wards, having 120 parishes, one city, Durham, the see of a Bishop, which sends 2 members to parliament, and 9 market-towns, viz. Barnard Castle, which gives the title of Viscount to the Fane family, Darlington, which gives the title of Earl to the same family, Stanhope, which gives the title of Baron to the family of the same name, Sunderland, which gives the title of Earl to the Spencer family, Stockton, Hartlepool, Auckland, Marwood, Walsingham, and Staindrop. Among the villages, Lumley gives the title of Baron to a family of the same name, as does Harrington in the same manner. The principal rivers are the Tees, Tyne, Were, Tame, Lune, Derwent, Gaundless, and Skern. The most noted places, Sunderland and Hartlepool Points, the Tees Mouth and Tynemouth Harbour and Bar, the Lune and Teesdale Forests, Weredale, and several considerable Hills, Oxenhall Pits, with the Cataract of the Tees River. The soil is various, the South part rich, but the Western rocky and moorish. It produces lead, abundance of coals, iron, excellent corn, and fine pastures, has extensive manufactories of glass, salt, mustard, and fine ale. It sends but 4 members to parliament, viz. 2 for the county, and 2 for the city of Durham, as before mentioned, pays 3 parts of the land-tax, and provides 400 men to the national militia. The air of the county is healthy, but severely cold in winter.

The most remarkable Seats in this county are,

Axwell Park, near Newcastle
Bishop Auckland.
Brancepeth Castle, near Durham
Gateshead Park, near Newcastle.
Grofide, near Newcastle
Hardwick, near Stagefield.
Helton le Hole.
Hilton Castle, near Sunderland
Lambton House, near Durham.
Lumley Castle, near Durham.
Raby Park, near Staindrop.
Ravensworth Castle, near Newcastle
Stanhope Castle.
Streatham Castle, near Barnard Castle
Whitworth, near Bishops Auckland
Windleston, near Bishops Auckland
Wilton Castle, near Bishops Auckland.

The most extensive Views in this County are from

The Banks of the Were, near Durham
Gilygate Church-yard, above the Rare Field, and through Pellew Wood to Old Durham.
Butterby Hill, S of Durham.
The Force of Teesdale
Wilston on the Tees.
New Field, E of Were.
The Black Halls, six miles from Hartlepool.
Miggleswick Park, near the Derwent.

ESSEX

Is a maritime county on the Eastern side of the island, which gives the title of Earl to the Capel family, and during the heptarchy, was comprized in the kingdom of the East Saxons, it now belongs to the province or Canterbury, and diocese of London, and is included in the Home circuit. It is 46 miles long from East to West, 42 miles broad from North to South, and 200 in circuit, containing 1390 square miles, or 889,600 acres, divided into 19 hundreds, including 415 parishes, and 27 market towns, viz Colchester, which sends 2 members to parliament, Harwich, which gives the title of Baron to the family of Hill, and sends 2 members to parliament, Malden which sends 2 members to parliament, and gives the title of Viscount to the Capel family, Rochford gives the title of Earl to the family of Nassau de Zuleftein, Walden, which gives the title of Baron to the family of Griffin, also Chelmsford, where the county business is transacted, Manningtree, Witham, Epping, Barking, Rumford, Billericay, Harlow, Dunmow, Waltham Abbey, Bradfield, Braintree, Brentwood, Rayleigh, Ongar, Coggeshall, Dedham, Greys, Halstead, Hatfield, Horndon, and Thaxsted. The principal rivers are Thames, Black Water, Stour, Coln, Lea, Crouch, Chelmer, and Roding. It sends 8 members to parliament, 6 as above mentioned, and 2 for the county, pays 24 parts of the land-tax, and provides 960 men to the national militia. The most remarkable places are Epping or Waltham, Henhault, Dunmow, Hatfield, and Broad Oak Forests. Its product is saffron, corn, hay, oysters, variety of excellent ith, hops, game, cattle, butter, and wood, and has the manufactures of woollens, gunpowder, and coppers. The air moist, the soil clayey, it has 3 excellent havens, and a great number of elegant villas and parks, among which

The following are most remarkable.

Albury Hall, near Barking
Allyn's, near Chigwell
Arnold's, near Brentwood
Afndon, near Walden
Audley House, near Walden
Aythorp Roding, near Harnfeld
Barking
Barrington Hall, near Hatfield Broad Oak
Birch, near Colchester
Bower Hall, at Steeple Bumpstead
Braxtead, near Witham
Button's, near Rumford
Coptfold Hall, near Ingatstone
Copthall, near Epping
Dagnam Park, near Brentwood
Danbury Place, near Chelmsford
Debden Hall, near Thaxfted
Dew's Hall, near Chigwell
Doryland, near Colchester
Felix Hall, near Kelvedon
Gosfield Hall, near Halstead
Gofton Lodge, near Dunmow
Halingbury Place, near Hatfield Broad Oak
Hyde, near Ingatstone
Ilford, near Barking
Kelvedon Hatch, near Chipping Ongar
Langley's, near Chelmsford

Luxborough House, near Chigwell
Marks, near Rumford
Mistley, near Manningtree
Myles's, near Chipping Ongar
New Hall, near Chelmsford
Navestock Hall, near Chipping Ongar
Newport, near Thaxfted
St Olyth's Priory
Parslow, near Rumford
Pirgo, near Brentwood
Quendon Hall, near Thaxfted
Ravenhill Place, near Coggeshall
Ray Hall, near Chigwell
Rolls, near Chigwell
Shellow Bowell, near Chipping Ongar
Terling Place, near Witham
Thorndall Hall, near Brentwood
Tiptrabes, near Colchester
Vallence, near Rumford
Wilton's near Saffron Walden
Wansted House, Epping Forest
Weald Hall, near Brentwood
Widford, near Chelmsford
Willingale, near Chipping Ongar
Wivenhoe, near Colchester
Writtle Park, near Ingatstone

The most remarkable Situations and Views are,

Afhder Parsonage House, near Linton
Barlow Hills
Beaumont, near Walton
Borley Church, near Sudbury
Great Bradfield Church, near Thaxfted
Little Chesterford Manor House, near Walden
Between Billericay and Chelmsford
Chigwell Row, near Chigwell
Chingford, near Epping Forest
Corringham, near the Hope
Danbury Hill, near Boreham
Easton Lodge, near Dunmow
Horndon or the Hill
Kelvedon Hall, near Ongar
Langdon Hills, near Horndon
Lafton, near Sudbury
Mount Beres, near Earl's Colne
Ongar Castle
Purley, near Malden
Raleigh Castle
Southchurch Wick, near Rochford
Tolleshunt Knights, near Malden
Wansted on Epping Forest
Warley House, near Brentwood
Great Wigborough Church, near Colchester

GLOCESTERSHIRE

IS an inland county, which, during the Saxon heptarchy, belonged to the kingdom of Mercia. It is now in the province of Canterbury, the diocese of its own name, and is included in the Oxford circuit. It contains 1300 square miles, or 832,000 acres, being 63 miles long, 47 broad, and 260 miles in circumference, divided into 30 hundreds, 280 parishes, one city, Glocester, the see of a bishop, which sends 2 members to parliament, and gives the title of Duke to a branch of the Royal family. In this county is the greatest part of the city of Bristol, which is also a bishop's see, sends 2 members to parliament, and gives the title of Earl to the Hervey family, but, being a county by itself, does not belong to this county. It has 26 market-towns, viz. Tewksbury, which sends 2 members to parliament, Cirencester, which also sends 2 members to parliament, gives the title of Baron to the family of Bentinck, Berkeley, gives the title of Earl to the family of the same name, Fairford, gives the title of Viscount to the family of Hill, Campden, gives the title of Viscount to the family of Noel, and Dursley, the title of Viscount to the family of Berkeley; besides which towns there are the following, viz. Colford, Dean, Stow, Wickwar, Lechlade, Marshfield, Cheltenham, Sodbury, Minchin Hampton, Newent, Northleach, Painswick, Stanley, Stroud, Tetbury, Thornbury, Winchcomb, Wotton, and Bisley. Amongst the villages the following places give titles, viz. Avalon, that of Viscount to the Mordaunt family, Clarendon, that of Earl to the family of Villiers, Hardwick, that of Earl and Baron to the family of Yorke, Hawkesbury, that of Baron to the family of Jenkinson, Tortworth, that of Baron to the family of Moreton, Sherborne, that of Baron to the family of Dutton, and Sudley Castle, that of Baron to the Brydges family, and St. Leonard's, the same title to that of Townshend. The rivers are the Severn, Wye, Coln, Chern, Stroud, eminent for dying scarlet, Isis, Avons, Fromes, Swilate, Caron, Windrush, Evendole, Leven, Lache, Isbourne, Chilt, Badgworth, Evelm, Berkeley, and Trim. In the river Severn are the Isles of Condicote, and the Alney. The most noted places are Kingroad and the Pill, St. Vincent's Rocks, Cotswold Hills, 450 yards above the Severn, and Downs, Vale of Stroud Water, Vale of Evesham, Dean and Kingwood Forests, Mycklewood Chace, and Cross Wood. Its product is coal and iron, cattle, sheep, excellent wool, corn, timber, salmon, and other river fish. Its chief manufactures are excellent cheese, stockings, mustard balls, mens hats, leather, pins, paper, iron ware, tinned plates, brass, steel, and variety of woollens. There are mineral waters at Cheltenham, at St. Anthony's Well at Abenhall, at Barrow and Moreden near Rodington, at Ash-church near Tewkesbury, at Dumbleton near Winchcomb, at Lasington near Dursley, and those of Bristol Wells near Cliston. It sends 8 members to parliament, 2 for the county, and 6 for those above-mentioned, it pays 12 parts of the land-tax, and provides 960 men to the national militia.

The most considerable Gentlemens' Seats are,

Ampney, near Cirencester
Badminton, near Sodbury
Barnesley Park, near Cirencester
Berkeley Castle
Cirencester Park
Coberly, near Cheltenham
Compton Park, near Northleach
Cromehall, near Thornbury
Dean Magna
Doddington, near Sodbury
Fairford Park
Flaxley, near Little Dean
Hatherop, near Fairford
High Meadow, near Coleford
Highnam, near Glocester
King's Weston, near Bristol
Knowle, near Thornbury
Lidney, near Blakeney
Miserden, near Stroud
Pinbury Park, near Cirencester
Prinknash Park, near Glocester
Rendon Park, near Chichester
Rencomb Park, near Chichester
Sandywell Park, near Chelton
Sorbourne Lodge and Park, near Northleach

Spoonhall, near Coleford
Spring Park, near Leonard Stanley
Stowell, near Northleach
Tudington Park, near Winchcombe.
Whitecliffe Park, near Berkley
Welcome Park, near Glocester

The most remarkable Views, Scenes, and Situations are from,

Kambsborough Castle Hill, or Castle Godwin, near Painswick, S. of Glocester
Alveston, or Alniston, near Aust Ferry, on a Hill called the Old Abbey
Frocester Hill, S W of Stanley, on the Road from Bath to Glocester
The Road from Glocester to Newnham
St. Vincent's Rock and Clifton, near Bristol Hot Wells
Brandon Hill, near Bristol
Bibury, on the Road between Cirencester and Burford
Crickley Hill, on the Road from Oxford to Glocester
Stinchcombe Hill, near Dursley
May Hill, between Glocester and Ross.

Birdlip Hills, 5 miles S E of Glocester on the Road to Chester
Barrow Hill, near the Severn, N of Berkeley, near Bedington. From hence 36 churches are visible.
Churchdon, near Bristol
Painswick Hill, 4 miles S E of Glocester, and thence to the left through Painswick Wood into the Birdlip Road
Broad Bridge Green, near Hareshield, 4 miles S of Glocester
Blaise Castle, near Henbury, 3 miles N W of Bristol
Shunlow Hill, 4 miles N W of Banbury
Staunton Hill, 3 miles E of Monmouth
Tower Hill, near Tytherington, S of Thornbury
Wootton, 4 miles N of Cheltenham, 3 miles W of Winchcomb
Bromeway Hill, on the Road between Moreton and Evesham
Woolhope Hill, in the Malvern Road, 4 miles N W. of Glocester
Robin Hood's Hill, 2½ miles S E of Glocester
Lancrof Hill, on the Wye, 1½ mile from Chepstow.
Abenhill, near the Severn, 5 miles from Glocester
Little Dean.

HAMPSHIRE

Is a maritime county on the south coast of the kingdom, which, during the Saxon heptarchy, belonged to the kingdom of Wessex, is now included in the province of Canterbury, the diocese of Winchester, and the Western Circuit. Including the Isle of Wight, it is 55 miles long from North to South, 40 miles broad from East to West, and 220 in circumference. It contains 1540 square miles, or 985,600 acres, including also the Isle of Wight, divided into 39 hundreds, 250 parishes, one city, Winchester, which sends 2 members to parliament, and gives the title of Marquis to the Powlett family, and 20 market towns, viz. Southampton, which sends 2 members to parliament, and gives the title of Baron to the Fitzroy family, Portsmouth, which sends 2 members to parliament, and gives the title of Earl to the Wallop family, Andover, which gives the title of Viscount to the Howard family, and sends 2 members to parliament, Lymington, which sends 2 members to parliament, and gives the title of Viscount to the family of Wallop; Christchurch, which sends 2 members to parliament, as does Stockbridge, Whitchurch, and Petersfield, with Newport, and Yarmouth, in the Isle of Wight, but the following market towns do not send representatives, viz. Basingstoke, Alresford, Alton, Fareham, Havant, Kingsclere, Odingham, Ringwood, Rumsey, and Waltham. Among the villages Titchfield gives the title of Marquis to the Bentinck family, Portchester, the title of Baron to the Herbert family, and Basing, the title of Baron to the family of Powlett. Newton, in the Isle of Wight, sends 2 members to parliament though no market town. The Isles of Jersey and Guernsey are both subject to the jurisdiction of the Bishop of Winchester, and are included as parts of this county, the former of which gives the title of Earl to the family of Villiers, and the latter that of Baron to the Finch family. This county sends 26 members to parliament, viz. 2 for the shire, and the others as expressed above, pays 14 parts of the land tax, and provides 960 men to the national militia. Its principal rivers are the Ithing or Alre, the Tees or Test, Anton, Avon, Stour, Wey, Lodoon, and Auborn. It has the harbours of Spithead, Portsmouth, St Helen's, East Cowes, Hampton Water or Southampton Bay, Titchfield Bay, Langston and Hamble Havens, &c., with a great number of ports, headlands, isles, forts, castles, &c. This county has also New Forest, near 30 miles in circuit, Wulmer, and 7 others, with a great number of parks, downs, &c. Its chief product is corn, cattle, pastures, wood, iron, wool, fish, and hops. It is noted for its honey, and the best bacon in the kingdom. It has manufactures of woollen, and contains the extensive magazine of naval stores at Portsmouth. The air of this county is fertile and healthy and abounds with extensive views and elegant villas, among which

The following are the most considerable:

Appuldercomb, Isle of Wight
Ashley Lodge, near Fordingbridge.
Avington, near Alresford
Bedvere, near Southampton
Bevis Mount, near Southampton
Boltorn, New Forest
Bentwood, near New Forest
Bolderwood Lodge, New Forest
Bramble Hill, near Fordingbridge
Bramshill Park, near Heckfield.
Buttlesford, Isle of Wight
Buxley Lodge, New Forest
Cadland Park, upon the New Forest
Canton Park, near Kingsclere.
Chapman's Ford, near Winchester
Clinton Cardover
Dogmersfield, near Odiham
Dinny Lodge, New Forest
East Stretton
Evelham
Farnborough
Freemantle Park

Gatcombe House, Isle of Wight
Grange, near Alresford
Hackwood Park, near Basingstoke
Havant Park
Headly Park, near Alton
Heckfield Park, near Odiham
High Cliff, near Christ Church.
Holmesley, New Forest
Hurstley Lodge, near Winchester
Ive Lodge, near Fordingbridge
Idsworth Park
Maliwood Lodge, near West Minsted.
New Park, New Forest
Pi Place, Isle of Wight
Pilton, near Rumsey
Ringfield Lodge, New Forest
Rotherfield, near Alton
Southwick Park, near Fareham
North Stoneham, near Southampton
Red Rice, near Andover
Stratfield Saye Park, near Odiham
Stubbington, near Crofton.

Sydmonton, near Kingsclere.
Tilney Hall, near Odiham
Walbury, near Comb.
Wulverton, near Winchester

The most remarkable Views and Situations are,

Portsdown, five miles North of Portsmouth
West Lodge, in Bere Forest.
The Needle Rock and the West End of the Isle of Wight, seen from the sea, with the Cavern
From Freshwater, six miles from Yarmouth
Between Cowes and Newport, and thence to Hurst Stoke
Shanklin Chine.
Ashley Down
Nunwell Down
From Ryde and Trobleheld, as well as from Appuldercomb Cliff
From Dur Nose on the South East Coast
From Carisbrook Castle

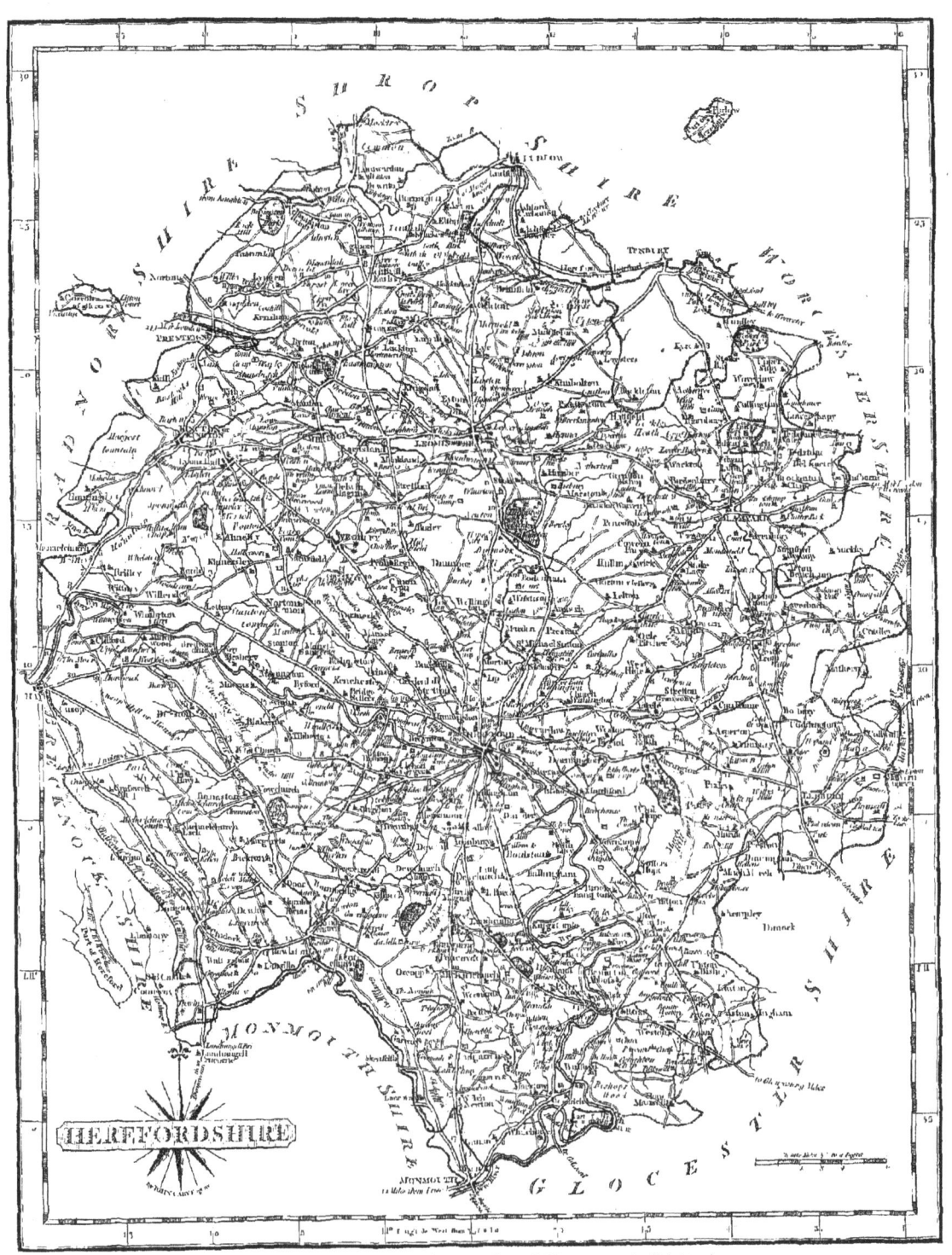

HEREFORDSHIRE

Is an inland county, which, during the Saxon heptarchy, belonged to the kingdom of Mercia. It is now in the province of Canterbury, the diocese of its own name, and in the Oxford circuit, being 46 miles long, 40 miles broad, and 220 miles in circumference, containing 1200 square miles, or 768,000 acres, divided into 11 hundreds, 176 parishes, one city, Hereford, which is the fee of a bishop, gives the title of Viscount to the family of Devereux, and sends 2 members to parliament, and 7 market-towns, viz. Leominster or Lempster, which gives the title of Viscount to the family of Fermor, and sends 2 members to parliament, Ross, which gives the title of Baron to the Herbert family, Weobley, which sends 2 members to parliament, Pembridge, Lidbury, Bromyard, and Kineton. Its rivers are the Wye, Lugg, Munnow, Arrow, Frome, Don, Leddon, and Tame. The most noted places are Marsha Hill, Malvern Hills, Hatterd Hills, Frome Hill, Black Mount, Gilden Vale, Bringwood Chace, Hawood and Derefold Forests, Creden Hill, Brynmaur Wood, and several Castles. It sends 8 members to parliament, 2 for the county, and 6 as abovementioned, pays 5 parts of the land-tax, and provides 480 men to the national militia. Before the Conquest, this county was reckoned a part of Wales, and being then a frontier between England and Wales, it had 28 strong castles, a few of which now remain. It boasts that it exceeds in wood, wheat, wool, and water, and the best cyder of all the counties in England. Its principal manufacture is in iron. The climate is very healthy, and the county abounds with ancient encampments. It enjoys some medicinal springs, particularly near Leominster and Malvern Hills.

The principal Gentlemens' Seats are,

Alienfmoor, near Hereford.
Benington, near Leominster
Bill Mill, near Ross
Brompton Bryan, near Presteign.
Bucknall, near Bromyard.
Cannon Bridge, near Hereford.
Crof Castle, near Leominster
Devereux Park, near Hereford
Laton Bishop, near Hereford.
Eywood, near Kineton
Foxley, near Weobley
Garnstone, near Weobley
Hampton Court, near Leominster.
Harewood, near Ross
Hay Park, near Ludlow
Haywood House, near Hereford.
Hill, near Ross.

Holm Court, near Hereford
Hom, near Weobley
Kinnerfley, near Kineton
Lyons Hall, near Kineton
Meend Park, near Hereford
Moccas.
Morehampton Park, near Hereford.
Newport, near Kineton
Pengethley, near Ross
Slebdon Court, near Presteign.
Street, near Pembridge
Tillington, near Hereford.
Urifh Hay
Whitefield, near Hereford
Woverlow Park, near Bromyard.

The Views that are most remarkable are from,

Hampton Court Park
The Gilden Vale on the Dore, W of Hereford
Creden hill, near Kenchester
The Ambrey in Croft Castle Park, on the Lugg, W. N W of Leominster
Copley-hill, near Holm Lacy
Ross Church
Sutton Walls from the Hill on the Lugg, N. of Hereford.
Brynmour Wood, near Hereford
The Road from Ross to Monmouth, viz.
Goodrick Castle
Coldwell Rocks
Symond's Yate.
River Dean Church
New Wear.
Longstone.

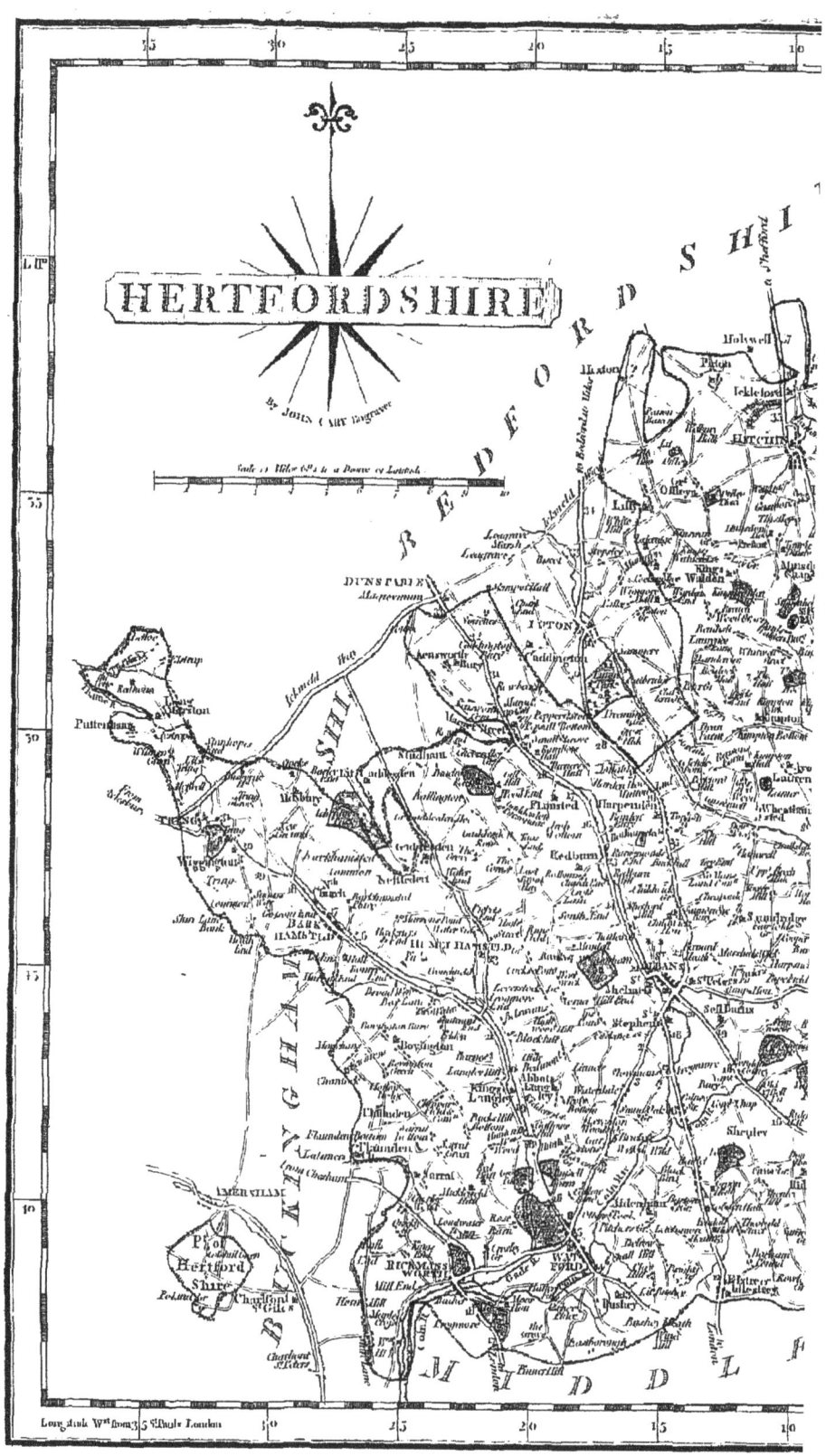

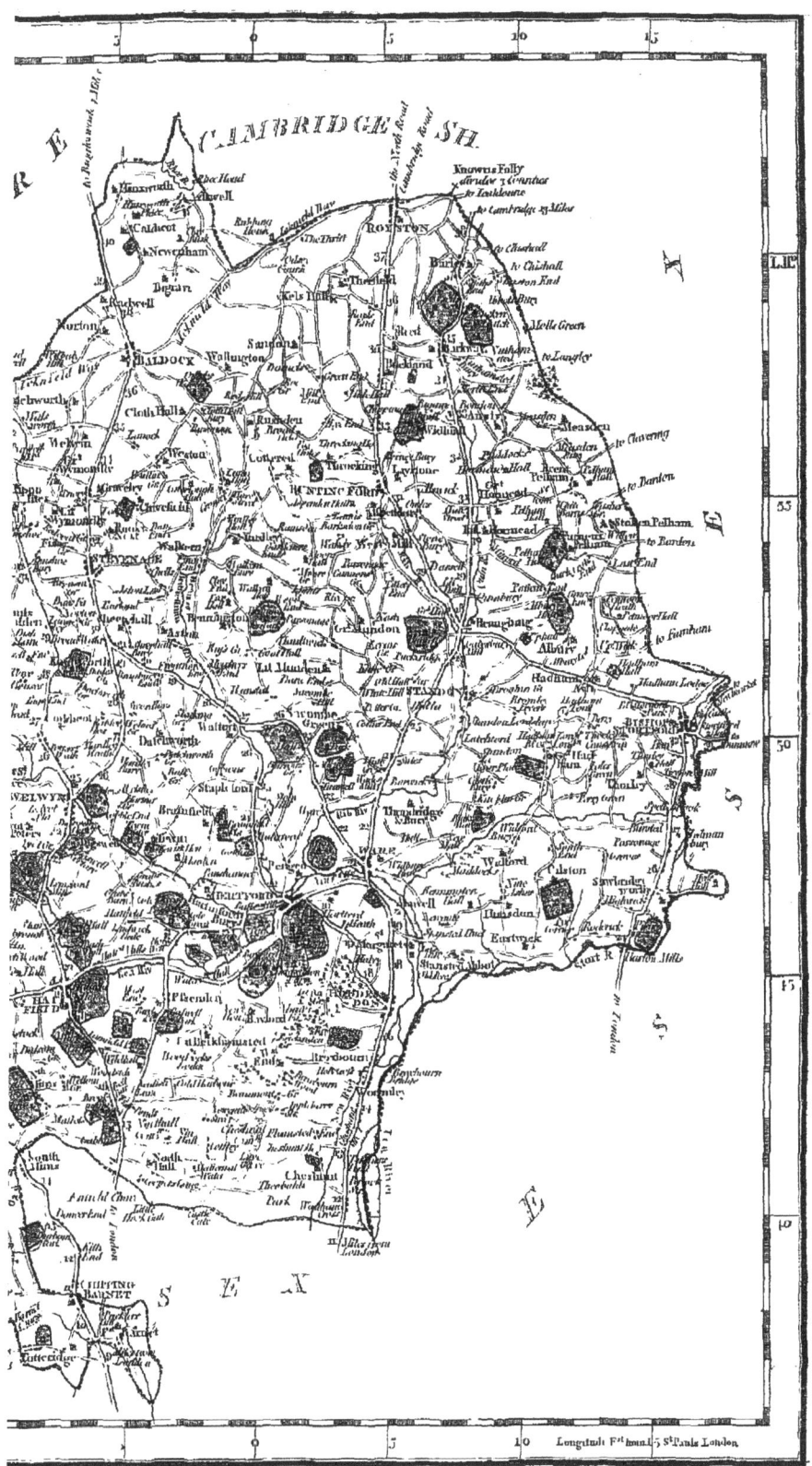

HERTFORDSHIRE

Is an inland county, which, during the Saxon heptarchy, belonged part to the kingdom of East Saxons, and the other part to the Mercians. It is now included in the province of Canterbury, in the dioceses of Lincoln and London, and in the Home circuit. Its form is nearly circular, being 35 miles from East to West, 27 miles from North to South, and 190 in circuit, containing 660 square miles, or 422,400 acres, divided into 8 hundreds, 120 parishes, and 18 market towns, viz. Hertford, the county town, which sends 2 members to parliament, and gives title of Earl to the Conway family; St Alban's, which sends 2 members to Parliament, and gives the title of Duke to the Beruclerk family; part of Royston, which gives the title of Viscount to the family of Yorke, and part of Barnet, with Ware, Hitchin, Baldock, Bishop's Stortford, Berkhamstead, Buntingford, Hemel Hampstead, Hatfield, Hoddesdon, Rickmansworth, Standon, Stevenage, Tring, and Watford. The principal rivers are the Lea, Coln, Stort, Gade, Bean, Tame, Rib, and the New River, which supplies London with water. This county sends 6 members to parliament, 2 for the shire, and the other 4 as above shewn; pays 11 parts of the land tax, and provides 560 men to the national militia. It has several fine woods, mineral springs, and a great number of beautiful parks, &c. Its products are fat cattle, sheep, and river fish. Its air being temperate, sweet, and healthful, and the soil fertile and rich, it abounds with elegant seats.

The most remarkable of which are,

Albury Hall, near Albury
Ashridge Park, near Gaddesden
Balls, near Hertford
Bayford Bury, near Hertford
Beechwood Park, near Gaddesden
Bedwell Park, near Essenden
Blake's Ware, near Ware
Brainfield Place, near Hertford
Buckerdonbury, near Hertford
Brocket Hall, near Wheathampstead
Brookman's, near North Mims
Broxbournbury, near Hoddesdon
Bury Park, near Rickmansworth
Bush Hall, near Hatfield
Camfield Place, near Hatfield
Cashiobury Park, near Watford
Cheshunt House
Chivefield Lodge, near Stevenage
Cockennatch, near Barkway
Cole green Park, near Hertford
Digswell, near Welwyn
Gobions, near Welham Green
Goldens, near Hertford
Gothambury, near St Alban's
Grove Park, near Watford

Hamells, near Watford
Huntingfordbury Park, near Hertford
Hatfield House, near Hatfield
Hoo, near Kimpton
King's Walden Park, near Preston
Knebworth Place, near Stevenage
Lamer Place, near Welwyn
Lockey's, near Welwyn
Millie's Park, near Hatfield
Moor Park, near Rickmansworth
Moor Place, near Bishop's Stortford
New Place, near Ware
Newsell's, near Royston
North Mims Place
Offley Place, near Hitching
Panshanger, near Hertford
Pelham Hall, near Pelham
Pishobury, near Sawbridgeworth
Pope's, near Hatfield
Porter's, near Shenley
Quick's Wood, near Watlington
Rothamsted, near Redburn
Roxford, near Hertford
Russel's Farm, near Watford
Sacombe Park, near Ware

Stagenhoe Park, near Stevenage
Temple, near Ware
Tewin House, near Welwyn
Tewin Water, near Welwyn
Tittenhanger, near London Colney
Totteridge, near Barnet
Tring House
Throcking, near Buntingford
Ware Park
Wood Hall, near Hatfield
Wood Hall, near Ware
Woolman's, near Hertford

The most remarkable and extensive Views are from

Bushy Heath, N W of Edgworth
Brockley Hill, near Stanmore
Little Gaddesden
Ashridge Park
Kingworth Green, S of Dunstable
A little S E of Ivinghoe
Brookman's, near North Mims
Knebworth, near Stevenage

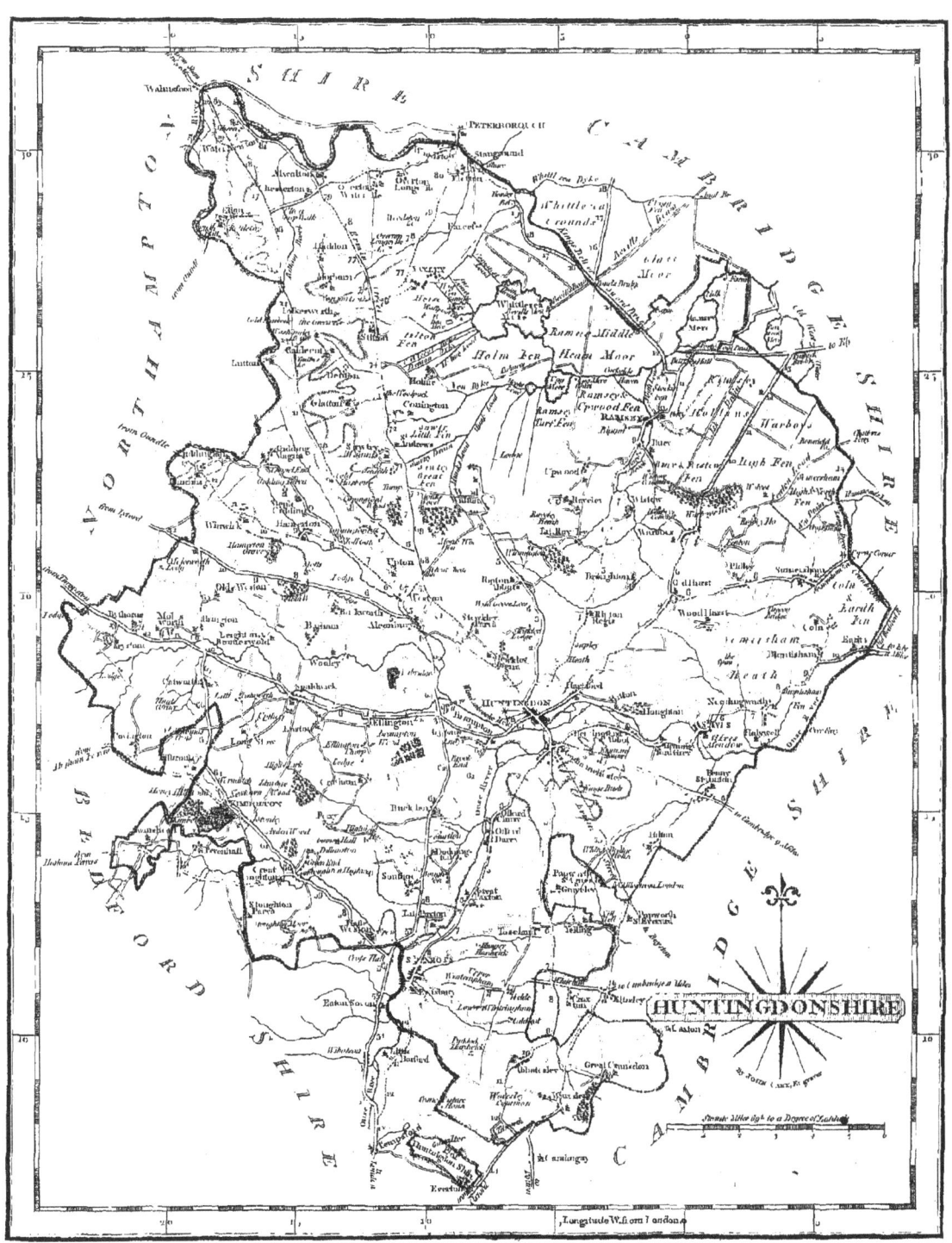

HUNTINGDONSHIRE

Is an inland county, which, during the Saxon heptarchy, belonged to the kingdom of Mercia; it is now in the province of Canterbury, diocese of Lincoln, and included in the Norfolk circuit. It is 30 miles long, 24 broad, and 130 in circuit, containing 414 square miles, 264,960 acres, divided into 4 hundreds, 78 parishes, and 6 market towns, viz Huntingdon, the county town, which sends 2 members to parliament, and gives the title of Earl to the family of Hastings; Kimbolton, which gives the title of Baron to the Montagu family; St Neots, which gives the title of Baron to another branch of the Montagu family; Ramsey, Yaxley, and St Ives among the villages, Hinchinbroke gives the title of Viscount to another branch of the Montagu family. It sends 4 members to parliament, 2 for the county, and 2 as shewn above; pays 4 parts of the land-tax, and sends 350 men to the national militia. The principal rivers are the Ouse, Nen, and Cam, with some smaller streams. The most remarkable places are King's Delf and Dykes, Ramsey, Whittlesea, Benwick, Brig, and Ug Meers, Wabridge Forest, with Salom and Alconbury Woods. This is one of the 7 counties that are contiguous without a city in either, viz Bedford, Huntingdon, Bucks, Berks, Hertford, Essex, and Suffolk. The products of this county are corn, cattle, wood, game, fish from the meers, rich pasture, excellent cheese, and fine butter. The soil is rich, and the air, except in fenny parts, good. Huntingdon is remarkable for having been the birth-place of Oliver Cromwell, and St. Ives for the largest market in England for cattle, except Smithfield, and at Warbois are the most beautiful meadows on the banks of the Ouse that are to be seen in England. This county formerly was the greatest part of it forest land, and peculiarly adapted to the Chase, whence the name of the county took its rise.

The most considerable Gentlemens' Seats are,

Brampton, near Huntingdon	Godmanchester, near Huntingdon	Little Paxton, near St Neots
Bugden Palace, near Huntingdon	Grafham, near Kimbolton	Longthorpe, near Peterborough.
Bushmead, near Stoughton Parva	Great Stoughton	St Neots.
Caststerton, near Alwalton	Hertford, near Huntingdon	Overton Longville, near Peterborough.
Doddington	Hinchinbroke House, near Huntingdon	Ramsey Abbey
Elton Hall, near Elton	St Ives.	Ripton Abbots, near Stewkley
Fenney Staunton, near St Ives.	Kimbolton Castle.	Washingley House, near Caldecot.

KENT

Is a maritime county, at the south east extremity of the kingdom, being separated from Flanders and Holland by the Straits of Dover. During the Saxon heptarchy, this county was an entire kingdom, and its kings kept their court at Canterbury, which now is an archbishoprick, and the primary of all England. It is in the dioceses of Canterbury and Rochester, and is included in the Home circuit. Its form is an irregular oblong, 65 miles long from east to west, 37 broad from north to south, and 195 miles in circuit, containing 1500 square miles, or 960,000 acres, divided into 5 laths, that are subdivided in 62 hundreds, comprizing 418 parishes, and 2 cities, viz. Canterbury, the seat of the metropolitan see, which sends 2 members to parliament, and Rochester, the see of a bishop, that sends 2 members also to parliament, 35 market-towns, viz. Maidstone, the county town, sends 2 members to parliament, and gives the title of Viscount to the Finch family; Chatham, which gives the title of Earl and Baron to the family of Pitt, one of the completest arsenals in the world for naval stores. Queenborough, which sends 2 members to parliament; Dover, a cinque port, where the packets are stationed for France, &c.; Sandwich, another cinque port, which gives the title of Earl to the Montagu family; Romney, also a cinque port, which gives the title of Baron to the Marsham family; Hythe, which is also a cinque port, each of which, as cinque ports, sends 2 members to parliament; Tunbridge, remarkable for its medical waters, gives the title of Viscount to the Nassau de Zulestein family; Fordwich, which gives the title of Viscount to the Cowper family; Feversham, Folkstone, which gives the title of Viscount to the family of Bouverie; Aylesford, gives that of Earl to the Finch family; Greenwich, distinguished by its royal Park, and observatory, and a most noble hospital for superannuated seamen, gives the title of Baron to the Townshend family; Woolwich, eminent for its dock-yards, elaboratory, &c. and being the mother-dock of the royal navy of Great Britain; Deal, where Cæsar landed in his descent on Britain; Gravesend, whence all shipping from London take their departure for foreign voyages; Milton, remarkable for its oysters sent to London; Appledore, Dartford, Ashford, which gives the title of Baron to the Keppel family; Bromley, Cranbrook, Eltham, Goudhurst, Lenham, Lidd, Malling, Sevenoak, Smarden, Tenterden, Westram, Wrotham, Wye, Northfleet, and Eleham. among the numerous considerable villages, Sundridge gives the title of Baron to the Campbell family; Lewisham, that of Viscount to the Legg family; Eastwell, that of Baron to the Finch family; Camden, which gives the title of Earl and Baron to the Pratt family, and the Isle of Thanet gives the title of Earl to the Tufton family. Its rivers are the Thames, Medway, Stour, Rother, Darent, Tun, Ravensbourne, and Wantsham. The most noted places are the North and South Forelands, Dungeness, Oxney, Thanet and Shepey Isles, Isle of Grains, the Downs, Godwin Sands, Sheerness Fort, and several castles, more particularly that of Dover, and St Margaret, Hope, and Hythe Bays, &c &c. It produces cattle, sheep, wild-fowl, iron, corn, hops, wood, cherries, and all other fruits and garden stuffs, excellent fish, chalk, timber, sand for the glass manufactories, &c. &c. The most remarkable places are Shooter's Hill, Mount Zion, Mount Ephraim, Idle Hill, Camphurst and Randall Woods, Blackheath, where is Morden College, with Greenwich Park, Romney Marsh, Weald of Kent, &c. &c. It has a great number of Roman, Saxon, and Danish encampments, and other antiquities, and the waters of Tunbridge are much resorted to by invalids. In the large space that this county covers there is a great diversity of soil. It sends 18 members to parliament, 2 for the county, and 16 as above shewn, pays 22 parts of the land tax, and provides 960 men to the national militia.

This county abounds with Gentlemens' Seats, the most remarkable are,

Aylesford Place.
St Alban's
Bedgebury, near Goudhurst
Beverley Park, near Canterbury
Boughton Place, near Maidstone
Chepsted Place, near Sevenoak.
Chilham, near Wye.
Chiliton, near Lenham.
Cobham Hall, near Rochester
Como Bank, near Sundridge
Danson Hall, near Dartford
Dean Park, near Canterbury
Eastwell Park, near Ashford
Ford Park, near Wye.
Gabriel's House, near Edenbridge
Greenwich
Goddington, near Ashford
Great Ollantigh, near Wye.
Gunston Place, Gunston
Halsted Place, near Sevenoak
Hayes, near Bromley
Hothfield Place, near Ashford.
Hunton Park, near Maidstone
King's Oaks, near Ramsgate

Knole, or Knowl Park, near Sevenoak
Knowlton Court, Knowlton
Langley, near Bromley
Lee House, near Bleakburn.
Lee Place, near Greenwich
Leed's Abbey, near Lenham
Leed's Castle, near Lenham
Linton Lodge, near Feversham.
Linton Place, near Boughton Monchelsea
Lillingstone Park
Mereworth Castle, East Peckham
Mersham Hatch, near Ashford.
Mote Park, near Maidstone
The Mote, near Canterbury
Nash, near Feversham.
Ottesden Place, near Lenham
Penshurst Place, near Tunbridge.
Roydon Hall, near East Peckham
Smethe Field, near Ashford
Somer Hill, near Tunbridge
Squerries near Westerham
Surrenden, near Ashford
Walde sham, near Dover
Walmer Castle, near Deal

The most remarkable Situations for extensive Prospects are,

Beachborough, near Folkstone
Boughton Hill, W of Canterbury
Boxley Hill, four miles from Maidstone to Rochester
Dover Castle and Cliffs
From Ramsgate to Broadstairs
Frendsbury to Upnor on the Medway.
Greenwich Park
Goudhurst, on every side
The High Grounds near Chatham
Macam's Court Hill, near Sevenoak
Minster Church Yard in the Isle of Shepey.
Northfleet, S. W. of Gravesend
Otford Palace, near Sevenoak.
The Ramparts at Sheerness
Rivers, a village near Dover
St Margaret's Bay, N E of Dover
Shooter's Hill
Shorne and Tarong, near Rochester
Windmill Hill, near Gravesend.

LANCASHIRE

IS a maritime county and a county palatine, which, during the Saxon heptarchy, belonged to the kingdom of Northumberland; it is now in the province of York, the diocese of Chester, and Northern circuit. It is 73 miles long, 41 broad, and 230 in circumference, containing 1,700 square miles, or 1,088,000 acres, divided into 6 hundreds, 61 parishes, and 26 market-towns, viz. Lancaster, the county town, which sends 2 members to parliament, as does Preston, Liverpool, Wigan, Newton, and Clitheroe; Manchester, which gives the title of Duke to the Montagu family; Blackburn, Bolton, Warrington, Burnley, Bury, Chorley, Colne, Garstang, Haslingden, Hawkeshead, Leigh, Ormskirk, Poulton, Kirkham, Prescot, Rochdale, Ulverston, Dalton, and Cartmel. Its principal rivers are the Duddon, Crake, Leven, Winster, Lon or Lune, Wyer, Calder, Hodder, Wenning, Ribble, Douglass, Yarrow, Darwent, Irwell, Roch, Alt, Mersey, Tame, Medlock, and Irk. The most remarkable places on its coast are Sunderland and Formby points, the isles of Walney, Barrow, Roe, Streen, Foulney, and Pile of Foudre, bay of Morecambe, Duddon, Ribble, Mersey, and Wyer Mouths. Other remarkable places are Pendle and Clougho Hills, Cartmel, Fourness, and Lorgridge Fells, Blackstone Edge, Wulf and Warton Craggs, and Warton Beacon, Wyersdale, Bolland, and Simonswood Forests, the lakes called Winander Meer and Coniston Water, Fourness Abbey near Ulverston, Latham Park, Spaw and the burning well near Wigan. On the coast near Poulton, and between Bespham and Layton, is Black-Pool, heretofore an inconsiderable place, but much resorted to for sea-bathing, on account of the pureness of the sea; of late years it has been much improved, and several elegant houses have been built. This county produces corn, flax, hemp, salmon, and a variety of river and sea fish, besides char, which are caught in the lakes or meers, canel coal, turf, and a variety of stone. Its chief manufactures are those of Manchester goods, with kersies, checks, and bedding. It enjoys great intercourse by the various canals, particularly those from Liverpool and Manchester. It sends 14 members to parliament, 2 for the shire, and 12 as above shewn, pays five parts of the land-tax, and provides 800 men to the national militia. The air is in general very healthy. The soil may be considered under three different classes, the hilly parts are stony and barren, the level ground produces plenty of corn, and there is a vast quantity of moss ground, which affords little else but turf and trees, that are frequently found lying under the surface to a considerable depth.

The most considerable Gentlemens' Seats are,

Adlington Hall, near Chorley
Aigburgh Hall, near Liverpool
Ardwick, near Manchester
Ashton, near Lancaster
Atherton Hall, near Wigan
Blakeley Hurst, near St Helen
Chadderton Hall, near Manchester
Childwall House, near Liverpool
Dunken Hall, near Haslingden
Eton House, near Haslingden
Garswood Hall, near St Helen
Hall on the Hill, near Chorley
Haigh Hall, near Wigan
Heaton House, near Manchester
Holker Hall, near Cartmel

Hornby Castle, near Hornby
Hulton Hall, near Bolton
Ince Blundell, near Ormskirk
Kirby Hall, near Broughton
Knowsley Hall, near Liverpool
Latham Hall, near Ormskirk
Leve Hall, near Bolton
Little Crosby, near Ormskirk
Newton
Park Hall, near Lancaster
Pennington Hall, near Wigan
Speak Hall, near Liverpool
Stanish Hall, near Ormskirk
Strangeway Hall, near Manchester
Stonyhurst, near Clithero

Tonge, near Manchester
Trafford Hall, near Manchester
Townley Park, near Burnley
Walton Hall, near Preston
Warrington

The principal Views and Situations are,
Bigland, North of Cartmel, over the Ken and Leven
Dunold Mill Hole, 3 miles from Lancaster, near the Road from Kirkby Lonsdale
Easegill Kirk, a Cavern near Leek, East of Kirkby Lonsdale
Road from Lancaster to Hornby
Road from Ulverston to Kendal

LEICESTERSHIRE

Is an inland county, which gives the title of Earl to the Townshend family. During the Saxon heptarchy it belonged to the kingdom of Mercia; it is now in the province of Canterbury, in the diocese of Lincoln, and in the Midland circuit. It is nearly of an elliptical form, being 35 miles long, 30 miles broad, and 170 in circuit, containing 790 square miles, or 505,600 square acres, divided into 6 hundreds, 200 parishes, and 12 market towns, viz. Leicester, the county town, which sends 2 members to parliament; Hinckley, which formerly gave title to the hereditary lord high stewards of England; Harborough, which gives title of Earl to the Sherrard family; Loughborough, which gives title of Baron to the family of Wedderburn; Melton Mowbray, Bosworth, Lutterworth, Ashby de la Zouch, Mount Sorrel, Hallaton, Bilsdon, and Waltham on the Wold; among the villages, that of Carleton gives the title of Baron to the Boyle family. Its chief rivers are the Stour, Welland, Wreck, Avon, Anker, Swift, Seme, and the Eye. The most noted places are Mount Sorrel, Charnwood and Leicester Forests, Dalby Wood, the Vale of Belvoir, and the memorable Bosworth field. It sends 4 members to parliament, pays 9 parts of the land-tax, and provides 560 men to the national militia. The chief products are corn, beans, cattle, hogs, fine sheep, large horses, rich pastures, long wool, and pit-coal. The air is gentle, mild, and temperate, the soil fertile. There is a mineral water at Ashby de la Zouch.

The most considerable Gentlemens' Seats in this county are,

Alton Grange, near Ashby de la Zouch
Bosworth, near Bosworth
Bromgate, near Leicester
Staunton Harold, near Ashby de la Zouch
Gopf, N W of Bosworth
Donnington Park, near Kegworth
Garendon, near Loughborough
Belvoir Castle, N of Melton Mowbray
Goadby, near Belvoir

Croxton, near Goadby
Edmond Thorp, E of Melton Mowbray
Stanford Hall, near Lutterworth
Tooley Park, near Leicester
Kirkby Mallory, near Bosworth
Stapleford, E of Melton Mowbray
Beaumont Leys, near Leicester
Frith Hall, near Leicester
Brickman Hall, near Leicester

Burbach House, near Hinckley
Grcby, near Leicester

The of remarkable Places in this County are,

Brandon Hill
Charnwood, or Charnley Forest, W of Mount Sorrel

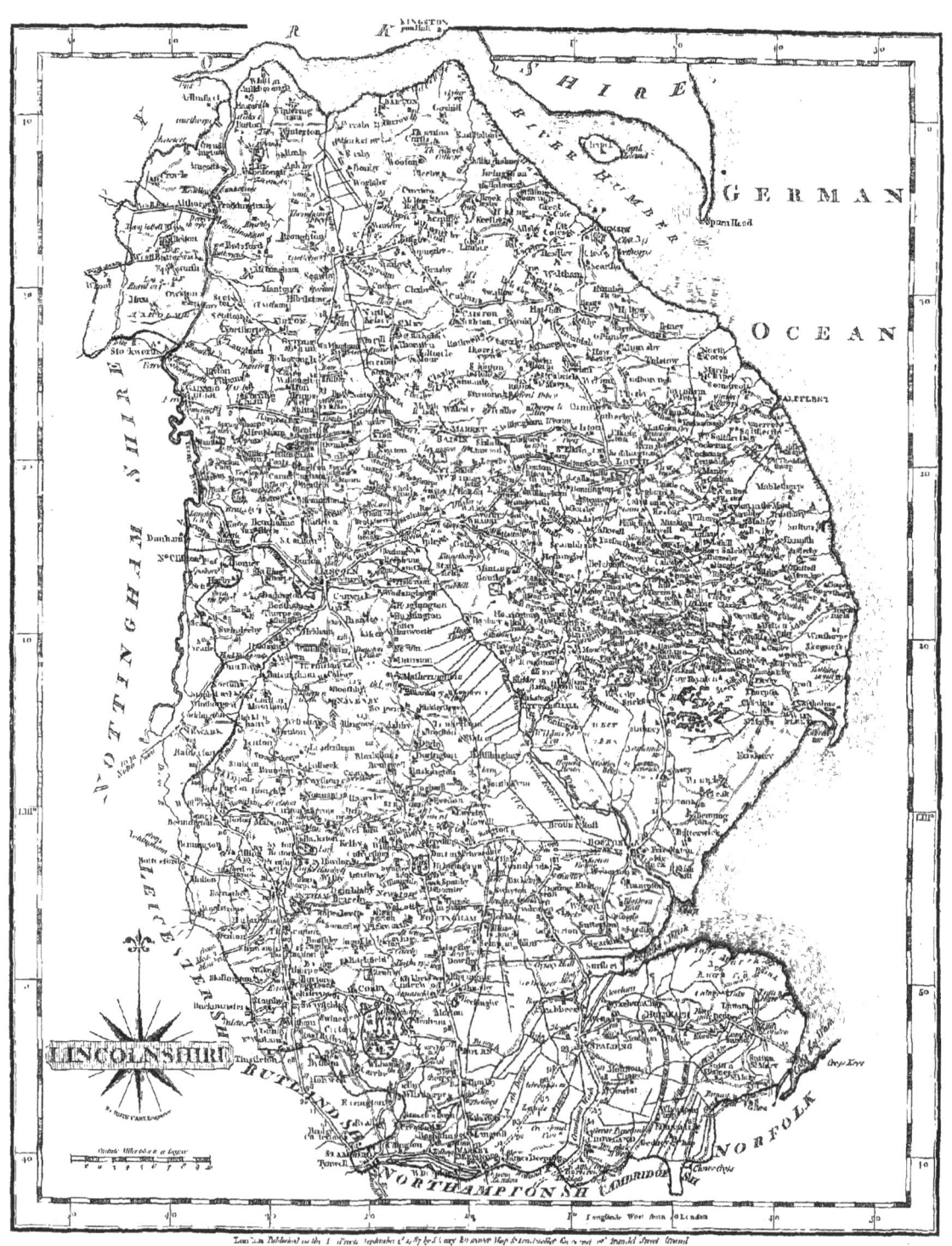

LINCOLNSHIRE

Is a maritime county, which, during the Saxon heptarchy, belonged to the kingdom of Mercia. It is now in the province of Canterbury, and diocese of Lincoln, and is included in the Midland circuit. It is 77 miles long, 48 broad, and 300 miles in circumference, containing 2958 square miles, or 1,893,120 acres, divided into three provinces, namely, Holland, which gives the title of Baron to the family of Fox; Kesteven and Lindsay, the former of which gives the title of Duke, and the latter that of Marquis and Earl, to the family of Bertie, the last of which divisions is far the largest, including all that lies North of the city of Lincoln, and the Fosse Dyke, which Henry I. cut between the Witham and the Trent, these provinces are sub-divided into 30 hundreds, containing 630 parishes, one city, Lincoln, which is the see of a bishop, sends 2 members to parliament, is the county town, and gives the title of Earl to the family of Clinton, and has 31 market-towns, viz. Stamford, which sends 2 members to parliament, and gives the title of Earl to the family of Grey, Boston, the title of Baron to the family of Irby, and sends 2 members to parliament; Grantham, the title of Baron to the family of Robinson, and sends 2 members to parliament, Gainsborough, the title of Earl to the family of Noel, Burton, the title of Baron to the family of Monson, Grimsby, which sends 2 members to parliament, Barton, Dunnington, Alford, Binbroke, Bolinbroke, Bourne, Burgh, Saltfleet, South Folkingham, Kirton, Caistor, Crowland, Deeping, Glandford Bridge, Holbeach, Horncastle, Raisin, Sleaford, Spalding, Spilsby, Stainton, Tattershall, Wainfleet, and Crowle. Among the villages, Ancaster gives the title of Duke to the Bertie family; Belton, that of Baron to the Brownlow family, Belvoir, the same dignity to the family of Manners, Harrowby, the like dignity to the Rider family, and Eresby, the same dignity to the Burrell family. The most noted places are Axholm Island, a light-house near East Fen, Boston and Lynn Deeps, the Humber Mouth, the Fosse Dykes, Lincoln Heath, East and West Holland Fens, Bourne and Wilcot Spaws, and part of the Vale of Belvoir. The principal rivers are the Humber, Trent, Witham, Welland, Ancam, Bane, Nen, Dun, and Idle. This county produces fine sheep, large oxen, a fine breed of horses, corn, pastures, hemp, remarkable fine wool, fish in great plenty, and all kinds of wild fowl, puettes, godwits, knotts, dotterels, &c. The air in some parts is thick and foggy, yet wholesome. The soil in the North and West parts abundantly fertile, pleasant, and rich, but the South and East are brackish and barren. The antiquities of this county are very numerous, particularly in religious foundations. It sends 12 members to parliament; viz. 2 for the county, and the others as above shewn, it pays 19 parts of the land-tax, and provides 1100 men to the national militia.

The most remarkable Seats in this County are,

Aswarby, near Folkingham.
Belton, near Grantham
Bloxholm, near Sleaford
Burton, near Lincoln
Blankney, near Lincoln.
Branston, near Lincoln
Brocklesby, near Grimsby.
Burwell Park, near Louth
Caswick, near Stamford
Culverthorpe, near Grantham.
Doddington, near Lincoln
Elsham, near Barton
Grimsthorpe, near Bourne.
Gunby, near Wainfleet.
Glentworth, near Kirton.

Goutby, near Horncastle
Haydor Lodge, near Grantham,
Hanby, near Folkingham.
Hainton, near Wragby
Haverhome Priory
Irnham, near Folkingham
Kettlethorpe, near Lincoln
Langton, near Spilsby.
Norton Place, near Kirton
Ormsby Park, near Spilsby
Panten House, near Wragby.
Riby, near Caistor
Revesby Abbey, near Horncastle.
Scrivelsby, near Horncastle.

Summer Castle, near Lincoln.
Somerby, near Glandford Bridge
Syston, near Grantham
Thonock, near Gainsborough.
Temple Bell Wood, in the Isle of Axholm.
Uffington, near Stamford.
Well, near Alford.

The most extensive Views are from,

Belvoir Castle, near Grantham
On the Road between Uppingham and Stamford
Coston Church steeple.

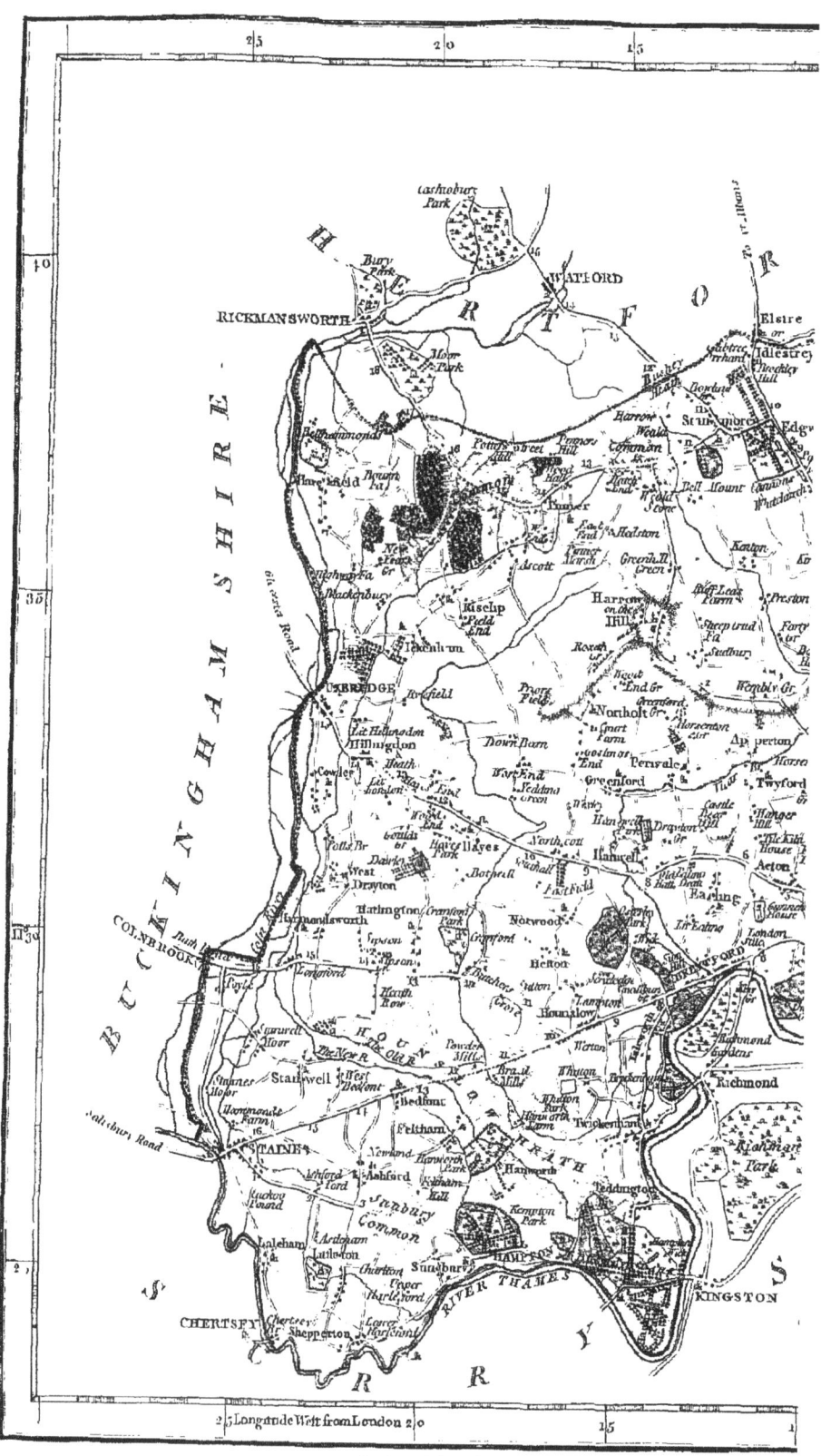

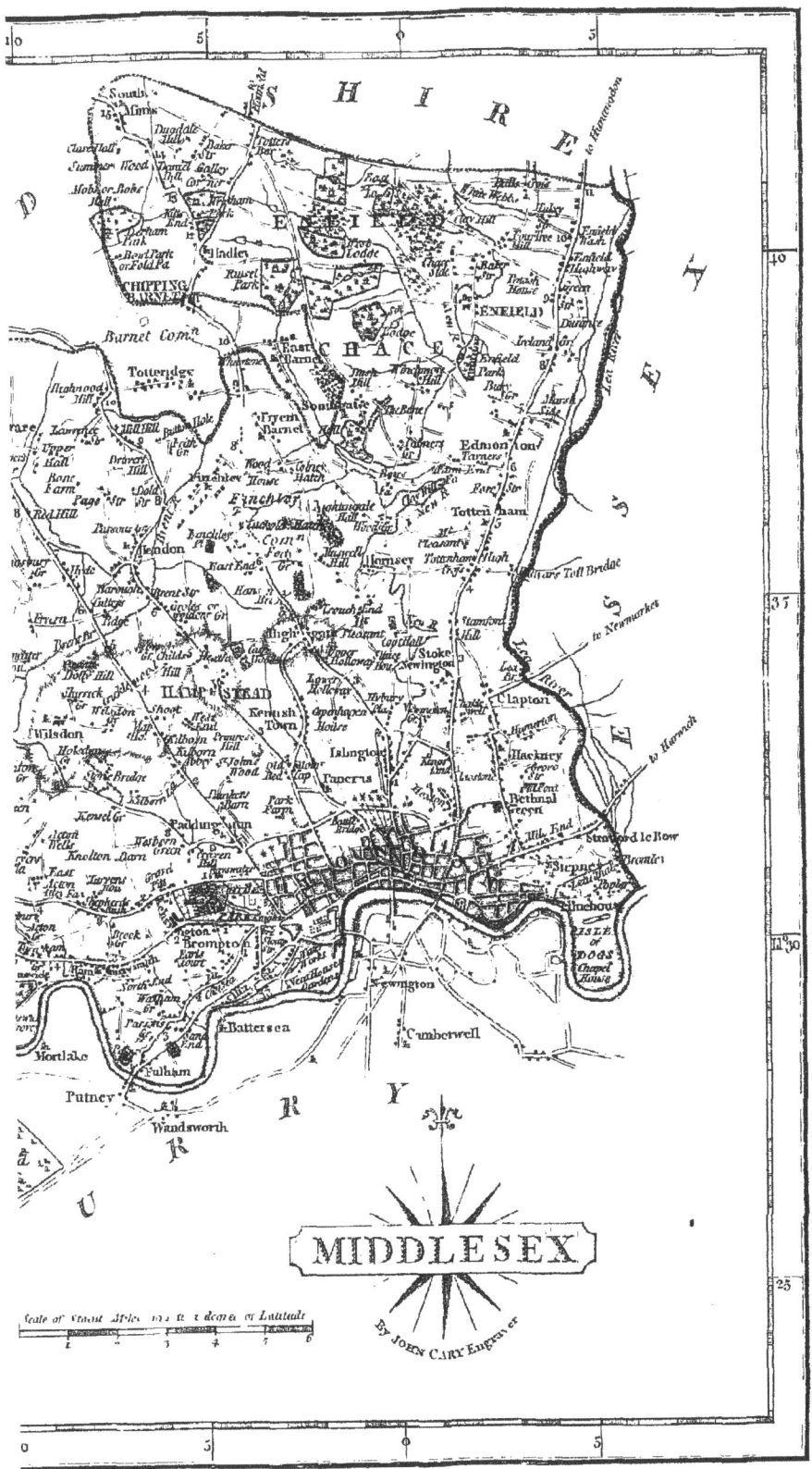

MIDDLESEX

Is situated near the center of the principal part of the kingdom, gives the title of Earl to the family of Sackville, and, during the Saxon heptarchy, belonged to the kingdom of the East Saxons; is now in the province of Canterbury, and diocese of London. It contains 240 square miles, or 217,600 square acres, is 23 miles long, about 14 broad, and nearly 115 miles in circuit; is divided into 6 hundreds and 2 liberties; has nearly 200 parishes, besides those in London and Westminster, with 41 vicarages, 2 cities, London and Westminster, the former the metropolis (to enumerate whose particulars, as to buildings, manufactures, &c. would fill a volume) the latter the residence of the King and his court, the courts of justice, nobility, &c.; it has 7 market towns, viz. Uxbridge, which gives title of Earl to the family of Paget, Brentford, the county town, where are chosen the members for the county, Enfield, disused, which gives title of Baron to the family of Nassau de Zulestein, Barnet, Staines, Edgeworth, and Hounslow, with a considerable number of villages, many of which are larger than some market towns. It sends but 8 members to parliament, 4 London, 2 Westminster, 2 for the county. It is one of the smallest counties in the kingdom for extent, yet, on account of London, &c. it pays 80 parts out of 513 of the land tax. It provides 1600 men to the national militia, besides the Trainbands and Artillery Company of the city of London. Its principal rivers are the Thames (whose tide flows above 70 miles from its mouth, and so extensive a trade is by it carried on, that in some years there have arrived 10,000 British and Foreign vessels) the Lea, the Coln, the Brent, and the New River, with whose water the greatest part of London, &c. are constantly supplied. The only navigable canal in this county is from Limehouse to the river Lea at Bromley. From London Stone, in Cannon Street, all the Roman roads took their center, and proceeded to the extremities of the kingdom in every direction. The principal natural product of this county is the best of all vegetables and eatables of every kind, but the production of artists and manufactures exceed comprehension. There are mineral waters at Hampstead, Islington, Barnet, Kilbourne, Bagnigge, and Acton. Amongst the numerous elegant Villas belonging to noblemen, gentlemen, &c. we shall mention the following as most conspicuous

Bruce Castle, near Tottenham
Belhammonds, near Rickmansworth
Boston House, near Old Brentford
Bush Hill
Bushy Park, near Hampton Court
Caen Wood, near Hampstead
Cranford Place, near Colnbrook
Cannons, near Edgware
Chiswick House
Dawley, near Hayes
Derham Park, near Barnet.
Enfield Park, near Enfield
Fitzroy Farm, near Highgate
Fortey Hall, Enfield
Fulham Palace
Grove House, near Chiswick

Gunnesbury House, near Brentford.
Hampton Court Palace
Hanwell Park, near Brentford
Hanworth Park, near Hounslow
Harefield House
Holland House, near Kensington
Ickenham, near Uxbridge
Kensington Palace
Kempton Park, near Sunbury
Littleton, near Laleham
Marble Hall, near Twickenham
Minchingdon Hall, near Southgate
Osterley Park, near Brentford
Russel Park, near Barnet
Sion House, near Brentford
South Lodge, on Enfield Chace.

West Lodge, on Enfield Chace
Twickenham Park
Whitton Park, near Hounslow
Wortham Park, near Barnet

The most remarkable Places for extensive Prospects, are,

Highbury Place, near Islington
Canonbury House, near Ditto
Harrow on the Hill
Mill Hill, near Hendon
Twickenham
Highgate Hill
Hampstead Heath
Datchet Bridge
Bushy Heath, near Edgware

MONMOUTHSHIRE,

WHICH is a maritime county, formerly part of Wales, is now reckoned part of England, but was not included in the Saxon heptarchy. It is in the province of Canterbury, diocese of Llandaff, and in the Oxford circuit. It is 30 miles long, 26 broad, and 110 in circumference; divided into 6 hundreds, containing 550 square miles, or 352,000 acres; having 127 parishes, and 7 market-towns, viz. Monmouth, which gives the title of Earl to the Mordaunt family, is the county town, and sends one member to parliament; Abergavenny, which gives the titles of Earl and Baron to the family of Neville, Usk, Chepstow, Newport, Caerleon, and Pontypool. The noted places are Goldcliff-point, Denny Island, Charlton Rock, St. Treacle Chapel, the Severn Mouth, and Usk Mouth, with the Hatteral, Peny-Vale, and Valure Hills; Erses and Wentse Woods. The principal rivers are the Severn, Monow, Wye, Usk, Rimney, and Avon. It produces wood, corn, cattle, sheep, goats, swine, salmon, trout, and pit coal. The chief manufacture is plated and Japan iron-ware. It is hilly and woody, but healthy and fertile. The tide rises at Chepstow frequently 60 feet perpendicular, which is higher than any other place in Europe. It sends 3 members to parliament, 2 for the county, and one for Monmouth; pays three parts of the land-tax, and provides 84 men to the national militia. The village of Ragland gives the title of Baron to the Somerset family; and that of Cardiffe the same honour to the family of Stuart.

The principal Gentlemens' Seats are,

Argoed, near Monmouth
Catchmayd, near Monmouth.
Clytha, near Usk
Etton, near Chepstow
Fetaplece, near Caerleon
Landilo, near Abergavenny.
Langibby, near Usk
Langstone, near Caerleon
Lanvihangle Crucornau, near Abergavenny.
Penhow Castle, near Caerleon.
Piercefield, near Chepstow.
Tredegar, near Newport
Troy House, Monmouth
Usk Castle.

Wentwood Lodge, near Caerleon.
Woneslow, near Monmouth

The most remarkable Views are, from,

The Road from Chepstow to Ragland and Monmouth.
The Sugar Loaf Mountain
On the Wye from Monmouth to Chepstow.
The Vale of Abergavenny
Colebrooke Park
Pena-y-Vale, 21 miles from Chepstow
At Whitbrook, Pilfan, or Llandagger.
Tintern Abbey Orchard

NORFOLK

Is a maritime county, which gives the title of Duke to the noble family of Howard, the first peer of the realm, and was, during the Saxon heptarchy, included in the kingdom of the East Angles. It is in the province of Canterbury, diocese of Norwich, and in the Norfolk circuit. This county is nearly an island of an elliptical form, being surrounded by the sea and four rivers. It is 70 miles long, 46 broad, and 210 miles in circumference, containing 2350 square miles, or 1,504,000 acres, divided into 31 hundreds, 660 parishes, one city, Norwich, which gives the title of Earl to the family of Gordon, sends 2 members to parliament, is the residence of its bishop, and is one of the first cities in the kingdom for trade, &c. containing 36 parish churches, besides its cathedral, and is 6 miles in circumference. It has 31 market-towns, viz. Thetford, in part, which gives the title of Viscount to the family of Fitzroy, and sends 2 members to parliament, Lynn, or King's Lynn, which gives the title of Baron to the family of Townshend, and sends 2 members to parliament, Walsingham gives the title of Baron to the family of Grey, and Yarmouth, which sends 2 members to parliament also, Burnham, Aylesham, North Walsham, Buckenham, Harleston, Harling, Attleborough, Fakenham, Loddon, Caston, Clay, Cromer, Dereham, Diss, Downham, Foulsham, Hickling, Hingham, Holt, Methwold, Reepham, Steeching, Snetsham, Swaffham, Watton, Windham or Wymondham, and Worsted. Amongst the villages, Castle-Rising gives the title of Baron to the family of Howard, and sends 2 members to parliament, Wolverton gives the title of Baron to the Walpole family, and Raynham that of Marquis to the family of Townshend. The rivers are the Great and Lesser Ouse, Wisbeach, the Yare, Waveney, Windsor, Thyrn, Lynn, and some lesser streams. The most remarkable places are Winterton Ness, Easton Ness, Yarmouth Sands, Boston and Lynn Deeps, Well's Harbour, Clay Harbour, Haven's Mouth, Hitcham Haven, Weyborne Hope, Yarmouth Roads, Cromer Bay, the Salt Marshes, several Meers, and Laden Trees near Deepham. This county produces rich pastures, corn, honey, saffron, great plenty of various game and water fowl, all kinds of river and sea fish, rabbits, sheep, cattle, wood, &c. It abounds with heaths; the marshy and watery places are aguish and unwholesome, but in the sandy or clayey part it is pleasant and healthy. The villages are large and well-inhabited, particularly in the eastern part, and the soil in this county is more various than perhaps in any other county, and comprehends all the sorts that are to be found in the island. It sends 12 members to parliament, 2 for the county, and 10 as above shewn, pays 22 parts of the land-tax, and provides 960 men to the national militia.

The most considerable Gentlemens' Seats in this County are,

Beeston, near Norwich.
Bixley, near Norwich.
Blickling, near Aylsham.
Carlton, near Wymondham.
Cotesley, near Norwich.
Crostwick, near North Walsham.
Ditchingham, near Bungay.
Felbridge, near Cromer.
Garboldisham, near New Buckenham.
St. Giles's, near Norwich.
Gunton, near Aylsham.
Hillington Hill, near Castle Rising.
Holkham, near Burnham.

Houghton, near Lynn.
Kimberley Park, near Hingham.
Kimble Hall, near Wymondham.
Melton Constable, near Holt.
Narford, near Swaffham.
Oldham, near Thetford.
Oxburgh, near Stokeferry.
Raynham.
Ringsted, near Hunstanton.
Snetsham Lodge.
Sprowston, near Norwich.
Stow, near Downham.
Suffield, near North Walsham.

Tasborough, near Shottisham.
Walsingham.
Wolverton, near Aylsham.

The most extensive Prospects are from,
The Church at Swaffham.
Holkham.
Norwich Castle.
Buckenham Castle.
Yarmouth.
Easton, N. W. of Norwich.

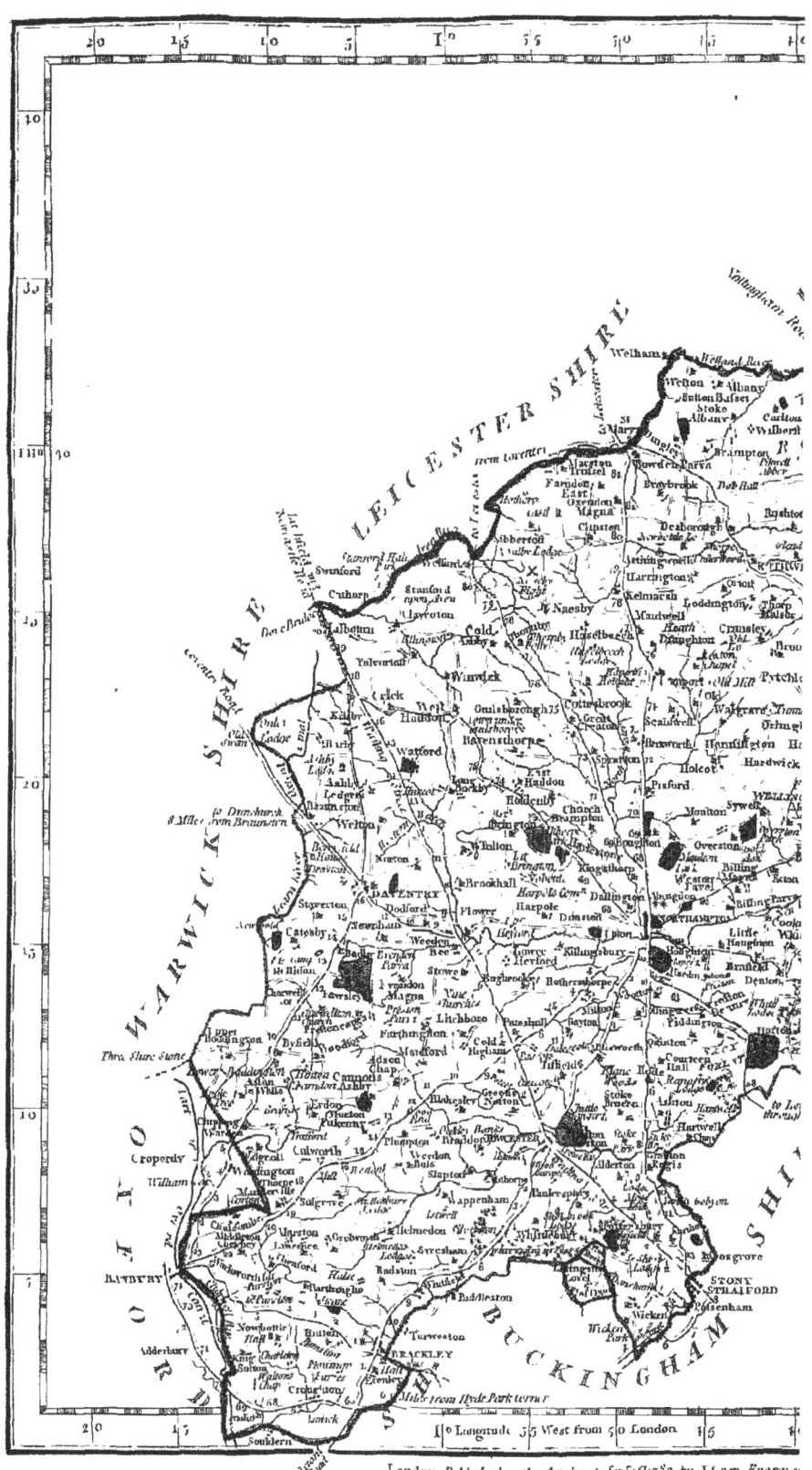

NORTHAMPTONSHIRE

Is an inland county, near the center of the kingdom, which, during the Saxon heptarchy, belonged to the kingdom of Mercia, it is now included in the province of Canterbury, the diocese of Peterborough, and in the Midland circuit. It is 68 miles long from North East to South West, 24 miles broad, and 230 miles in circuit, containing 1000 square miles, or 640,000 acres, divided into 20 hundreds, 330 parishes, with one city, Peterborough, which sends 2 members to parliament, and gives the title of Earl to the family of Mordaunt, also 12 market towns, viz. Northampton, the county town, which sends 2 members to parliament, and gives the title of Earl to the Compton family, Brackley, which likewise sends 2 members to parliament, and gives the title of Marquis and Viscount to the Egerton family, and Higham Ferrers, which sends one member to parliament, Rockingham, Wellingborough, Thrapston, Oundle, Cliffe, Kettering, Rothwell, Towcester, and Daventry, which gives the title of Baron to the family of Finch, the village of Boughton gives the title of Baron to the Brudenell family, Burleigh, the same title to the Cecil family, Althorpe, the title of Viscount to the Spencer family, Thornhaugh, the title of Baron to the Russel family, and Grafton, the title of Duke to the Fitzroy family. The principal rivers are the Ouse, Nen, Welland, Cherwell, and the Learn. This county sends 9 members to parliament, viz. 2 for the county, and the others as expressed above, it pays 12 parts of the land tax, and provides 640 men to the national militia. The most remarkable places are Audvery Mounts, Sacy and Rockingham Forests, Dunsmore Heath, Naseby Field, Holmeby House, where Charles I was confined, and Fotheringay Castle, where Mary Queen of Scots was beheaded. Its chief product is corn, cattle, and stone.

The most considerable Seats in this county are,

Abingdon, near Northampton.
Althorp Park, near Harlestone
Ashby Lodge, near Daventry
Blatherwick, near Kingscliff
Burghley Hall, near Stamford
Canon's Abbey, near Towcester
Carlton
Castle Ashby, near Northampton.
Dean upon Rockingham Forest
Delapre Abbey, near Northampton
Dingley
Drayton House, near Thrapston
Laston Mauduit, near Bozeat
Laston Neston, near Towcester
Fawsley, near Daventry.

Furtho, near Stony Stratford
Harlestone, near Northampton
Harringworth Park, Rockingham Forest
Higham Park, near Higham Ferrers.
Horton, Yardley Chace
Knuston Hall, near Knuston
Moulton Park, near Northampton.
Milton Park, near Peterborough
Newbottle Hall, near Brackley
Newbottle Lodge, near Desborough
Overston Park, near Wellingborough
Steane, near Brackley
Stoke Park, near Towcester
Upton, near Northampton.
Wadford, near Daventry

The most remarkable Views are from,

Between Great Biblington and Overton,
Near Kettering
Hard Mill Meer, between Kingsteid and Rame.
Bush Hill, near Wellingborough
From Clifford to Eston Mill
On the Welland from Stamford,
A little West of Naseby
Burrow Hill, West of Daventry
Near St. Martin's Stamford, and on towards Easton.

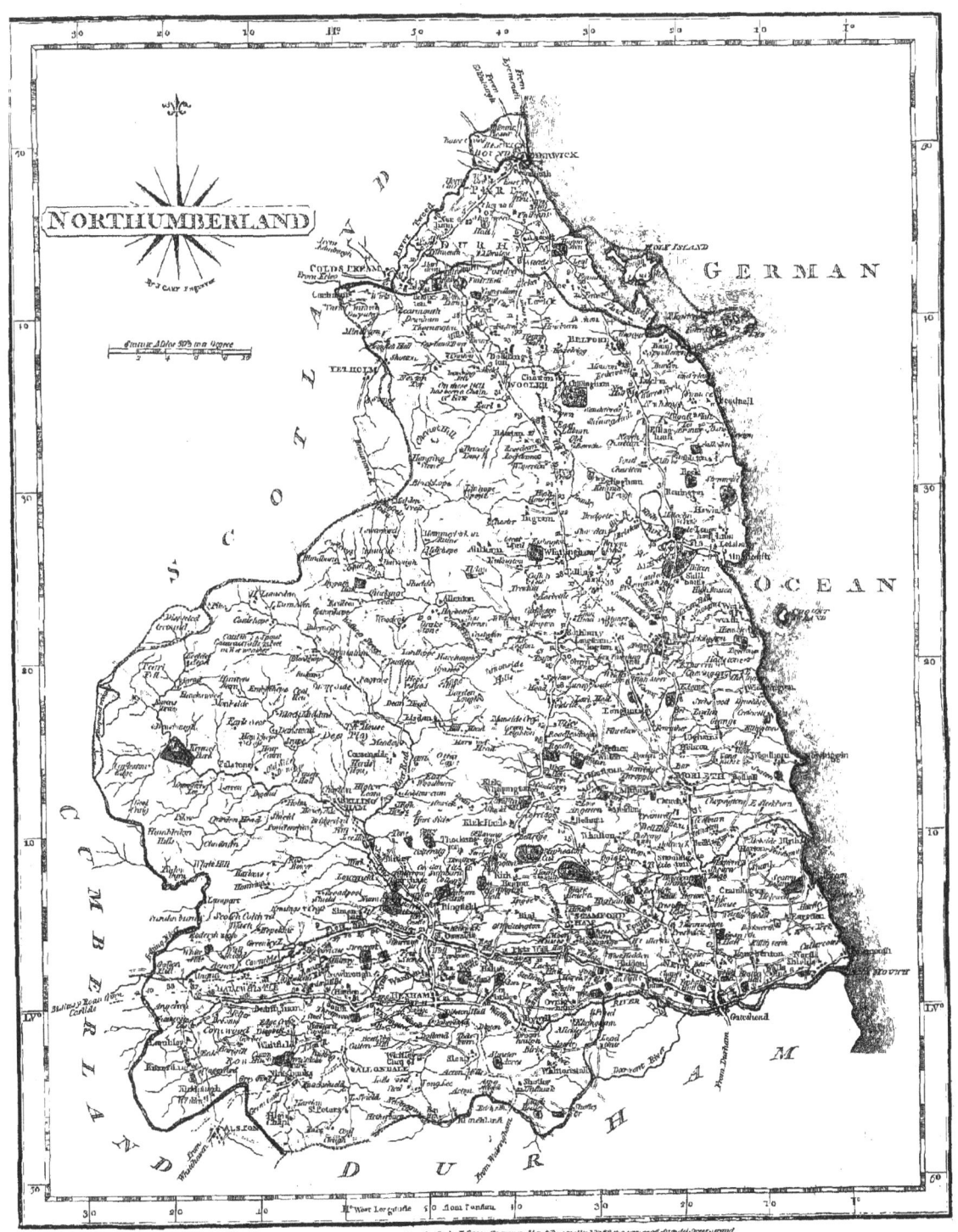

NORTHUMBERLAND

Is a maritime county, which gives the title of Duke and Earl to the family of Percy, during the Saxon Heptarchy it belonged to the kingdom of the Northumbrians, it is now in the province of York, diocese of Durham, and in the Northern circuit. It is 66 miles long, 47 broad, and 230 miles in circumference, containing 1700 square miles, or 1,331,200 acres, divided into 6 wards, 460 parishes, and 12 market-towns, viz. Newcastle, the county town, which gives the title of Duke to the Clinton family, and sends 2 members to parliament, Berwick, sends 2 members to parliament, and gives the title of Baron to the family of Hill, Morpeth, also sends 2 members to parliament, and gives the title of Viscount to the Howard family, Alnwick gives the title of Baron to the Percy family, Belford the same honour to the family of Graham, also Hexham, Billingham, Woller, Rothbury, Haltwesel, Elleston, and Learmouth. Among the villages, Tyndall gives the title of Baron to the family of Scott. The rivers are the Tweed, Tyne, North and South Tyne, Alne, Wensbeck, Coquet, Bramish, Urway, Blythe, Till, East and West Alon. The most noted places are Sunderland Point, Holy, Fern and Coquet Isles, Staple's Rocks, Black Middens, Clifford's Fort, Dunstanburgh Castle, Bamburgh and Tinemouth, and several other Castles, Tweedmouth, Alnemouth, Tinemouth, and Wensbeck mouth Havens, Felton Bridge, Cheviot, Flodden, and Stainmore Hills, Hexham and Lowes Forests, with the Picts' Wall. The product of the county is game, corn, salmon, malt, alum, iron, and lead, with an inexhaustible fund of coals. Its chief manufactures, glass, wrought-iron, and salt. The air is sharp and cold, subject to boisterous winds, frost and snow. It sends 8 members to parliament, 2 for the county, and 6 as before shewn, pays 4 parts of the land-tax, and provides 500 men to the national militia. It abounds with Roman antiquities, and affords an infinite fund for the Antiquarian.

The principal Gentlemens' Seats are,

Abby of Alnwick
Alnwick Castle
Aydon, near Hexham
Backworth, near Earsdon
Bavington, near Stamfordham
Beaufort, near Hexham
Beanridge, near Ponteland
Belford
Belsay Castle, near Stamordham
Benwell, near Newcastle
Biddleston, near Allenton
Blagdon, near Stannington
Broom Park, near Alnwick
Callaly Castle, near Whittingham
Capheaton Castle, near Stamfordham
Cartington Castle, near Rothbury
Caraway Park, near Morpeth
Cheeseburn Grange, near Stamfordham
Chirlington, near Wooller
Chirton, near North Shields
Close House, near Ovingham
Cletswell Hill, near Woodham
Egling, near Alnwick
Esllington, near Whittingham
Etall Hall, near Tod
Falloden, near Alnwick
Fenham, near Newcastle
Fiand Hall, at Ponteland
Ford Castle, at Ford
Gosforth Hall, near Newcastle
Greenhen, near Shotley
Hallington Hall, near Stamfordham
Haukey, near Warkworth
Hazelyside, near Beltingham

Henton Hall, near Newcastle
Heppel, near Rothbury
Henscot, near Morpeth
Highamd kes, near Ponteland
Howick, near Alnwick
Kennell Park
Kirkley, near Ponteland
Lanchoe, near Hexham
Lee Hill, near Birtley
Longhorsley
Matsen, near Stamfordham
Minster Acres, near Shotley
Mitford, near Morpeth
Morpeth
Newbrough, near Hexham
New Hall, near Belford
Newton Hall, near Rothbury
North Leaton, near Woodham
Oakenland, near Hexham
Ogle Castle, near Whalton
Pallinsburn Hall, near Branxton
Ridley Hall, near Beltingham
Rondley Castle, near Hartburn
Rock, near Alnwick
Roddam, near Ildeston
Rosedean, near Ildeston
Seaton Delavel, near Earsdon
Shotley Hall
Stob Hall, near Newcastle
Sevansfield Hall, near Alnwick
Swarland Hall, near Rothbury
Swinburn Castle, near Chollerton
Tareepwood, near Hexham
Tone, near Beltingham

Willington
Whitley, near Earsdon
Widdington Castle
Witton, near Hartburn
Woolsington, near Ponteland

The extensive Views and Situation are,

Vale of Tyne from Newcastle to Hexham
Reedsdale, and the fall of the Chedlup, which falls 70 feet, near Catchigh and Reedilne
Cheviot Hills, S W of Wooller
Christenbury Crag, on the borders of Cumberland, S W of Bew Castle
Crag Lough, to the N of the Roman Wall, and the 31 Mile-stone on the Military Road
Tacket, near Simondburn, N W of Walwick, the fall of the Rivult and Caven
Staward le Pool, E of the Allen
High Stward along the Allen, S S E of Beltingham
Newbigger, from the Church Yard on the Coast E of Bothall
Kitley, five miles N of Belford, on the Berwick Road
Cornhill, S of the Tweed, and near the New Bridge
Tilmouth Chapel, at the junction of that River and the Tweed
Shidlaw Hill, near Carnam and Wark Castle
Watchlaw Hill, four miles from Etall
Glanton Pike, near the Wooller Road and Whittingham
Linel Law, near Eslee, N B of Morpeth
Finington on the River Ering

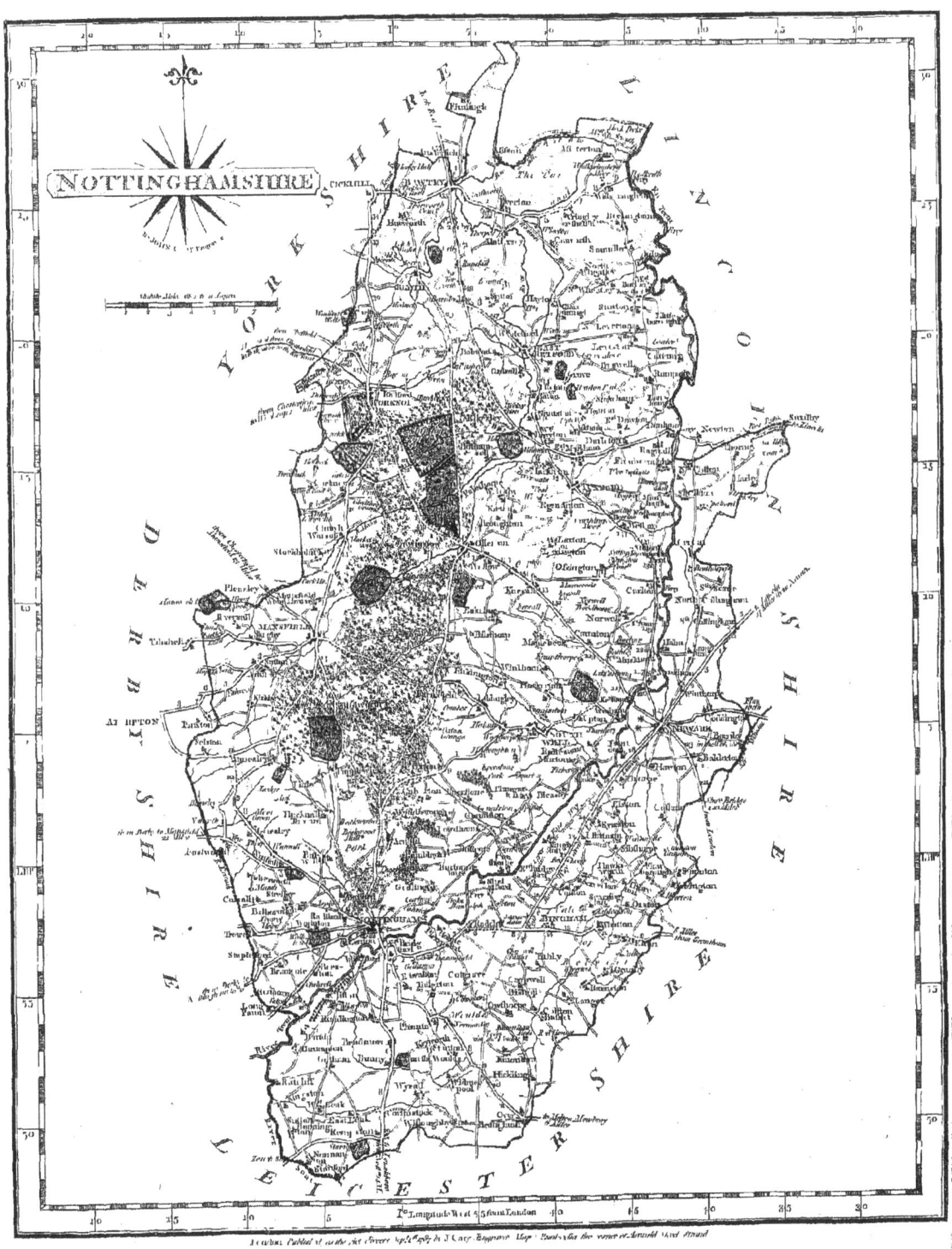

NOTTINGHAMSHIRE

Is an inland county, which, during the Saxon heptarchy, belonged to the kingdom of Mercia. It is now in the province of York, and the same diocese, and in the Midland circuit. It is 48 miles long, 25 broad, and 76½ in circumference, containing 778 square miles, or 77,800 square acres, is nearly of an oval form, divided into 8 hundreds, 168 parishes, and 9 market-towns, viz. Nottingham, the county town, which gives the title of Earl to the family of Finch, and sends 2 members to parliament, as does Newark, and Retford, 2 members each, Mansfield, which gives the title of Baron and Earl to the Murray family, Bingham, Southwell, Workſop, Tuxford, and Blith, among the villages, Langar, gives the title of Viscount to the family of Howe, and Granby, that of Marquis to the family of Manners. The principal rivers are the Trent, Idle, Erwaſh, Meden, and Maun. It sends 8 members to parliament, viz. 2 for the county, and 6 others as above mentioned, pays 7 parts of the land-tax, and provides 480 men to the national militia. The most noted places are the Cells near Nottingham, the Forest of Sherwood, Vale of Belvoire, and Thorney and Lindhurst Woods. It produces corn, hops, lead, coals, alabaster, liquorice, wood, game, and flax, and the chief manufactures are ſtockings, ale, and malt, the air is very pleaſant and wholeſome, and the soil fruitful towards the eaſt, and, towards the weſt, is well furniſhed with wood and canal coal. The Cheſterfield Canal, which joins with the Trent, paſſes through the northern part of the county.

The principal Seats in this county are,

Anneſley, near Mansfield.
Aveſham Park, near Newark.
Brenny
Clifton, near Nottingham
Clipſton Park, near Olleiton.
Clumber Park, near Workſop.
Eaſt Stoke, near Newark
Grove, near Eaſt Retford.
Haughton Park, near Eaſt Retford.
Headon Hall, near Ditto.
Langar
Newſtead Abbey, near Mansfield.

Norwood, near Southwell
Nottingham Caſtle.
Nuthall, near Nottingham
Rufford, near Ollerton
Serlby, near Blyth
Shire Oak, near Workſop.
Stanford Hill, near Remſton
Thoreſby Park, near Ollerton
Welbeck Abbey, near Workſop.
Winthorp, near Newark
Wollaton Hall, near Nottingham.
Worksop Manor

The moſt extenſive Views are from

Clifton, Three Miles from Nottingham
Nottingham Caſtle
Creſwell Crag, W. of Wellbank
Road from Newark to Nottingham, near the Trent
Wollaton Hall, Three Miles from Nottingham.

OXFORDSHIRE

Is an inland county, which, during the Saxon heptarchy, belonged to the kingdom of Mercia, is now in the province of Canterbury, and in the diocese and circuit of Oxford, containing 435,200 square acres, or 680 square miles, is 45 miles long, 26 broad, and 190 miles in circuit, being divided into 14 hundreds, 280 parishes, and 92 vicarages, having one city, Oxford, which gives title of Earl to the Harley family, is an University in high estimation, containing 20 colleges and 5 halls, wherein upwards of 3000 students complete their education. It has also 12 market towns, viz. Woodstock, which gives title of Viscount to the Bentinck family, Burford, which gives the title of Earl to the Beauclerk family, besides Banbury, Chipping Norton, Henley, Witney, Charlbury, Doddington, Bicester, Bampton, Tame, and Watlington; and 451 villages. The villages of Ricot give the title of Baron to the Bertie family, Stanton Harcourt, that of Viscount and Baron to the Harcourt family, as does Newnham that of Viscount to the same family. It sends 9 members to parliament, viz. 2 for the county, 1 for Banbury, 2 for Oxford city, 2 for the University, and 2 for Woodstock, pays 10 parts of the land tax, and provides 560 men to the national militia. Its principal rivers are the Thames, Cherwell, Isis, Tame, Swere, Glin, Rea, Oke, Windrush, Evanlode, and Sorbrook. The most remarkable places are, the Chiltern Hills, Whichwood Forest, Astrop Wells, Rollrich Stones, and several other antiquities. This county produces rich pastures, corn, wood, cattle, game, and fruits of every kind, and the rivers fine fish. Its chief manufacture is coarse woollens and blankets. The air is healthy and the soil dry, abounding with streams of excellent water. There are mineral springs at Aston and Somerton. A canal goes from Oxford in a north direction to Warwickshire, which is of considerable advantage to the county, particularly to Oxford.

The most remarkable Seats in this county are,

Alderbury, near Banbury
Blandford Park, near Charlbury
Blechingdon, near Islip
Blenheim, near Woodstock, built by Parliament, and given to the late Duke of Marlborough.
Breuern Abbey, near Lynchum
Caversham Park, near Caversham
Charlbury
Cockthorp, near Stanton Harcourt
Cornwall House, near Chipping Norton.
Crowsley Park, near Henley
Ditchley Park, near Charlbury
Great Tew Park, near Deddington.
Grey's Court, near Henley
Heythorp, near Chipping Norton
Holton, near Wheatley
Hanwell Park, near Banbury
Kirklington Park, near Woodstock
Middleton Park, near Middleton Stony.
Newnham Courtney
Ricot Park, near Thame
Rousham, near Woodstock
Shirburn Castle, near Watlington
Swinbrook, near Burford
Thame Park, near Thame
Wittingen Park, near Watlington.

The most remarkable Places for extensive Prospects, are,

Teynton, near Burford
Shiplake on the Thames, near Henley
Stokenchurch Hill, N E of Watlington
Whitcham Hill, N W of Oxford
Quinton Hill, near Aylesbury
Edgehill, near Banbury
Nettlebed Hill, supposed the highest in England.
Shotover Hill, near Wheatly

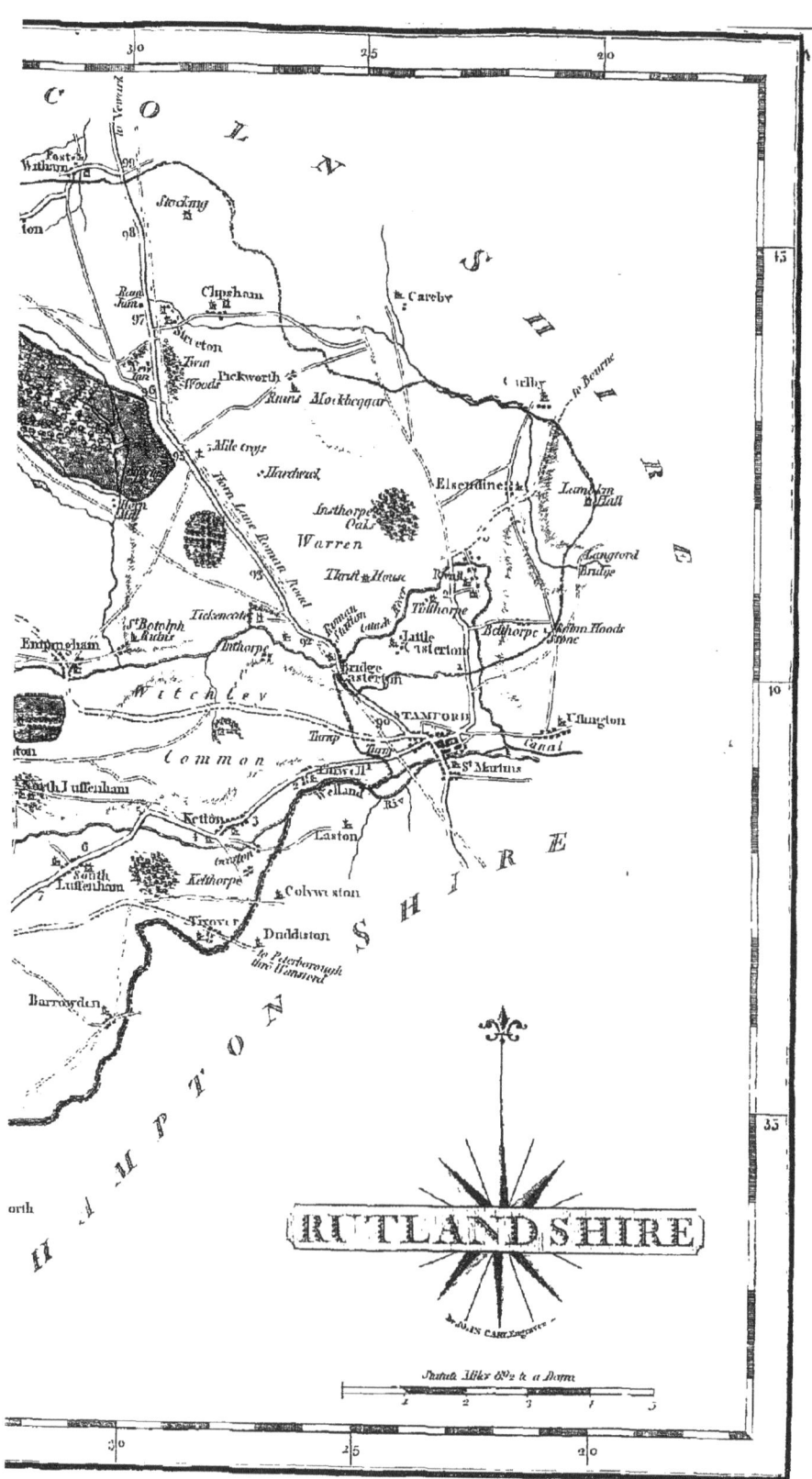

RUTLAND

Is an inland county, which gives the title of Duke to the Manners family, and, during the Saxon heptarchy, belonged to the kingdom of Mercia. It continued, from Alfred's division of England into counties, to the reign of Henry II. as part of Northamptonshire. It is in the province of Canterbury, the diocese of Peterborough, and belongs to the Midland Circuit. It is 19 miles long, 18 broad, and 70 miles in circumference, containing 210 square miles, or 134,400 acres, divided into 5 hundreds, containing 48 parishes, and 2 market-towns, viz. Oakham, the county town, and Uppingham. Among the villages, Essenden gives the title of Baron to the family of Cecil, as does Bidlington the same dignity to that of Noel. The most remarkable places are the Quarries, the old Forest of Liefield, the Vale of Catmos, Witchley Heath, and Five Mile Cross. The rivers are the Guash, Eye, Chater, and Welland. This county produces limestone, corn, cattle, sheep, wood, &c. It sends only 2 members to parliament, viz for the Shire, pays 2 parts of the land-tax, and provides 120 men to the national militia. This is the smallest county in the kingdom, but the most fruitful. The air is good, and the soil rich, especially the Vale of Catmos. Its form is nearly circular. There is an old custom established at Oakham, when a Nobleman comes, for the first time, within its precincts, he is obliged to pay homage of a shoe from one of his horses, or to commute for it in money.

The most considerable Gentlemens' Seats are,

Burley House, near Oakham.
Exton, near Oakham,
Northmanton, near Oakham.
Pilton, near Uppingham
Overton.

The beautiful and extensive Views are from,
North Luffenham, near Stamford
The Road from Stamford to Uppingham,

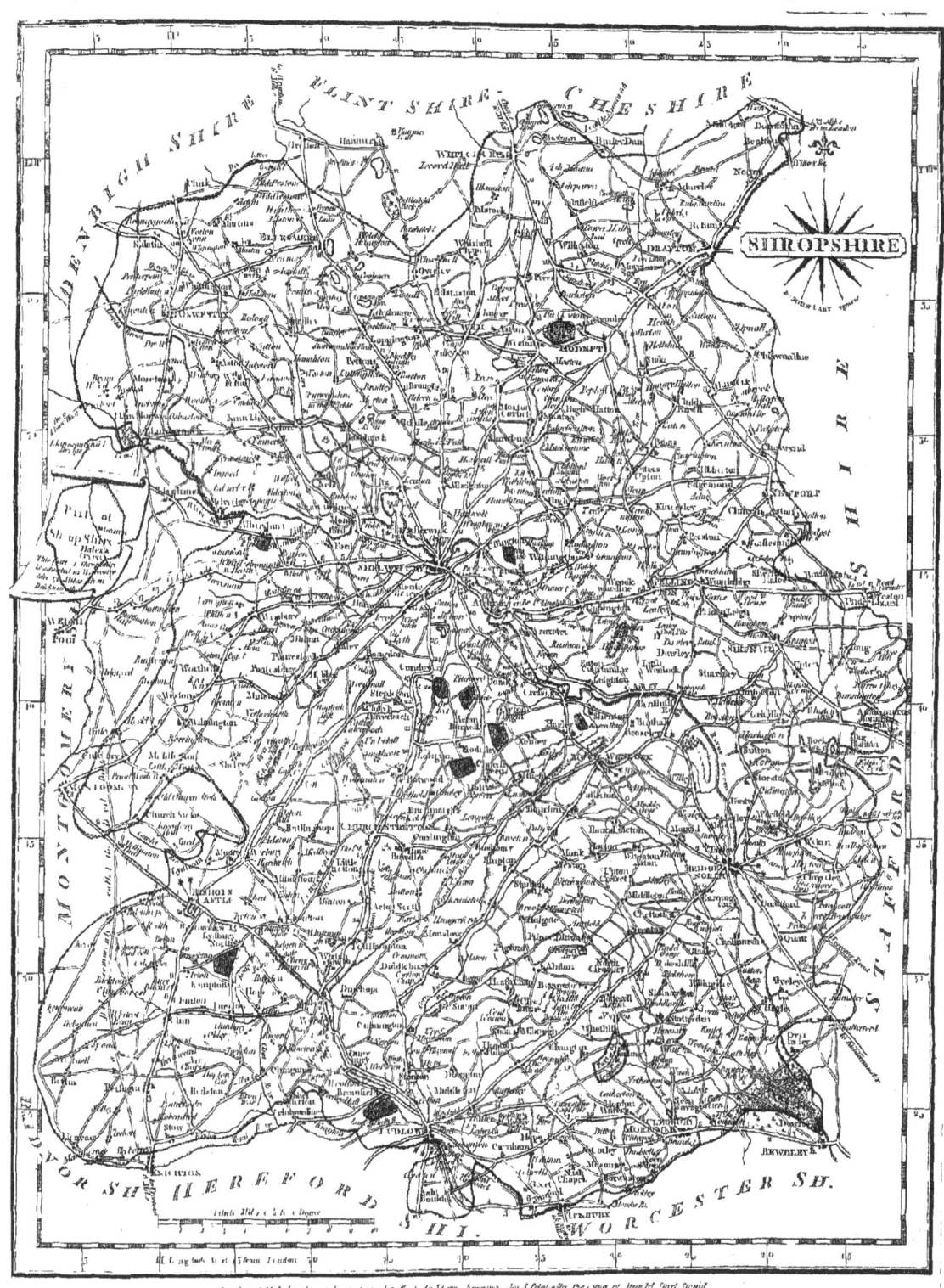

SHROPSHIRE

Is an inland county, which, during the Saxon heptarchy, belonged to the kingdom of Mercia, it is now in the province of Canterbury, the diocese of Hereford in part, and the remainder in that of Litchfield and Coventry, and is included in the Oxford circuit. It is 47 miles long, 38 broad, and 210 in circumference, containing 1320 square miles, or 844,800 acres, divided into 15 hundreds, 170 parishes, and 15 market towns, viz. Shrewsbury, the county town, which sends 2 members to parliament, and gives the title of Earl to the Talbot family, Ludlow, which gives the title of Viscount to the family of Herbert, and sends 2 members to parliament, as does Bridgenorth, Wenlock and Bishop's Castle, 2 members each, besides which, there are Drayton, Wem, Whitchurch, Church Stretton, Cleobury Mortimer, Newport, Shefnal, and Wellington, with Ellesmere, which gives the title of Baron to the Egerton family, and Oswestry which gives the same honour to the Howard family. The following villages give titles to noble families, viz. Clun, that of Baron to the family of Howard, Chesbury, the same title to that of Herbert, Harley, to that of Harley, and Powis, that of Earl and Baron to the family of Herbert. The principal rivers are the Tweed, Severn, Teem, Clun, Ony, Warren, Torn, Corve, Rea, Kemlot, and Mele. The most remarkable places are Wire, Morf and Hockflo Forests, St. Gilbert's Caradock, Wrekin, Stiperston, Titterston Hill, Brownclee, Breteen, Cleobury Mount, Burning-Well, Bishop's Mott, Corvesdale, and Blaze Heath; Botcobel House and Grove, Caractacus's Camp, Acton Burnell Castle and Barn. It sends 12 members to parliament, 2 for the county, and 10 as before shewn, pays 7 parts of the land-tax, and provides 640 men to the national militia. The air of this county is healthy, but cold. The soil in the vallies produces different sorts of grain, and upon the hills pasture for black cattle and sheep, besides which its chief product is fruits, river fish, pit-coal, copper, lead, iron, stone, lime-stone, pitch and tar. Its manufactures are gloves and stockings, woollen cloths, flannels, and cannon. It is reckoned the largest inland county in the kingdom.

The most remarkable seats are,

Acton Burnell, near Shrewsbury
Adderley Hall, near Drayton
Attingham House, near Shrewsbury
Bellport, near Drayton
Belsidine, near Shrewsbury
Buntingsdale Hall, near Drayton
Canlover Park, near Shrewsbury
Chetwynd Park, near Newport
Cleobury Park, near Bridgenorth
Cond Hall, near Shrewsbury
Coweshall Hall, near Drayton
Edesmere
Frodesley Park, near Shrewsbury
Harcott Park, by Hadicot
Haughton Hall, near Shifnal
Hawkstone Hall, near Wem
Kinlet Hall, near Mortimer
Longnor Park, near Shrewsbury
Loton Hall, near Shrewsbury
Oakley Park, near Ludlow
Pitford Park, near Shrewsbury
Ryton Hall
Sanfaw Hall, near Lee
Shawbury Park, near Shrewsbury
Shavington Hall, near Drayton
Tong Park, near Albrighton
Weston, near Hodnet

The most extensive and beautiful Views are from,

Bridgenorth, on the Banks of the Severn
Quarloc Hill, near Church Stretton
Wrekin Hill, 1398 feet high, near Shrewsbury
Colebrooke Dale, near Shifnal
Endless Woods, near Bridgenorth
The Road from Kidderminster to Bridgenorth
Quatford Church Yard
The Road from Ludlow to Montgomery
Stipperston Clee, near North Cleobury, 1800 feet high
Ellesmere Bowling Green
Arson Hill, five miles from Shrewsbury
Between Ludlow and Church Stretton
Titterston Clee Hill, or the Glee, between Ludlow and Bewdly
Pim-hill Hill, near Shrewsbury
Between Welchpool and Oswestry
The Morf, near Bridgenorth
The Edge, near Wenlock
The Puthy, near Ellesmere.

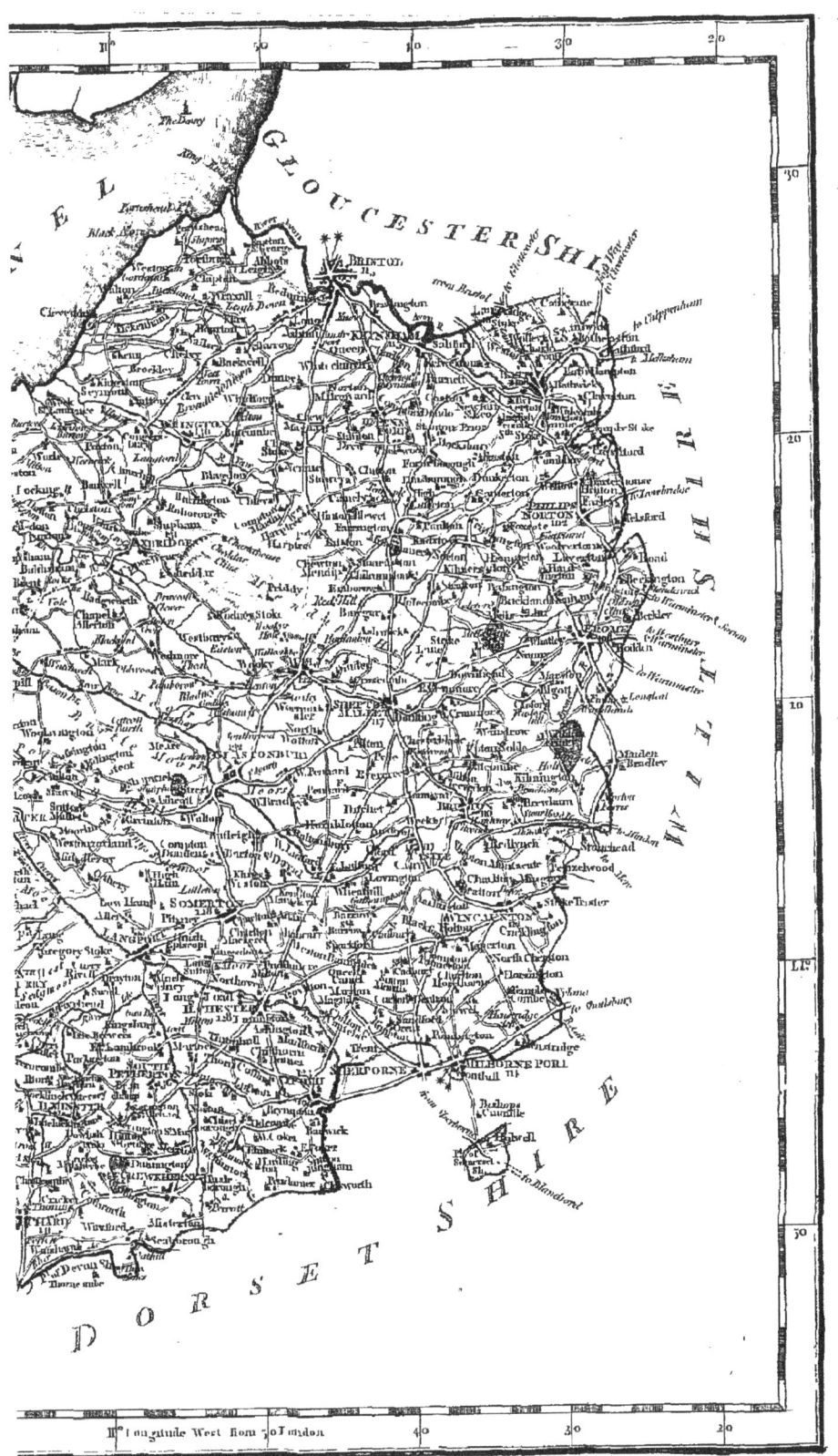

SOMERSETSHIRE

Is a maritime county, and gives the title of Duke to the ancient family of Seymour. During the Saxon heptarchy it belonged to the kingdom of the West Saxons; it is now in the province of Canterbury, in the diocese of Bath and Wells, and is included in the Western circuit. It is 68 miles long, 47 broad, and 240 in circumference; containing 1520 square miles, or 972,800 acres, divided in to 42 hundreds, 385 parishes, 2 cities entire, viz. Bath, which sends 2 members to parliament, and Wells, which also sends 2 members, and, in conjunction with Bath, is a bishoprick that comprehends the county, besides which, this county contains a part of the city of Bristol, which is also a bishoprick, a county of itself, gives the title of Earl to the family of Hervey, and sends 2 members to parliament. It has 31 market-towns, viz. Taunton, which sends 2 members to parliament, Bridgewater, also sends 2 members to parliament, and gives the title of Duke to the Egerton family, Ilchester, gives title of Earl and Baron to the family of Strangeways-Fox, and sends 2 members to parliament, as does Minehead and Milborne Porte, 2 members each; Somerton, from whence the county had its name, gives the title of Baron to the Legg family; besides these, there are the market-towns of Pensford, Frome, North Curry, Bruton, Langport, Philip's Norton, Wincaunton, Wellington, Dunster, Dulverton, Axbridge, Castle Cary, Chard, Nether Stowey, South Petherton, Crewkerne, Glastonbury, Wrington, Wivelescomb, Watchet, Ilminster, Keynsham, Porlock, Shepton Mallet, and Yeovil. Among the villages, Lansdown gives the title of Marquis to the family of Petty; Poulet, gives title of Earl, Viscount, and Baron to the family of the same name, and that of Baron to the family of Cooper; Redlinch and Stoverdale the title of Baron to the family of Strangeways-Fox, Rodney-Stoke, the title of Baron to that of Rodney; Hinton St. George, the titles of Viscount and Baron to the Poulet family; Burton Pynsent, the title of Viscount to the family of Pitt, and Enmore Castle, that of Baron to the Perceval family. Its principal rivers are the Severn, Avon, Ivel, Axe, Cai, Exe, Frome, Brue, Parret, Brue, and Tone. The Points of Land and Isles are Portis-head, Anchor-head, St Thomas's-head, Start-point, Bolestall-point, Flatholms and Steepholm Isles, and the Isle of Athelney; Bridgewater Bay, Porlock Bay, Severn Mouth, and Hung Road. The most remarkable places are, the Wedding at Stanton-Drew, Wookey-hole, Cheddar Rocks and Caverns, Vallis Rocks near Frome, Cadbury Castle, Mendip Hills, Quantock, Blackdown and Poulton Hills, Burkley Comb near Wrington, Camalet Mount, Brent Knoll, Selwood and Neroche Forest, Sedgemoor, Exmore, Heathmore, Kingswood, and Odds Downs. The soil for the most part rich and fertile, particularly the S. and S W parts. The fertility of the Vale of Taunton Dean has long been proverbial. Its productions are various, and comprehends almost every thing necessary for the life of man, viz. pastures, corn, cattle, very large oxen, fruits cheese, and cyder; nor are its excellences confined to the surface, within its bowels are rich veins of coals, copper, lead, iron, lapis calaminaris, limestone, fullers' earth, very fine crystal, yellow ochre, excellent freestone, and alabaster, and its mineral waters of Bath, Bristol, Wells, Alford, and Glastonbury, are well known throughout the world. Its manufactures of woollens, flax, hemp, glass, and stockings are very considerable. It has a salt spring at East Chernock, 20 miles from the sea. It sends 18 members to parliament, 2 for the county and 16 as before shewn, pays 19 parts of the land tax, and provides 840 men to the national militia. It abounds with Roman encampments near Bath and Glastonbury, and has a great number of antique buildings within its limits.

The most considerable Gentlemens' Seats in this county are,

Ashton Court, near Bristol
Babington, near Frome
Barrow Court, near Bristol
Berkley, near Frome
Brewham Lodge, near Bruton
Brockley Court, near Wrington
Bruton Abbey, near Bruton
Burton Pynsent, near Langport
Butleigh, near Somerset
Camerton, near Bath
Charlton Adam, near Somerton
Chelcompton, near Bath
Cleeve Cottage, near Bristol
Comb Hay, near Bath
Compton Pauncefoot, near Castle Cary
Crickett, near Crewkerne
Crowcombe, near Stogumber
Dillington, near Ilminster
Dunster Castle, near Dunster
Enmore Castle, near Bridgewater
Evercreech, near Shepton Mallet
Farley, near Bath
Hilport, near Purton

Haswell, near Bridgewater
Hatch Beauchamp, near Taunton
Heatherton, near Taunton
Hill, near Taunton
Hinton St. George, near Crewkerne
Houndstreet, near Bath
Hestercombe, near Taunton
King's Weston, near Somerton
Langford Court, near Wrington
Marston Bigott, near Frome
Mells Park, near Frome
Midford Castle, near Bath
Mappefter House, near Wincaunton
Nettlecomb, near Taunton
Newton Park, near Bath
Orchardley, near Frome
Pill, near Shepton Mallet
Prior Park, near Bath
Pyrland, near Taunton
Redlynch, near Bruton
Roundhill, near Wincaunton
Shapwick, near Bridgewater
Spargrove, near Barton

Standerwick, near Frome
Stone Easton, near Wells
Stowey, near Pensford
Sutton Court, near Pensford
Vew, near Milborne Porte
Wellington Court, near Wellington
West Monkton, near Taunton
Wraxall Court, near Bristol

The most remarkable Views and Situations are,

Alfred's Tower, near Stour Head
Glastonbury Tor
Cothelston Lodge, near Taunton
Polden Hill
Camalet Hill, or Arthur's Palace, near Yeovil
Quantock Hills, near Watchet
Brent Knoll, near Huntspil
Mendip Hills
Lansdown and Claverton Down, near Bath
Noar Path, on the Upper Bristol Road
Stantonbury Hill, near Stanton Drew

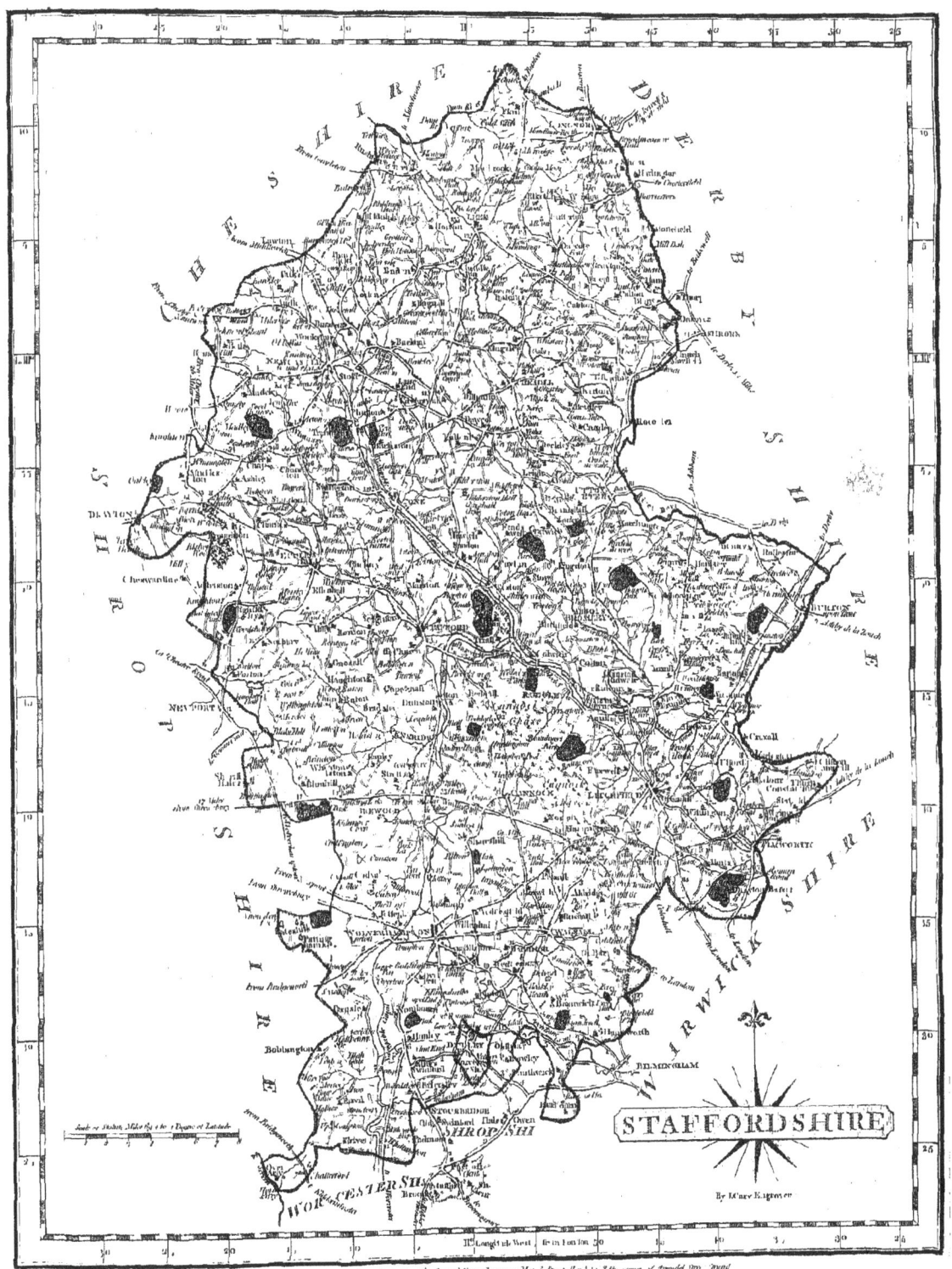

STAFFORDSHIRE

IS an inland county, which, during the Saxon heptarchy, belonged to the kingdom of Mercia, is now belonging to the province of Canterbury, in the diocese of Lichfield and Coventry, and is included in the Oxford circuit. It is in the form of a lozenge, being pointed at both ends, and the broadest in the middle, is situated near the center of England. It is 30 miles broad, 48 long, and 220 in circuit, containing 874 square miles, or 558,360 square acres, divided into 5 hundreds, 130 parishes. It has one city, Lichfield, which sends 2 members to parliament, and enjoys the see of a bishop in conjunction with Coventry, and 17 market towns, viz. Stafford, which gives the title of Marquis to the Gower family, and sends 2 members to parliament; Newcastle-under-line, which gives the title of Duke to the Clinton family, and sends 2 members to parliament; Tamworth, which gives the title of Viscount to the Ferrers family, and sends 2 members to parliament; besides those, there are Burton, Uttoxeter, Tutbury, Wolverhampton, Ecclesall, Cheadle, Abbot's Bromley, Betley, Brewood, Leek, Penkridge, Rudgeley, Stone, and Walsall. The village of Trentham gives the title of Baron to the Gower family, as does Beaudesert to the Paget family, Ingestre, the title of Viscount to the Talbot family, Audley, the title of Baron to the Touchet family, Stourton Castle, the title of Baron to the Stourton family, and Dudley Castle, the same honour to the family of Ward. Its principal rivers are the Trent, Manyfold, Churnet, Lime, Penk, Stour, Tern, Dove, Borne, Sow, Blyn, Tern, and Smestall, with very extensive navigable Canals. The most noted places are Ecton, Moon and Mowcap Hills, the Cloud, Needwood Forest, Cannock Wood or Chace, and Black Meer. It sends 10 members to parliament, pays 7 parts of the land-tax, and provides 560 men to the national militia, produces corn, fish, coals, iron, copper, lead, alabaster, stone, lime-stone, marble, &c., its manufactures are chiefly woollens, iron, and earthen-ware, and the town of Burton is famous for its ale. The air is good and very healthy, but sharp in the North and Moorlands.

The most principal Seats in this county are,

Byrot's Park, near Abbot's Bromley
Batchacre Park, near Ecclesall
Beaudesart Park, near Lichfield
Blithfield
Chartley Park, near Uttoxeter
Drayton Bark, near Tamworth
Juckhill
Jewel
Fisherwick Park, near Tamworth
Hatton Hall, near Brewood
Himley
Hoarcross Hall, near Abbot's Bromley
Ingestre Park, near Stafford
Loxley Hall, near Uttoxeter
Madley Park, near Newcastle

New Park, near Newcastle
Oakley, near Drayton
Pateshill Park, near Wolverhampton
Sandon
Sandwell Park, near Walsall
Slenston
Shuckborough, near Cornwich
Stourton
Swinin, near Lichfield
Toddesly coppice, near Rudgeley
Trentham Park, near Newcastle
Weston Park, near Brewood
Wichnor, near Lichfield
Wolsey Park, near Stafford
Womburn Park, near Dudley

Wooten Park, near Cheadle
Wrottesley

The most remarkable Views are from,

Stafford Castle Hill
Narrowdale, N W of Onecover
Abbot's Castle, near Wolverhampton
Leek Hills, in the road to Congleton
Ecton Hill, between Newcastle and Leek
Barbican de Miles, N of Birmingham
Snow Park
Tutbury Castle.

SUFFOLK

Is a maritime county, which gives the title of Earl to the family of Howard, and, during the Saxon heptarchy, belonged to the kingdom of the East Angles. It is now in the province of Canterbury, diocese of Norwich, and is included in the Norfolk Circuit. It is 55 miles long, 35 broad, and 230 miles in circumference, containing 1460 square miles, or 984,400 square acres, divided into 22 hundreds, 575 parishes, and 30 market-towns, viz. Ipswich, the county town, which sends 2 members to parliament, and gives title of Viscount to the family of Fitzroy, Bury, which sends two members to Parliament, and gives the title of Viscount to the family of Keppel, Sudbury, which sends 2 members to parliament, and gives the title of Baron to the family of Fitzroy, Orford, which gives the title of Earl to the family of Walpole, Brandon, which gives the title of Duke to the family of Hamilton, Eye, which sends 2 members to parliament, and gives the title of Baron to the family of Cornwallis, Ickworth, which gives the title of Baron to the family of Harvey; Alborough, which sends 2 members to parliament, Dunwich, which also sends 2 members to parliament, Clare, which gives the title of Duke to a branch of the Royal Family, Leostoff, Woodbridge, Bilston, Southwold, Budesdale, Bungay, Beccles, Hadley, Stowmarket, Debenham, Halesworth, Lavenham, Menulesham, Mildenhall, Needham, Saxmundham, Woolpit, Neyland, Framlingham, and part of Haverill; among the villages, Ashfield gives the title of Baron to the family of Thurlow, Bolebrook, the same honour to the family of Germaine, Euston, that of Earl to the family of Fitzroy, Houghton, that of Baron to the Walpole family, and Susfield, the same dignity to the family of Harboard. The principal rivers are the Stour, Bret, Larke, Little Ouse, Orwell, Deben, Butley, Alde, Waveny, and Blyth. It produces corn, cattle, rye, hemp, salt, game in great plenty of all kinds, fish of every sort, timber, wood, &c. It has manufactories of bone-lace, woollen goods, fine and coarse, &c. and carries on an extensive commerce to Holland, Germany, Denmark, Sweden, Russia, Prussia, &c. It sends 16 members to parliament, 2 for the county, and 14 for the different boroughs, as above shewn, pays 20 parts of the land-tax, and provides 960 men to the national militia. On its coast are Leostoff Point, Easton Ness, Orford Ness, Burgh Castle, &c. with Sowl Bay, Misinere, Ortord, Baudsey and Orwell Havens, with Alborough Harbour. The most noted places are Angill Hill, Slaughden Valley, several Woods and Stour Meer.

The most remarkable Seats in this county are,

Acton Place, near Sudbury
Ampton, near Bury St Edmunds
Ash Park, near Wickham Market
Badmordesfield Hall, Lidgate
Barton Hall, near Bury St Edmunds
Benacle Park
Benhall Lodge, near Saxmundham
Botesdale
Great Boughton, Ipswich
Boxted Hall, near Clare
Bramford Hall, near Ipswich
Branches Hall, near Cooling
Bretenham Hall, near Sudbury
Cavenham Hall, near Mildenham
Christchurch, near Ipswich
Coldham Hall
Crowfield Hall, near Needham
Culford, near Bury St Edmunds
Dunston Hall
Easton, near Wickham Market
Euston, near Thetford

Flixton Hall, near Bungay
Gazeley, near Newmarket
Glenham Parva, near Saxmundham
St Genove
Felmingham, near Debenham
Hennave, near Bury St Edmunds
Herill an Park, near Southwold
Heisel, near Woolpit
Hevenningham Hall, near Halesworth
Hintlesham, near Ipswich
Holbrook, near Ipswich
Hoxne
Ickworth, near Bury St Edmunds
Kentwell Hall, near Sudbury
Loudhall Hall, near Wickham Market
Melford Hall, near Sudbury
Nacton, near Ipswich
Ousden Hall, near Newmarket
Polsted
Red House, near Ipswich
Rushbrook, near Bury St Edmunds

Great Sacham, near Bury St Edmunds
Shrubland Hall, near Needham
Sibton
Sotterly Hall
Sproughton Chauntry, near Ipswich
Sudourn Hall, near Orford
Stavender Park, near Orford
Thurlow Hall
Thorington Hall, near Halesworth
Welnetham, near Bury St Edmunds
Zoxord

The places most remarkable for beautiful and extensive views are,

Wickham Steeple, S of Framlingham
Burstall, W of Ipswich
Stoke Neyland, S E of Sudbury
From Ipswich to Harwich by Water
The High Grounds at Stoke

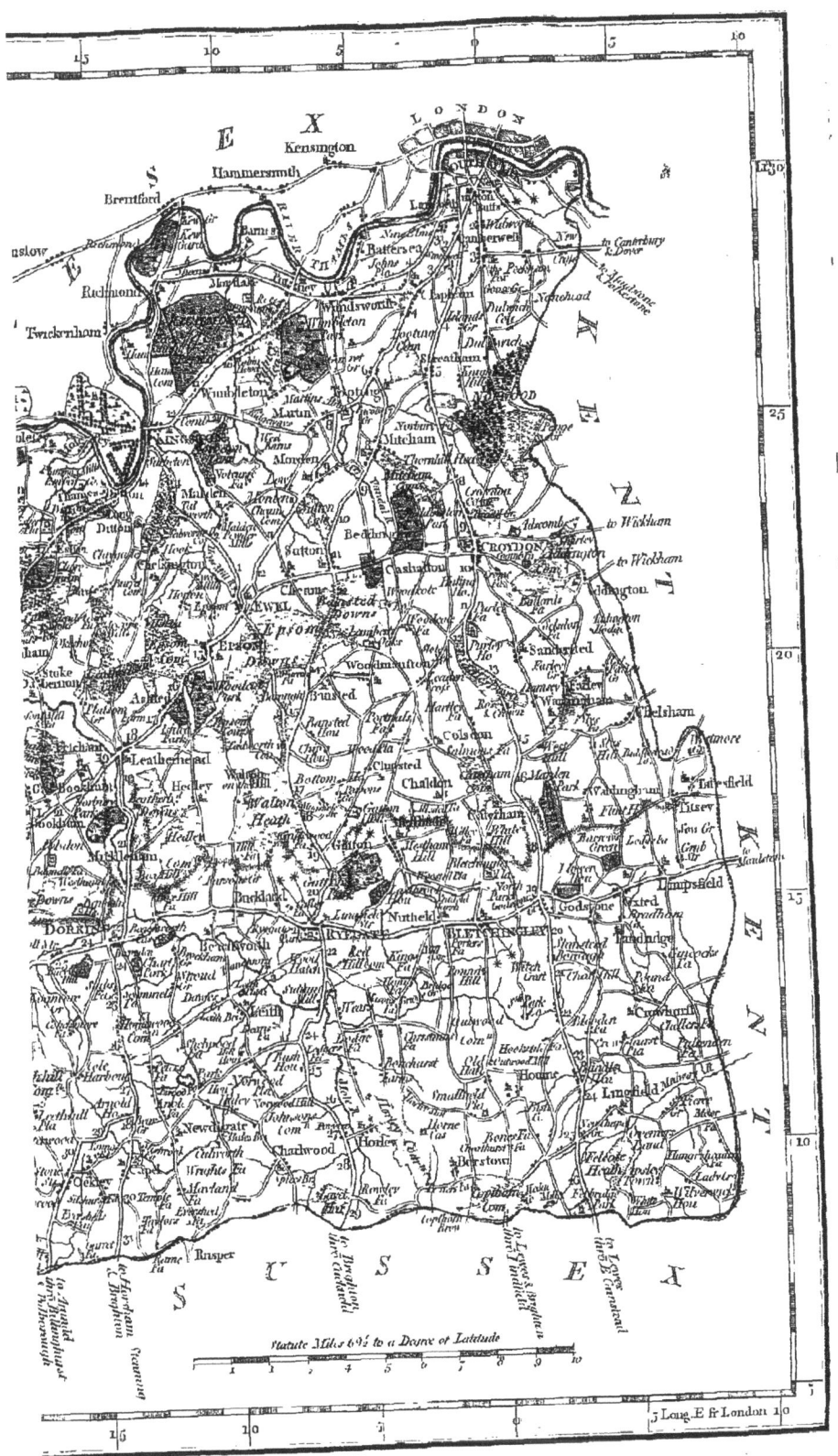

SURRY

Is an inland county, which gives the title of Earl to the family of Howard. During the Saxon heptarchy it belonged to the South Saxons, is now in the province of Canterbury, the diocese of Winchester, and is included in the Home circuit. It is 39 miles long, 26 broad and 146 in circuit, containing 499,200 square acres or 780 square miles, is divided into 13 hundreds, having 140 parishes, and 11 market towns, viz. Guilford, the county town, which sends 2 members to parliament and gives the title of Earl to the family of North, Kingston, Haslemere, which sends 2 members to parliament, Ryegate, which gives the title of Baron to the Mordaunt family, and also sends 2 members to parliament, Croydon, Epsom, Chertsey, Dorking, Ewell, Farnham, and Godalming. Southwark is a suburb to London, sends 2 members to parliament, as does Gatton and Bletchingly, neither of which enjoys a market. The village of Battersea gives the title of Baron to the family of St John, Compton, the title of Baron to the families of both Ferrars and Compton, Effingham, the title of Earl to the family of Howard, Streatham the title of Baron to the family of Russe, Petersham, the title of Baron to the Stanhope family, and Cranley, the title of Baron to the Onslow family. It is almost square in its form, the principal rivers are the Thames, Wandel, Mole, Wey, and Loddon, producing rich pasture, sheep, corn, hops, fruit, wood, game, poultry, fish, and abundance of every kind of garden-stuff. It has a great variety of extensive manufactures of glass, iron, &c &c. The S E. and N W parts have abundance of uncultivated grounds, but the other parts are remarkably fertile, and its air particularly wholesome and pleasant, which formerly induced several of our Kings to erect palaces in it for their residences. It sends 14 members to parliament, pays 18 parts of the land-tax, and supplies 800 men to the national militia, and, for its extent, has more gentlemens' villas than any other county in the kingdom, among whom the following are most remarkable.

Abury Park, near Abury
Ashted Park, near Epsom
Abbs Court, near Moulsey
Burrow's Green
Bagshot Park
Betchworth, near Ryegate
Bedington Place
Bletchingly Place
Bookham
Botley House, near Chertsey
Burwood Park
Busbridge, near Godalming
Byfleet, near Cobham
Bury Hill, near Dorking
Carshalton
Clare Park, near Dorking
Chertsey
Clandon Park, near Guilford
Clermount, near Esher
Cobham
Combe house, near Kingston
Comb Park
Comb
Deepden, near Dorking
Denbigh, near Dorking
Dudley Place, near Guilford

Esher Place, near Esher
Leatwick Park, near Leatherhead
Ember Court
Farnham Park
Felbridge Park
Fetcham Park, near Leatherhead
Flower House, near Godstone
Gatton Park, near Ryegate
Gatton, near Chipstead
Hatchland Park, near E Clandon
Henley Park
Hern Haw, near Chertsey
Horsley East, near Bookham
Horsley West, near Clandon
Kew Palace
Ledbroke House, near Gatton
Lambert Oaks, near Bansted
Marden Park, near Godstone
Mascall's Grove, near Chertsey
Mitcham
Moor Park, near Farnham
Norbury, near Leatherhead
Oatlands, near Weybridge
Oakham, near Ripley
Painshill Park, near Cobham
Pepper Harrow, near Godalming

Petersham, near Richmond
Pierpont Lodge, near Farnham
Polsdon, near Mickleham
Potter's Park, near Cobham
Rochampton
Shallingly Park
Slinne, near Bagshot
Waverley Abbey, near Farnham
Westbrook Place, near Godalming
Wimbleton Park
Woodcote Park, near Epsom
Woburn Farm, near Weybridge

The most remarkable Views are from,

Richmond Park and Hill
Terrace in Richmond Gardens
Wandsworth Hill
St Ann's Hill, near Chertsey
Box Hill, near Dorking
Leith Hill, near Wotton
Road from Dorking to Guilford
Bansted Downs
Hind Hill, near Godalming
Gracewood Hill near Godalming

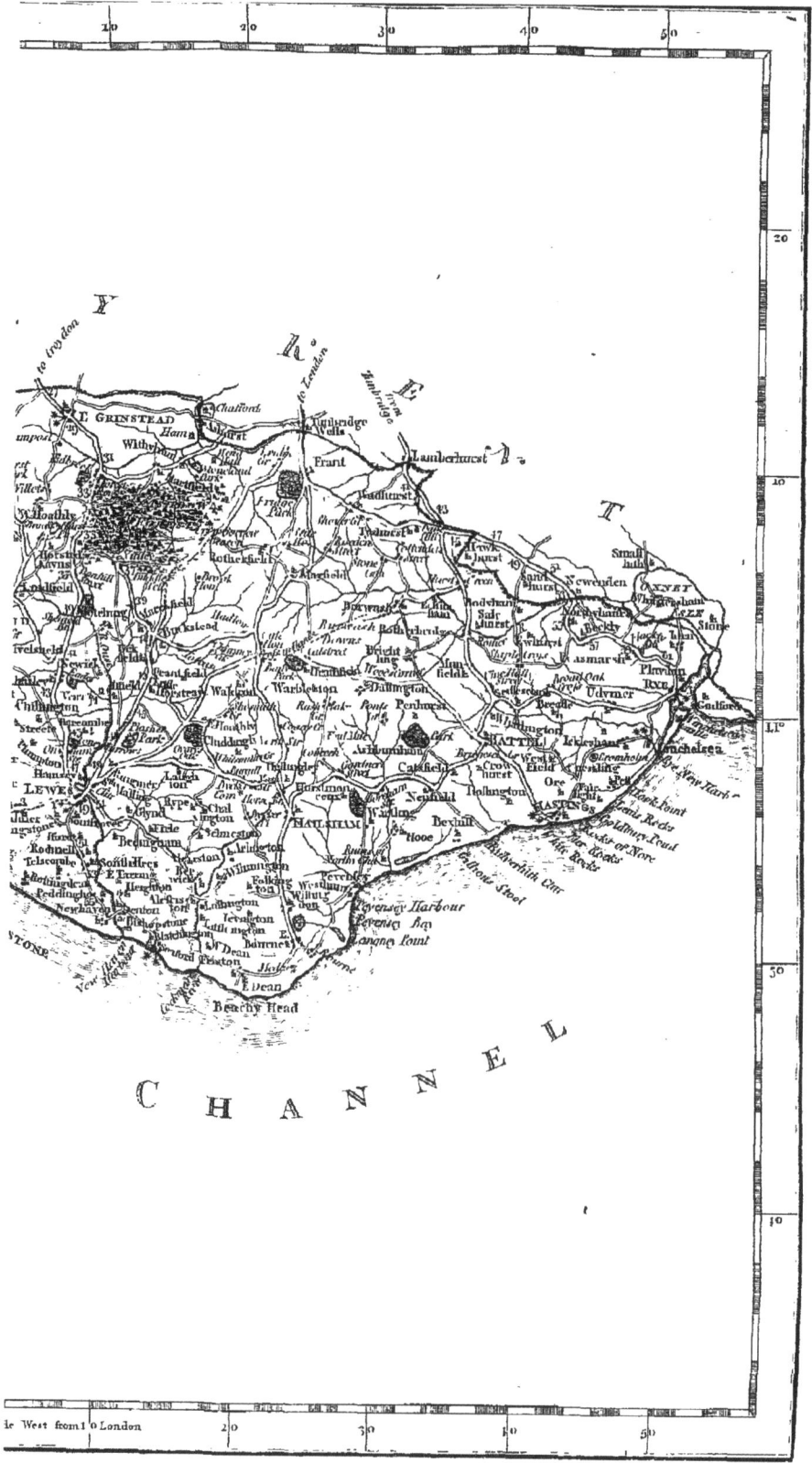

SUSSEX

Is a maritime county on the southern boundary of the kingdom, and gives the title of Earl to the family of Yelverton. During the Saxon heptarchy it belonged to the kingdom of the South Saxons, it is now in the province of Canterbury, in the diocese of Chichester, and is included in the Home circuit. It is 75 miles long, 28 broad, and 195 in circumference, containing 1444 square miles, or 924,160 acres, divided into 6 rapes, which are sub-divided into 65 hundreds, containing 342 parishes, one city, Chichester, which sends 2 members to parliament, and is the see of a bishop, and 16 market-towns, viz. Lewes, which sends 2 members to parliament, Arundel, which sends 2 members to parliament, and gives the title of Earl to the Howard family (and has the singularity of being the only local dignity in England, by conferring the dignity of an Earl on whoever is its possessor, without any patent of creation, but is annexed by parliament to the Dukedom of Norfolk), East Grinstead, which sends 2 members to parliament; as does Midhurst, Shoreham, Horsham, and Steyning, Bramber, sends 2 members to parliament, but enjoys no market, Winchelsea, Seaford, Hastings, which gives the title of Baron to the family of the same name, and the title of Earl to the family of Finch, and Rye, as Cinque Ports, sends each 2 members to parliament, the two latter enjoy markets, as does Chiddingford, Petworth, Battle, Brighthelmstone, Cuckfield, Haylsham, and Terring, the village of Ashburnham, gives the titles of Earl and Baron to the family of Ashburnham, Bayham, that of Viscount to the family of Pratt, Buckhurst, that of Baron to the family of Sackville, Heathfield to that of Eliot, and Tufton to that of Tufton. The most remarkable places in the county are, Thorney Isle, Chichester Harbour, Selsey Bill and Harbour, Bognor Rocks, Arundel, Shoreham, and Newhaven Harbours, Beachy Head, Langney Point, Pevensey and Rye Harbours, Crowborough and Beacon Hills, Ashdown, St. Leonard's, Tilgate, Waterdown, Dallington, Arundel and Worth Forests, Holm, Petlor, Dirum, and Vent Woods, the Dyke, the Downs, and watering or bathing places. The principal rivers are the Cockmere, Little Ouse, Rother, Adur, Rye, and Arun. Its product is sheep, corn, wood, timber, wild fowl, sea and river fish, and that delicate bird the Wheat-ear. The manufactures are charcoal, gunpowder, and iron-work. The air is various, as is also the soil, yet not unwholesome. It sends 20 members to parliament, 2 for the county, and 18 as above shewn, besides those for the Cinque Ports, pays 9 parts of the land tax, and provides 640 men to the national militia.

The principal Gentlemens' Seats are,

Arundel Park
Ashburnham Park, near Battel.
Buxly Park, near Hailsham
Brodhurst Park, near East Grinstead.
Buckingham House, near Shoreham.
Burton Park, near Petworth
Coombe, near Lewes.
Coney Burrows, near Lewes
Cowdrey Park, near Midhurst
Crowhurst Park, near Hastings.
Danfey, near Ditchling
Den Park, near Horsham.
Lade, near Lewes
Eartage Park, near East Grinstead
Finden, near West Tarring
Firle, near Lewes
Friston Place, near Hailsham.

Goodwood House, near Chichester
Halnaker House, near Chichester
Hookland Park, near Steyning
Horstmonceux Park, near Battel
Lavyhole, near Midhurst
Michelgrove, near Arundel
Muntham, near West Tarring
Offington, near West Tarring.
Petworth
Sedgwick Park, near Horsham
Selhurst Park, near Arundel,
Shillingby Park, near Midhurst.
Slaugham Park, near Cuckfield
Slindon House, near Arundel
South Bourne, near Hailsham
Stanstead House, near East Bourne
Stanmer, near Lewes.

Uppark, near Midhurst
Wakhurst Park, near East Grinstead.
Wellington Park, near Hailsham
West Grinstead Park, near Steyning
Wiston Park, near Steyning
Wormnghurst Park, near Steyning

The most extensive and beautiful Prospects are from,
Beachy Head
The Windmill, near Lewes
A Hill near Rye
South Downs.
Rooke Hill
Devil's Dyke.
Mountfield Cour Lodge.
Durford, near Petersfield.

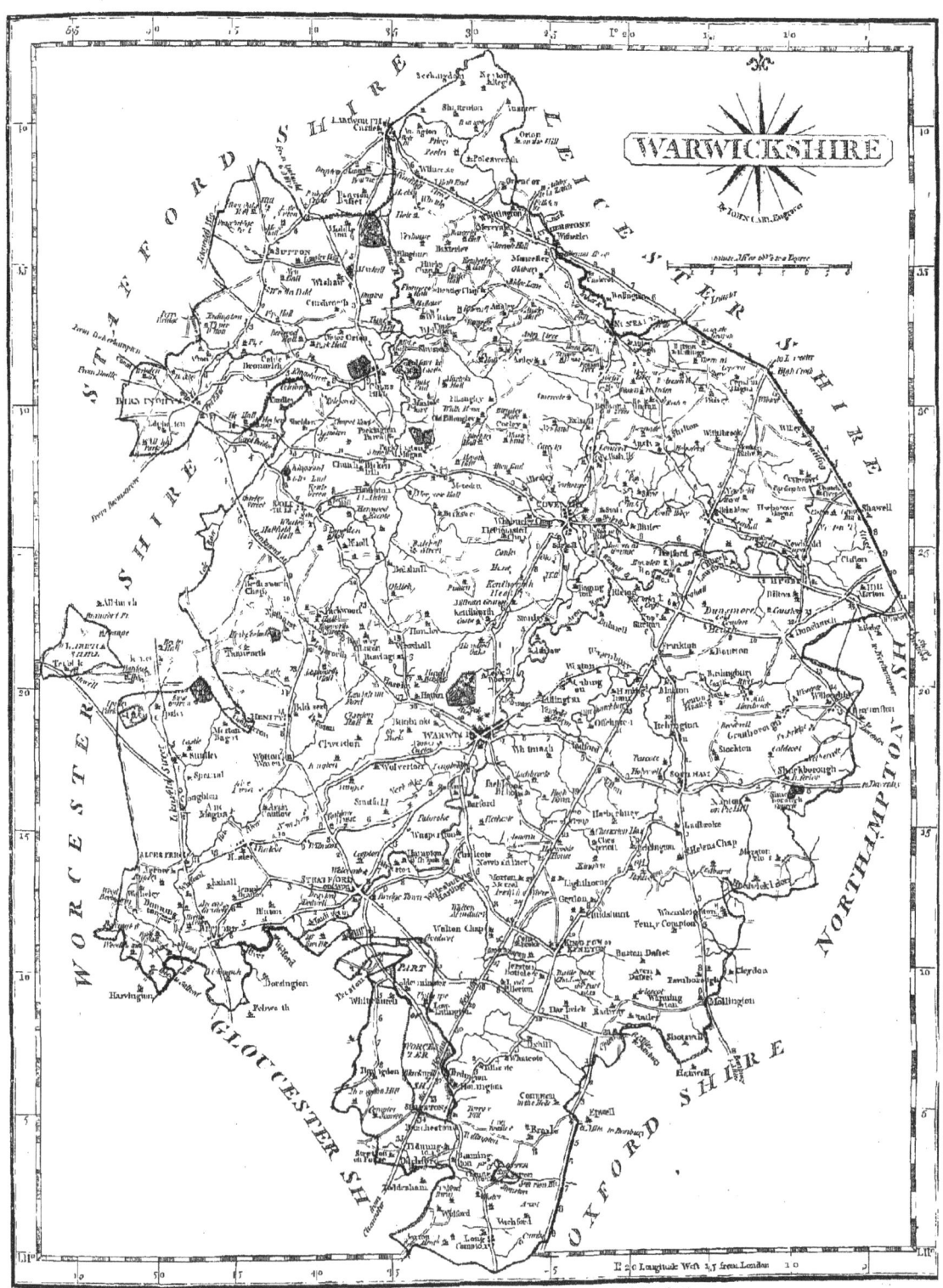

WARWICKSHIRE

Is an inland county, which, during the Saxon heptarchy, belonged to the kingdom of Mercia. It is now in the province of Canterbury, diocese of Worcester, Litchfield and Coventry, and is included in the Midland circuit. It is 50 miles long, 32 broad, and 210 in circumference, containing 980 square miles, or 627,200 square acres, divided into 4 hundreds and 1 liberty, 158 parishes, one city, Coventry, which sends 2 members to parliament, and, in conjunction with Litchfield, is the see of a Bishop, and gives the title of Earl and Baron to the family of Coventry, and 14 market-towns, viz. Warwick, the county town, which sends 2 members to parliament and gives title of Earl to the family of Greville, Tamworth, which is partly in this county, sends 2 members to parliament, and gives the title of Viscount to the family of Shirley, Birmingham, gives the title of Baron to the family of Ward, Stratford, Henley, Coleshill, Atherstone, Alcester, Kyneton, Nun-Eaton, Rugby, Southam, and Sutton-Colfield, among the villages, Beauchamp Court gives the title of Baron to the Greville family, Beauchamp, that of Viscount to the family of Conway, Middleton, that of Baron to the Willoughby family, Newnham-Paddock, those of Viscount and Baron to the Fielding family, Overlsey, that of Baron to the family of Wentworth, and Wormleighton the same dignity to the Spencer family. Its principal rivers are the Avon, Tame, Alne, Anker, and Cole. It produces corn, iron, cattle, has manufactories of thread, flannel, linen, pins, woollen stuffs, silks, the most extensive in iron-works, Japan-ware, plated goods, &c. and the water of Sherborn, noted for the best blue dye. This county sends 6 members to parliament, viz. 2 for the shire, and 4 for the towns as above mentioned, pays 10 parts of the land-tax, and provides 640 men to the national militia. This county is in the center of the kingdom, and has a most wholesome air, divided into two parts by the river Avon, which runs through it, called Feldon and Woodland. The soil is fruitful, especially the south parts. The most noted places are Lagehill, Aubury Mounts, Vale of Red Horse, Dunsmore Heath, and the antient Roman Military Withingstreet and Foss Way. This county enjoys great advantage from the inland navigable canals, which join the Severn and Humber.

The most eminent Seats in this county are,

Aiton End
Alkeby Park
Arbury, near Coventry
Baggington, near Coventry
Barsaley Hall, near Polesworth
Biton, near Rugby
Famcote, near Polesworth
P.ndon, near Coventry
Chadbam, near Kyneton
Charleston
Combe Abbey, near Coventry
Four Oaks Hall, near Sutton

Kenilworth Castle, near Warwick
Little Lawford, near Rugby
Mount Grevil, near Stratford
Newood Revel, near Rugby
Parkington, near Coleshill
Pagley, near Alcester
Stanley Abbey, near Warwick
Umberslade
Warwick Castle
Weston, near Coventry
Wolverhall,

The most extensive Prospects are from,

Aubury Mounts
Edgehill
Guy's Cliff
Ragley.

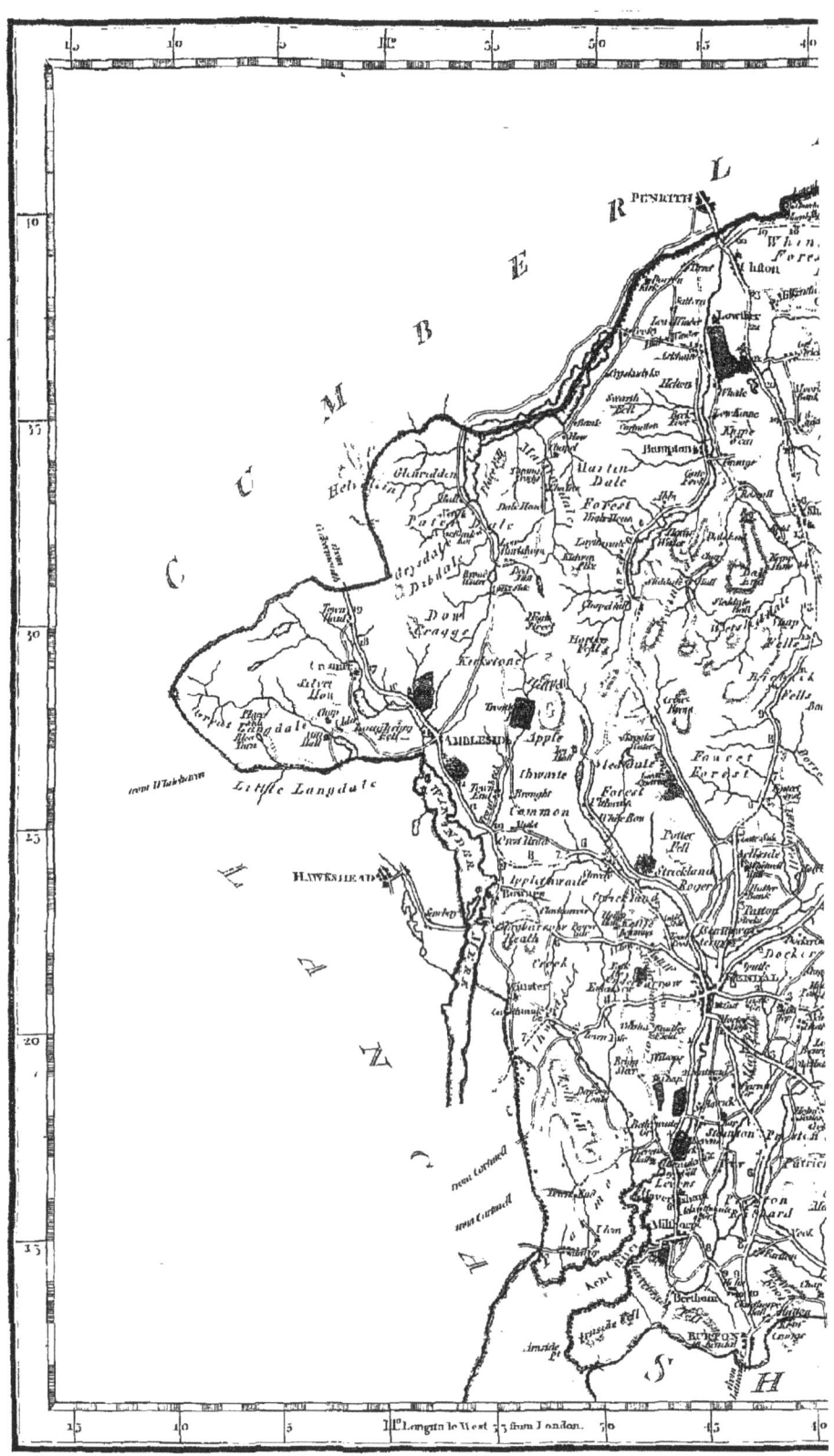

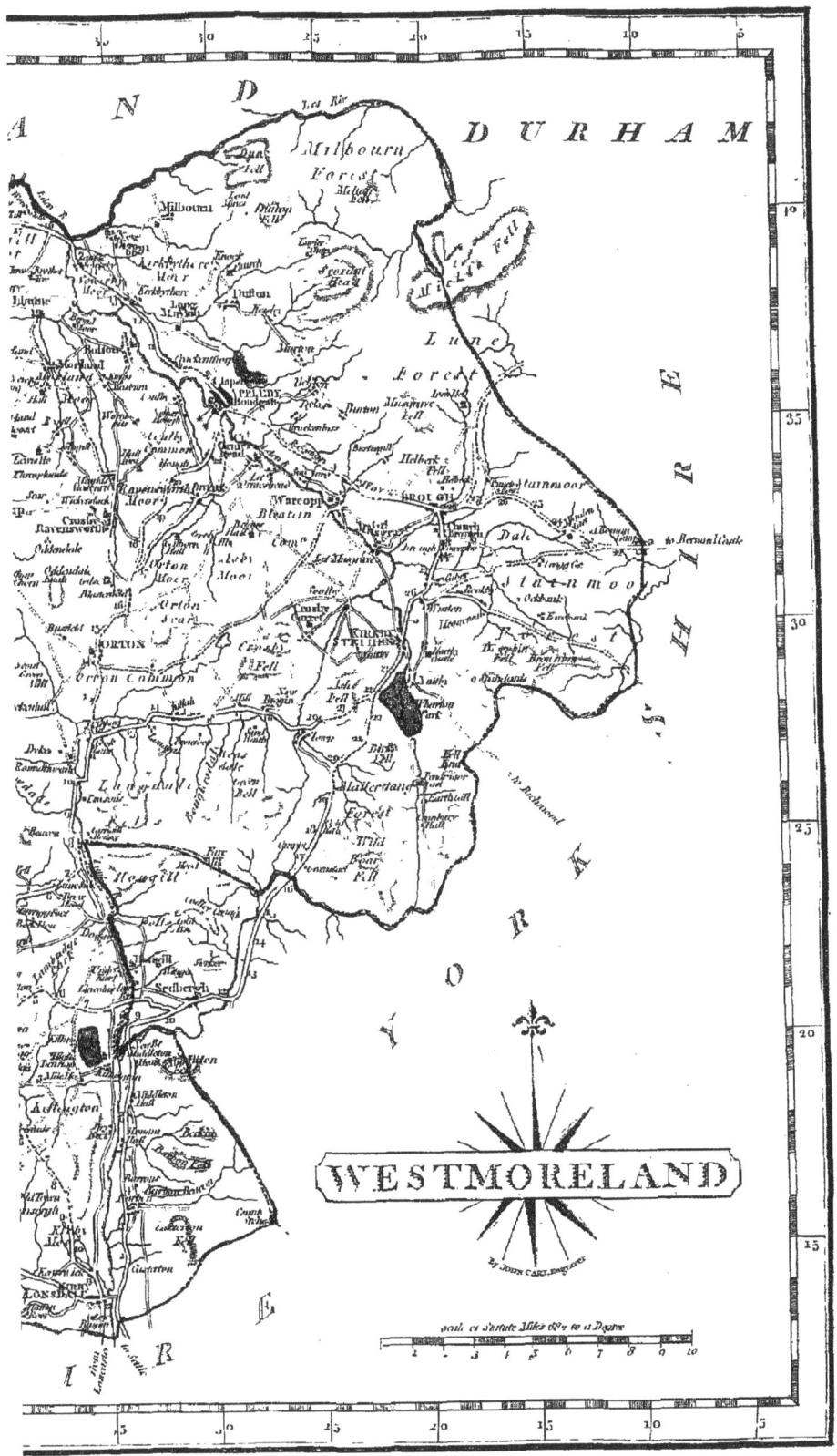

WESTMORELAND

Is an inland county, which gives the title of Earl to the family of Fane, and, during the Saxon heptachy, belonged to the kingdom of Northumberland. It is now in the province of York, dioceses of Carlisle and Chester, and is included in the Northern circuit. It is 40 miles long from east to west, 33 from north to south, and 130 miles in circumference, containing 770 square miles, or 492,800 square acres, divided into 4 wards, though generally into two baronies, 32 parishes, and 8 market-towns, viz. Appleby, which is the county town, and sends 2 members to parliament, and gives the title of Baron to the Southwell family; Kendal, which gives the same honour to the family of Herbert; Lonsdale, which gives the titles of Earl and Viscount to the family of Lowther; Brough, which gives the title of Baron to the same family; Ambleside, Kirkby-Steven, Burton, and Orton. The principal rivers are the Eden, Kent, Lune, Tees, Belo, Lowther, Rotha, and Emont. The chief products are corn, wood, sheep, copper mines, various river fish, particularly salmon, trout, char, &c. Its chief manufactures are woollens of various kinds, stockings, hats, and fine narns and cotton in a great many branches. Here are many noble stone-bridges, several cataracts, and some chalibeat-waters. There are Thornthwaite, Martendale, Melton, Mallerstane, Milburne, Stanmore and Winfield Forests, Ulles, Broad and Horns waters, and that extensive piece called Winander Meer, the largest in England, being 10 miles long, and 2 broad, with several islands in it, and its bottom one continued rock, Faileron-knot Hill, Winfield Hill, Murton, Dufton and Knock Points, Roman and Rumary Fells, Lonsdale and Stanmore Vales. The air of this county is sweet and pleasant, as well as healthy; but, in the mountainous parts, sharp and piercing. It sends 4 members to parliament, 2 for the county, and 2 for Appleby, as above mentioned; pays one part only of the land-tax, and supplies 240 men to the national militia.

The principal Gentlemen's Seats in this county are,

Appleby	Lowther	*The most extensive Views are from,*
Bigstur Park	Milthorpe	Rydale Hill and Head, N. of Ambleside
Cappiel wite, near Sedbury	Pendragon Castle, near Kirkby Steven.	The Falls of the Ken, Five Miles from Kendal
Clifton	Rydal, near Ambleside	The Road from Appleby to Penrith
Hartley Castle, near Kirkby Steven.	Shap	High Point of Land overlooking Winander Meer
Inpsture Hall, near Sedborg	Syzergh Park, near Kendal	The road from Ambleside to Kendal
Kidlington Park, near Sedborg	Troutbeck Park, near Ambleside	Falls of Water, near Ambleside
Kirkby Steven	Warcopp, near Brough	Greyridge Hill, between Brough and Kendal
Leven's Park, near Milthorpe	Wharton Park, near Kirkby Steven.	Grasmere Water, N. of Ambleside
		Whitbarrow seats, near Milthorpe

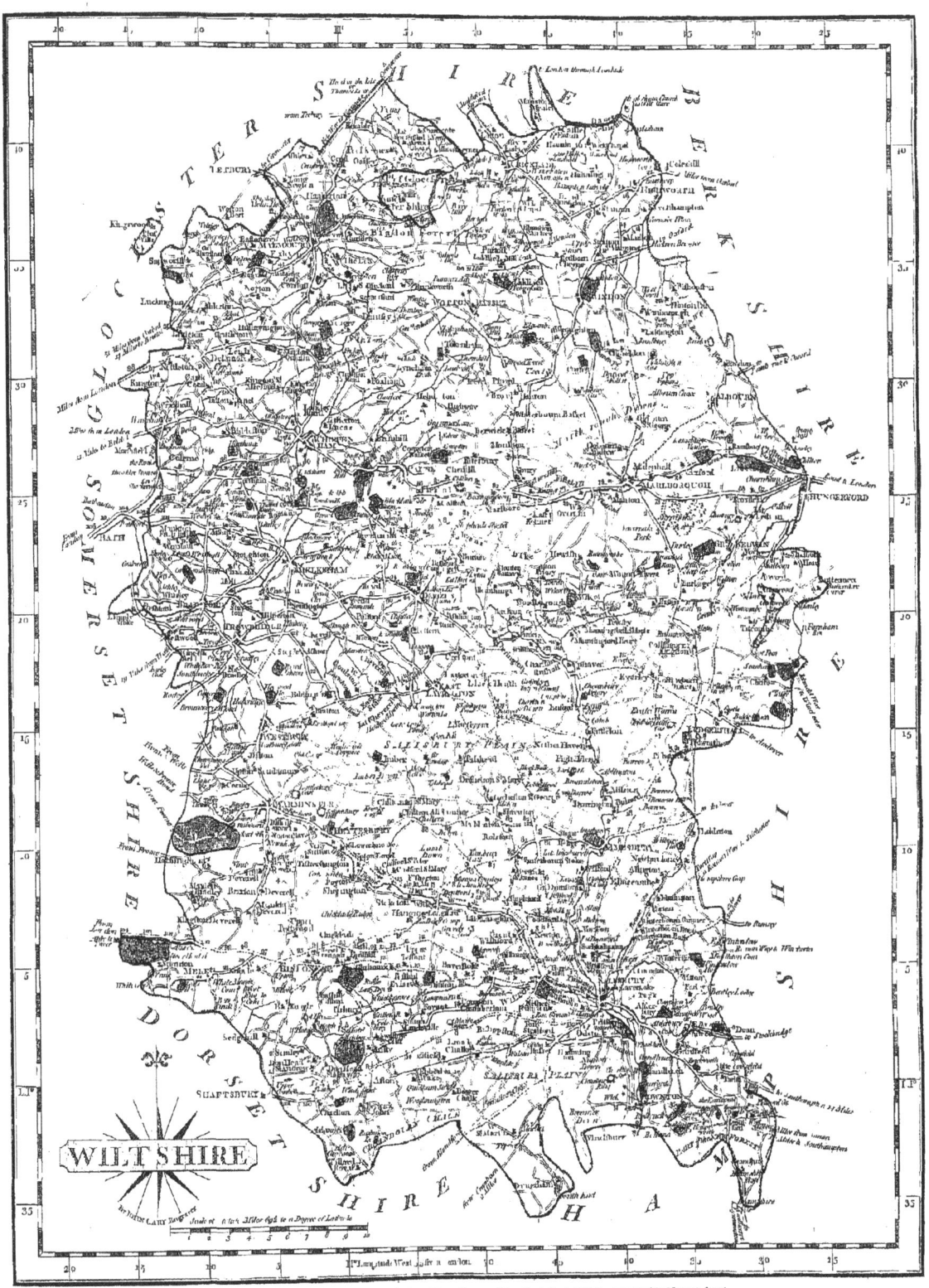

WILTSHIRE

Is an inland county, which gives the title of Earl to the family of Powlett, and sends 2 members to parliament. During the Saxon heptarchy it made part of the kingdom of Wessex, is now in the province of Canterbury, in the diocese of Salisbury, and is included in the Western circuit. It is 54 miles long, 34 broad, and 200 in circuit, containing 1200 square miles, or 760,000 square acres, divided into 29 hundreds, 304 parishes, 107 vicarages, about 950 villages, 1 city, Salisbury which sends 2 members to parliament, and gives the title of Earl to the family of Cecil, and 21 market towns, viz. Marlborough, which sends 2 members to parliament, and gives the title of Duke to the family of Spencer, Devizes, sends 2 members to parliament, Malmsbury, sends 2 members to parliament, Wilton, which gives the title of Baron to the Egerton family, and sends 2 members to parliament, Chippenham, sends 2 members to parliament, Calne, which sends 2 members to parliament, and gives the title of Viscount to the Petty family, Cricklade, sends 2 members to parliament, Downton, also sends 2 members to parliament, Heytesbury, sends 2 members to parliament, Hindon, sends 2 members to parliament, Luggershall, sends 2 members to parliament, Westbury, sends 2 members to parliament, Wotton Basset, sends 2 members to parliament, besides which there is Castle Comb, Warminster, Amesbury, Auburn, Bradford, Highworth, Lavington, Swindon, Trowbridge, and Mere, the villages of Old Sarum and Great Bedwin, though they enjoy neither market nor fair, send each 2 members to parliament, but Clarendon gives the title of Earl to the Villers family, Charlton, the title of Baron to the Howard family, Lydiard Tregoze, the title of Baron to the family of St John, and Wardour Castle, the title of Baron to the Arundel family. This county sends 34 members to parliament, pays but 13 parts of the land tax, and provides 800 men to the national militia. Its chief rivers are the two Avons, the Kennet, Willey, Adder, Nadder, Duril, Were, Calne, Isis, Rey, and Wellyborne. Wiltshire is generally divided into two parts, North and South. The most remarkable part of South Wiltshire is that extensive plain called Salisbury Plain, on which vast numbers of sheep are bred and depastured, and on which, near Amesbury, stands that noble and ancient monument of antiquity called Stonehenge. This part of the country produces vast quantities of corn supplying not only its own consumption, but frequently Bath and Bristol, and the eastern part of the county of Somerset. The Northern abounds with rich pastures, producing that most excellent cheese called North Wiltshire, and frequently (in London) Glocester cheese. The air is generally sharp on the Downs, but mild in the vales. Wiltshire carries on very large manufactures of different kinds of woollen goods, &c. viz. Salisbury, flannels and fancy goods; Wilton, carpets, marbled cloths, &c. Devizes, fancy goods and serges; Bradford, Trowbridge, Melksham, Warminster, Westbury, and Heytesbury, superfine and coarse broad cloths and kerseymeres, and about Mere a very large trade is carried on in dowlas, ticking, and other coarse linens. It has a great number of Roman, Saxon, British, and Danish encampments in different parts of the county, and three of the Roman roads pass through it. It has several antiquities remaining, and many Gentlemen's seats, the most remarkable are,

Amesbury Park, near Amesbury
Ashcombe, near Shaftsbury
Baynton, near Eddington
Bowood, near Calne
Boyton, near Heytesbury
Bradley House, at Maiden Bradley
Brimslade, near Marlborough
Bromham, near Devizes
Burltrop, near Swindon
Charlton Park, near Marlborough
Cleverel Park, near East Lavington
Chilton Lodge, near Chilton Folia
Chute Lodge, near Chute
Clarendon Park, near Salisbury
Cole Park, near Malmsbury
Comberwell, near Bradford
Compton House, near Calne
Compton House, near Wilton
Corsham House, near Corsham
Crow Wood, near Auburne
Cutteridge House, near North Bradley
Danzey House, near Danzey
Draycot House, near Chippenham
Eastwell House, near Devizes
Fern, near Shaftsbury
Foxley House, near Malmsbury
Fonthill, near Hindon
Groveley Lodge, near Wilton
Hartham, near Biddleston
Heytesbury House, at Heytesbury

Heywood House, near Westbury
Imber, near West Lavington
Ivy House, near Chippenham
Langford House, near Downton
Liddington Castle, near Chisseldon
Laycock Nunnery, near Corsham
Lydiard Tregoze, near Wotton Basset
Lydiard Millicent, near Purton
Littlecot, near Chilton Foliat
Longford Castle, near Salisbury
Longleat, near Warminster
Luckrim, near Biddleston
Lusbinger, near Downton
Maddenton, near Shrewton
Monkton Farley, near Bath
New House, near Downton
Oare, near Wotton
Overton, near Swindon
Park House, near Amesbury
Park House, near Devizes
Pinkey House, near East Shrenton
Ramsbury Park, near Marlborough
Rowd Ashton, near North Bradley
Rushmore Lodge, near Shaftsbury
Rusley, near Auburne
Salthorp, near Wotton Basset
Sandridge, near Melksham
Seagrey, near Stanton St. Quintin
Seend Green, near Seend
Spy Park, near Broomham

Sanalynch, near Downton
Santon S. Quintin
Stour Head, near Mere
Studley Hill, near Calne
Swindon House, at Swindon
Tokenham House, near Wotton Basset
Totenham Park, near Beswin
Wardour Castle, near Shaftsbury
Witham, near Calne
Wyck, near Sapworth
Welbury House, near Amesbury
Wilcot House, near Wilcot
Wilton House, near Wilton
Winterflow House, near Salisbury
Wraxhall House, near Monkton Farley
Wolf Hall, near Luggershall
Zeal's House, near Mere

The most extensive views are from,

Martinsall Hill, near Old Sarum
Alfred's Tower, at Stour Head
Roundaway Hill, near Devizes
Clay Hill, West of Warminster
Highworth Hill
Lush Hill, near Hannington Wick
Berry Hill, in Brandon Forest
Chidbury Hill Castle, near Luggershall

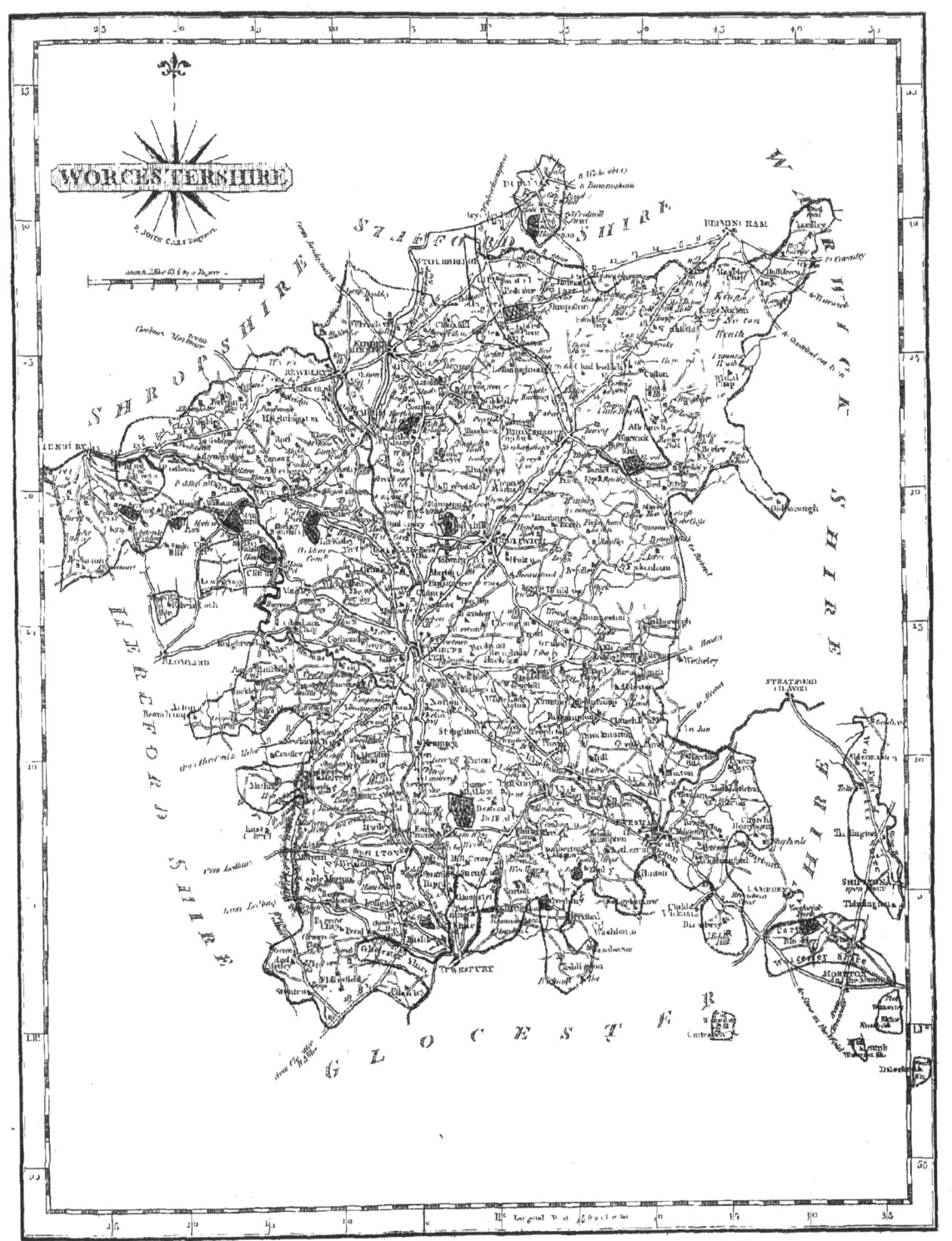

WORCESTERSHIRE

Is an inland county, which, during the Saxon heptarchy, belonged to the kingdom of Mercia, it is now in the province of Canterbury, the diocese of Worcester, and in the Oxford circuit. It is 34 miles long, 28 broad, and 220 in circumference, containing 660 square miles, or 158,400 acres, divided into 5 hundreds and 2 limits, containing 152 parishes, one city, Worcester, the fee of a bishop, which sends 2 members to parliament, and gives the titles of Marquis, Earl, and Viscount to the family of Somerset; and 11 market-towns, viz Kidderminster, which gives the title of Baron to the Foley family, Evesham, which sends 2 members to parliament, and gives the title of Baron to the family of Cocks, Droitwich, which sends 2 members also, and Bewdley, which sends one, Dudley, which gives title of Baron to the family of Ward, Bromsgrove, Upton, Pershore, Stourbridge, Shipton, and Tenbury. Amongst the villages, Omberfley gives the title of Baron to the family of Sandys, and Ragley, the same dignity to the family of Conway. The principal rivers are the Severn, Avon, Teem, and Stour, but, enjoying the benefit of some of the late constructed canals, it has, by the inland navigation, communication with the most considerable rivers in the kingdom, which navigation, including its windings, extends above 500 miles through different counties. The most remarkable places in this county are, Malvern, Aberley, Woodberg, Bredon, and Clent Hills, the vale of Evesham, Malvern Chace, Feckingham and Half of Wire Forest, several woods, and 2 medicinal springs on Malvern Hills. Its chief products are pasture, corn, cattle, sheep, wood, cyder, perry, coal, hops, very fine salt, river fish, fruit, and common meadow saffron. The county is of a triangular form, has a sweet and temperate air, and soil fertile, interspersed with hills that feed large flocks of sheep. The chief manufactures are carpetting, china and eathern ware, woollens, salt, and stockings. It sends 9 members to parliament, 2 for the county, and 7 as above-mentioned, pays 9 parts of the land-tax, and provides 560 men to the national militia.

The most considerable Gentlemen's Seats in this County are,

Bufhley Park, near Tewkesbury.
Cotheridge, near Worcester
Crome Park, near Pershore.
Dudley Lodge, near Dudley
Elmley Park, near Evesham.
Grafton.
Grafthampton, near Great Whitley.
Hadfor, near Droitwich.
Hagley Park, near Dudley
Ham Castle Park, near Clifton
Hanbury Hall, near Droitwich
Herslip, near Worcester
Hewell Grange, near Bromsgrove
Holdfast, near Upton

Holtcastle, near Worcester
Madersfield, near Great Malvern
Midlehill, near Broadway
Northwich Park, near Cambden
Omberfley Court, near Droitwich
Overbury, near Tewkesbury
Ribbesford, near Bewdley
Roufe Linch, near Droitwich
Saddington, near Bewdley
Shipoing, near Mathorn
Stenford Park, near Tenbury
Waftley Green, near Bewdley
Westwood Park, near Droitwich
Witley Park, near Worcester.

The most remarkable Views and Situations are,

Bewdley on the Severn
Perry Wood, near Worcester
The Road from Evesham to Worcester.
Clent Hill, near Hagley
Malvern Hills
Road from Bewdley to Worcester.
Red Hill, by Ribbesford
Poor's Hole
Hundred House and Witley.
Croukbury Hill, two miles from Worcester.
Cleeve Prior, near Evesham.

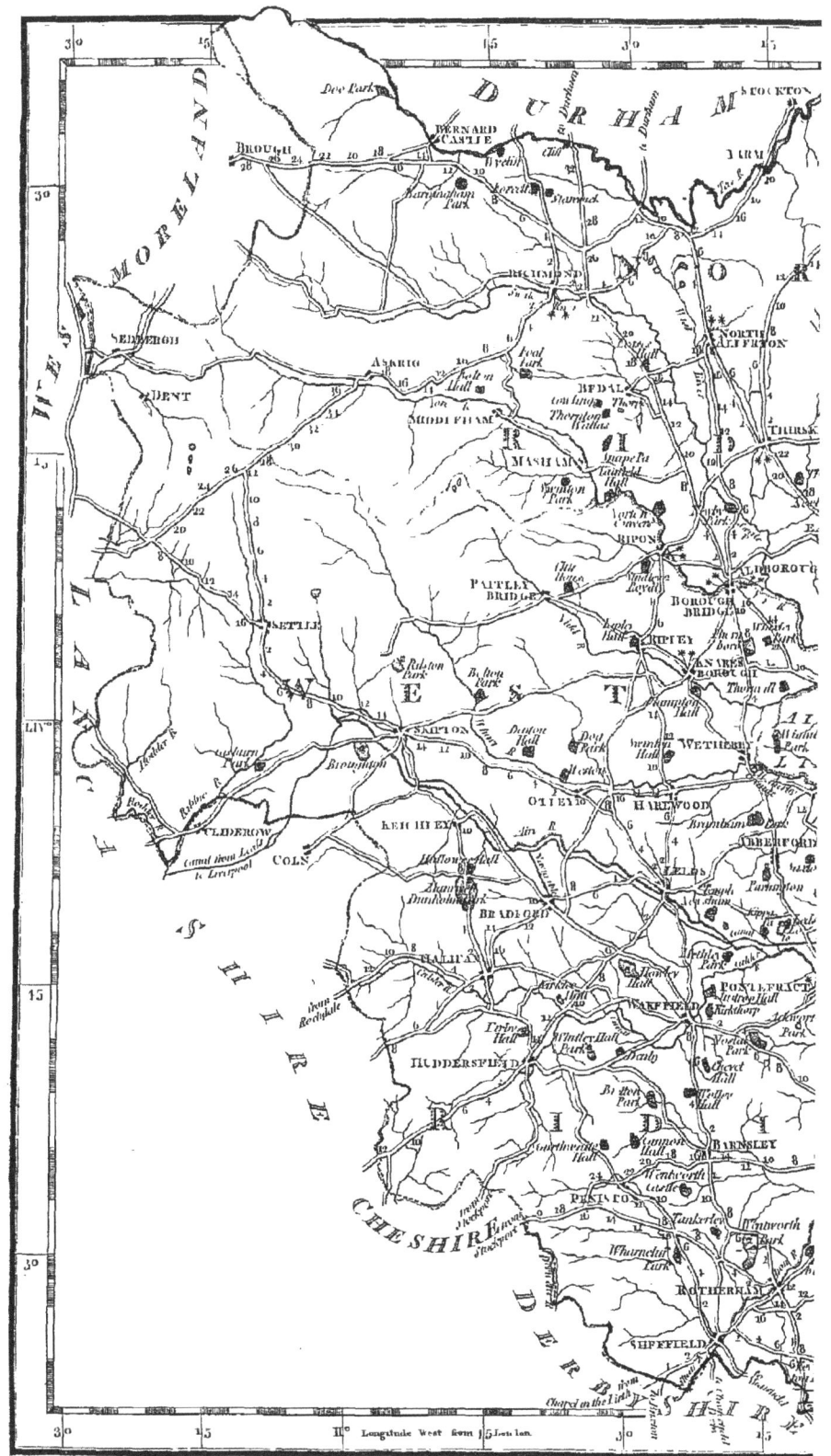

YORKSHIRE

Is a maritime county, which, during the Saxon heptarchy, was included in the kingdom of Northumberland, and at the division of England, by Alfred, into counties, it included those of Durham and Lancashire, though now, without them, it is bigger than any two counties in the kingdom, and in extent exceeds either the Dukedoms of Wirtemburg, Mecklenburg, Courland, Savoy, the Principality of Hesse Caffel, the Electorate of Mentz, the Dominion of Genoa, &c. and all the Seven United Provinces of Holland connected. It is in the diocese of York, and province of the same name, except Richmondshire in the North Riding, which belongs to the diocese of Chester. It is 130 miles long, 90 broad, and 460 in circumference, containing 5490 square miles, or 3,513,600 acres, in form nearly square, divided into Three Ridings, of which we have given distinct maps, viz. North, East, and West Ridings, of which the last-mentioned is both the largest and richest: besides these, there is a fourth division called Richmondshire; as also Cleveland, formerly a Dukedom, Holderness, which had the title of Earl, and Craven, formerly an Earldom, now a Barony, in the family of the same name, also a small division called Ainsty, wherein the city of York is situated. It is divided into 24 wapentakes or hundreds, including 563 parishes, 58 market-towns, which are mentioned in their distinct Ridings, and one city, York, the second in rank, whose cathedral is one of the finest in Europe, whose Archbishop is Primate and Metropolitan of England, and crowns the Queen, to whom he is perpetual chaplain. The Mayor of York has the title of Lord, like that of London. Henry VII. gave the title of Duke of York to his son, and ever since that time the title has been given to the second son of the Kings of England. This city was in great estimation in the time of the Romans, and is memorable for the death of two of the Emperors, Severus and Constantius-Chlorus, as also for the nativity of Constantine the Great. It abounds with venerable remains of religious structures. The city of York has the dignity of being a county of itself, and has the district that adjoins it called Ainsty Liberty. There are more antiquities in this county than any other part of England, and it abounds with Roman roads, camps, &c., among which are the remains of a temple at Godmanham, near Market Weighton, encampment at Castle Hill, near Almondbury, near Huddersfield, at Cockridge, near Otley, at Merton, near Bernard's Castle, at Aldborough, at Bain Brig, near Askrig; at Catterick, near Richmond, near Ripponden, on Toot-hill between Iland and Wakefield, near Old Richmond; at Middleton, near Stokesley, near Pickering, at Nutwith, near Tanfield, on Black hill, near Bramhope, at Castleford, on Brough-hill, near Rotherham, at Winco Baul, near Rotherham, on Barnby-Moor; Temple-brough, near Conisborough, and a Roman road from the Tees to the Swale river. The air and soil of this county varies extremely, which is shewn in the description of each Riding. The whole number of members of parliament is 30, 2 of which are for the county, 2 for the city of York, and 2 for each of the following boroughs, viz. Aldborough, Boroughbridge, Beverley, Hedon, Rippon, Scarborough, Thirsk, Knaresborough, Kingston upon Hull, Malton, Northallerton, Pontefract, and Richmond, pays 24 parts of the land tax, and provides 2360 men to the national militia. The principal places on the coast are Flamborough Head and Light house, Spurn Head and Light-house, Horsai, and Scarborough Castle, Whitby Harbour, Robin Hood's and Burlington Bays. The most remarkable places in the county are York Wolds, Asgarth Force, St Robert's Cave, Ingleborough, Pennigant, Hutton, Morvill, Wharnside, Pine, Pinnow, Cam, Whelpstones, and Hamilton Hills, Applegarth, Swaledale, Pickering, Bolland, New, Stanmore, Gautries, June, and Hardwick Forests, Blackstone Ridge, Peter's Post, Hatfield Chace, King's and Grange Woods, Heath Moor, Wensley, Shile Swale, Lune, Baulder and Whart Dales, Hambleton Down Races, Scarborough, Beverley, Harrogate and Knaresborough Spaws. Its rivers are the Humber, Ouse, Youre, Wharf, Swale, Tees, Nid, Calder, Aire, Hull, Don, Derwent, Rye, Wisk, Ribble, Esk, Skelter, Recall, Lune, Barnes, Went, Rother, Greta, Foulney, and Leven. It produces fine pastures, corn, cattle, deer, sheep, goats, excellent horses, river and sea fish, game, fowls, copper, brass, lead, iron, coal, wood, liquorice, rape-feed, free-stone, lime-stone, jet, alum, black amber, marble, copperas, and kelp, with the manufactures of woollens, alum, copperas, malt, fine ale, pins, bone lace stockings, cutlery wares, and iron work, which employs at least 40,000 hands. It has an extensive trade from Kingston upon Hull to Hamburgh, and all parts of the Baltick, Germany, Holland, &c. &c.

NORTH RIDING OF YORKSHIRE

Is one of the divisions of the most extensive county in Great Britain, which, with the other two divisions, will be more fully described under its general name. On the East it is bounded by the German Ocean, on the North by Durham, on the West by Westmoreland, but on the South extends over both East and West Ridings, the two other divisions of the county of York. This district is divided into 12 wapentakes, comprehending that district formerly termed Richmondshire. It is 85 miles long, 44 broad, and 280 miles in circumference, containing 2000 square miles, or 1,280,000 acres, and contains 18 market-towns, viz. Richmond, which sends 2 members to parliament, and gives the title of Duke to the family of Lenox, Scarborough, which also sends 2 members to parliament, and gives the title of Earl to the family of Saunderson, Thirsk, Malton, and Northallerton, each of which towns sends 2 members to parliament; besides these there are the following market-towns, viz. Whitby, Bedale, Asking, Thorn, Easingwold, Gisborough, Helmsley, Kirby Moorside, Middleham, Masham, Pickering, Stokesley, Thirsk, and Yarm. On its coast are Robin Hood's Bay, Whitby Harbour, Hun cliff, and Scarborough Castle. This Riding in general exceeds the other two in the salubrity and coldness of the air: the worst parts breed lean cattle; but on the sides of the hills, in the vallies and plains, it produces good corn and rich pastures for large cattle, nor is it wanting in subterraneous riches, as calamine, marble, pit-coal, copperas, alum, and between the clifts of the rocks on the sea coast is found the best sort of jet. The Eastern Part of this Riding is called Blackmoor, and consists of a hilly, rocky, woody country, and that part, termed Richmondshire, consists of one continued eminence or ridge of rocks and vast mountains. The principal rivers in this Riding are the Ure, Wharfe, Swale, Teese, Don, Lune, Rye, Wysk, Eden, Esk, Codleach, Leven, and Recal, with the North Bank of the Derwent.

The principal Gentlemens' Seats are,

Acklam, near Stockton.
Burningham Park, near Stockton.
Bolton Hall, near Middleham.
Castle Howard, near New Malton.
Cliff, a Conscliff
Constable Burton, near Bedale.
Cowling, near Bedale
Danby, near Middleham
Duncombe Park, at Helmsley
Forcett Hall, near Richmond.
Giling, near Helmsley
Hoiling House, near Rippon
Hornby Castle, near Richmond
Kirkleaton Park, near Gisborough
Mulgrave Castle and Hall, near Whitby.

Newby Park, near Masham
Newbrough Park, near Easingwold
Ness, near Kirby Moorside
Norton Conyers, near Rippon
Pleringford, near Rippon
Ravensworth Castle, near Richmond.
Sedbury, near Richmond
Snape Park, near Masham
Stanwick, near Richmond
Studley Park, near Rippon
Swinton, near Masham
Tanfield Hall, near Masham
Thirkleby, near Thirsk
Thomson Widlas, near Masham.
Thorp, near Bedale.

The most remarkable Situations and extensive Views are,

Aigarth Force, E. of Asking, near Swinwate
Bolton Castle
Cam Fell, W. of Asking, from its summit
Cotter Hill, on the Borders of Westmoreland, and its highest part called Shunner Fell, the Head of Swale dale, where rise the Rivers Eden, Swale, and Ure
Hardrow Force, W N W of Asking, with Whitnoid Gill and Mill Gill Forces, or Cataracts near Asking
Hackness Vale, 3 miles N W of Scarborough
Hell Gill, near the Head of the Eden, N W. of Asking, on Cotter Hill
Jarvis Abbey
Middleham Castle
Rosberry Topping, near Gisborough.
Rowcliff on the Coast, N E of Gisborough
Southwick, W of Richmond, near the Asking Road.
Wensleydale, on the Ure of Asking
Whiston Cliff, on Black Humbleton, near Thirsk

EAST RIDING OF YORKSHIRE

BORDERS on the German or British Ocean, being one of the divisions of the very extensive county of York, which is fully described under its general name. It is separated by the Ouse from the West Riding, and is the smallest of the three Ridings which the county is divided into, and is separated from the North Riding by the river Derwent. It is 55 miles long from North-west to South-east, and 33 from North to South, and 175 in circumference, containing 1040 square miles, or 665,600 acres. In this division are 12 market-towns, viz. Kingston upon Hull, Beverley, and Hedon, sending each 2 members to parliament, Bridlington, or Burlington, Hunmanby, Frodingham, Hornsey, Howden, Kilham, Patrington, Pocklington, and Wighton. On the Coast are the Spurn Head and Flamborough Head, with Fley Bay, Bridlington Bay, and Kingston upon Hull Harbour. The most considerable rivers in this division are, the Humber, Hull, Ouse, Derwen, and Foulness. It has the Meer of Hornsey, together with York Wolds. The air of this Riding, on account of its neighbourhood to the German Ocean and the great estuary of the Humber, is less pure and healthy than that of the other two, yet on the hilly parts towards the North-west, in the large tract called the Wolds, the air is less affected by the waters. The soil, however, is in general dry, sandy, and barren, but the sea coast and vallies are fruitful. The Wold produces corn, and feeds great numbers of black cattle, horses, and sheep, whose wool is reckoned equal to any in England. This division yields plenty of wood, pit-coal, turf, jet, and alum stone, with great plenty of all kinds of sea and river fish. Its principal manufacture is woollen cloth. This Riding includes that division of the county named Ainsty Liberty, wherein stands the city of York, as described in the general account of Yorkshire.

The following are the most considerable Seats.

Burton upon Kingston
Everingham, near Market Weighton
Londesborough, near Market Weighton.
Moorby, near Cawood.
Nun Appleton
Risby, near Beverley.

Rise, near Hornsey
Scampston, near New Malton.
South Dalton
Wassand, near Hornsey
Wighill Park, near Tadcaster
Winestead Hall, near Patrington.

The most remarkable and extensive Views are,

Flamborough Head and its Caverns
Spurn Head

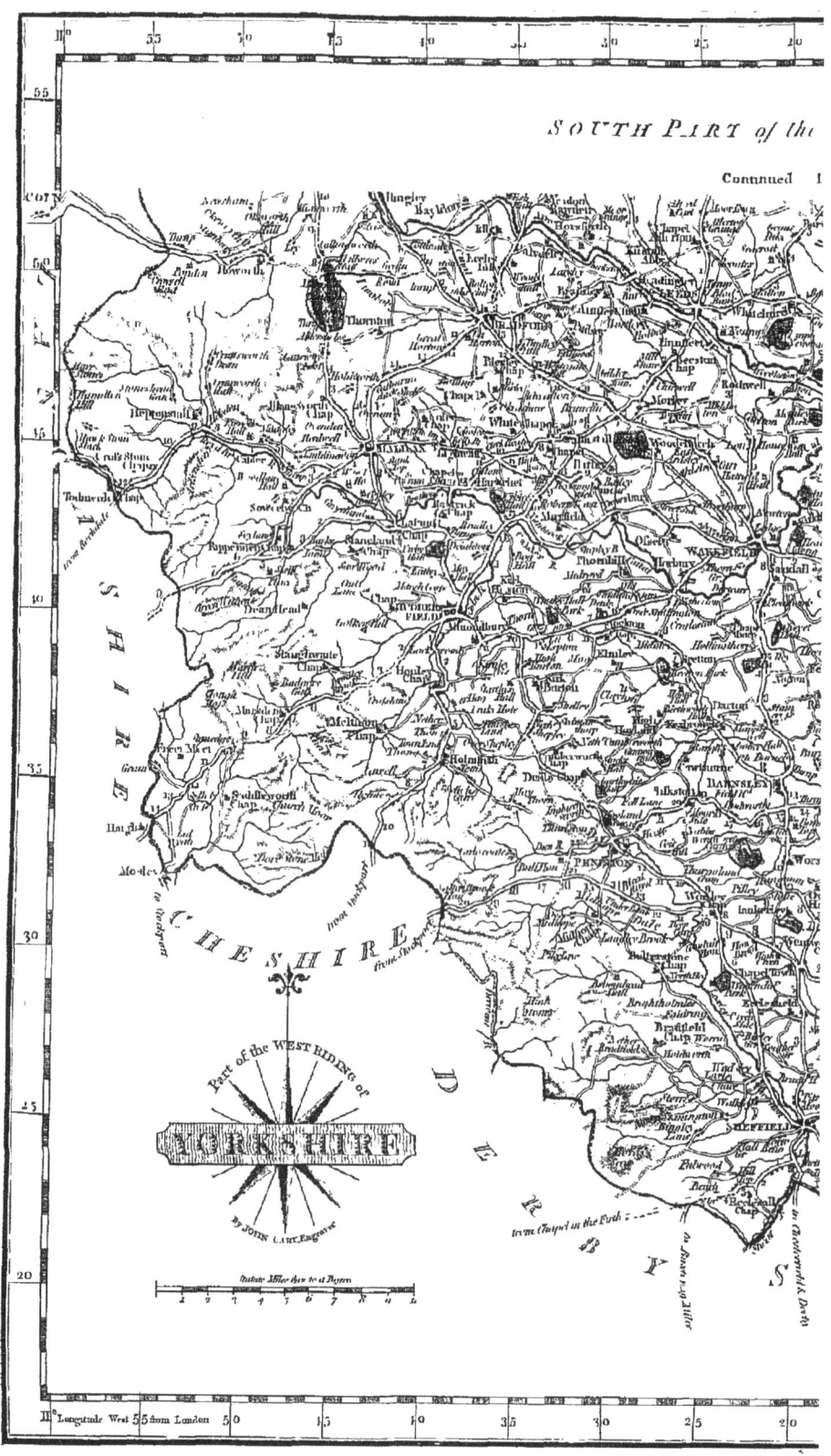

WEST RIDING OF YORKSHIRE.

THIS is the most inland division of this extensive county, and by far the largest and richest. It is divided from the East Riding by the river Ouse, and is bounded on the North by the North Riding. It is 95 miles long, 48 miles broad, and 320 in circumference, containing 2450 square miles, 1,568,000 acres, divided into 10 wapentakes or hundreds, containing 29 market-towns, viz. Leeds, which gives the title of Duke to the family of Osborne, Wakefield, the titles of Earl and Baron to the family of Kerr, Skipton, the title of Lord of the Honour of Skipton to the Tufton family, Doncaster, the title of Earl to the family of Scott, Pontefract, or Pomfret, the title of Earl to the Fermor family, with Rippon, Boroughbridge, Aldborough, and Knaresborough, which sends 2 members each to parliament, Halifax, Sheffield, which gives the title of Baron to the family of Baker Holroyd, Bawtry, Barnsley, Aberford, Sherborne, Bradford, Cawood, Gisborne, Huddersfield, Otley, Ripley, Rotherham, Selby, Settle, Snaith, Tadcaster, Tickhill, Wetherby and Ferrybridge. Among the numerous villages the following give titles, viz. Stratford, that of Earl to the family of Wentworth, Stainsborough, that of Baron, and Wentworth, that of Viscount to the same family, Wentworth also gives the titles of Viscount and Baron to the Noel family, Kiveton, the title of Baron to the Osborne family, Rawdon, the title of Baron to the family of the same name, Towton, the same Honour to the Hawke family, Wortley, the like Honour to the Stuart family, Markenfield, the dignity of Baron to the family of Norton, the Tract called Craven, gives the honour of Baron to a family of that name. The chief rivers are the Ure, Don or Dune, Went, Calder, Are, Ribble, Wharfe, Dearn, Nidd, and Hodder, with a variety of smaller streams. The most considerable hills are the Ingleborough, Pendle, Pennigant, Whelpstones, Cam, Wharnside. Here are mines of pit-coal, lime-stone, alum, &c. The air is sharper and healthier than either of the other two divisions of the county, the soil on the western side is hilly and stony, but the vallies afford the very best pasture and meadow ground. It is famous for fine horses, &c. It abounds with parks and chaces, and its chief manufactures are cloth and iron wares, which by means of canals that this division of the county has lately been enriched with, it has communication with the inland parts of the kingdom, and has considerably enlarged its trade. There is a petrifying spring at Knaresborough.

The most considerable Gentlemens' Seats in this Division are,

Ackworth, near Pontefract
Allerton Mauleveer, near Knaresborough.
Attrington, near Harewood
Afton
Bawtry
Bramham Park, near Tadcaster.
Breton Park, near Barnsley
Broughton, near Skipton
Burley House, near Otley
Byrom, near Ferrybridge
Cowick, near Snaith
Cusworth, at Doncaster
Denton House, near Otley
Dunholme Park, near Keighley
Farnby Hall, near Huddersfield.
Farnley Hall, near Otley
Gisbourne Park, near Gisbourne.
Goldthrough, near Knaresborough
Grange Park, near Huddersfield
Grantley Hall, near Rippon
Grove Hall, near Pontefract
Gunthwaite Hall, near Penistone.
Harewood House, at Harewood.
Heaton, near Sheffield
Helaby Hall, near Rotherham.
Holling Hill, near Rippon
Holme, near Rotherham
Hooky Hall, at Chapeltown
Howley Hall, near Wakefield
Kiveton Park, at South Afton.

Kirklees Hall, near Halifax
Kippax, near Pontefract
Kirkthorpe, near Wakefield.
Leathley Hall, near Otley
Ledstone Lodge, near Pontefract.
Melton on the Hill, near Doncaster.
Methley Park, near Wakefield
Newland Hall, near Wakefield.
Park Hill, near Tickhill
Parlington, near Aberford
Plumpton Hall, near Knaresborough.
Ravenfield, near Rotherham
Ripley Park, at Ripley
Rudding Hall, near Harewood
Sandbeck Park, near Tickhill.
Saxton, near Aberford
Skelbrook, near Pontefract
Skipton Castle.
Stapleton Park, near Pontefract.
Studley Royal
Tankersley Park, near Chapeltown.
Temple Newsham, near Leeds
Thornvill, near Wetherby.
Thribergh, near Rotherham
Walding Wells, near Tickhill
Wentworth Park, near Rotherham.
Wentworth Castle, near Barnsley
Weston Hall, near Otley
Wooley Park, near Barnsley.

The principal Scenes, Situations, or extensive Views are at
Skipton in Craven
The Vale about Aberforth, N. of Pontefract.
Kilnsey Crag on the Wharfe, near Skipton
Gordale, 6 miles S E of Settle, near Malham
Michael Haw Hill and Laver Banks to Hackfall, W. of Rippon
Laughton, near Sheffield
Blackstone Edge, near Halifax
Otley Chevin from the Bradford and Leeds Road, in the Wharfedale
The Pyramid at Wentworth House
From a Ridge of Rocks, near Leyburn and Middleham, called Scarthnick, in the road from Richmond to Alkrig
Apperley Bridge N W of Leeds
Steeton Bank, S of Skipton.
Vale of Calder
Elland Edge, near Halifax
Harwood Castle, N of Leeds on the Wharfe
Brimham Crags, N W of Ripley, near Pateley Bridge Road to Rippon
Pendle and Pennigant Hills, near Wakefield
From Skipton to Otley, through Wharfedale
From a Field near Rotherham
From Ingleton to Clapham, and from Clapham to Settle, between which last places there is an ebbing and flowing Well, arising under a long chain of Limestone Rocks.

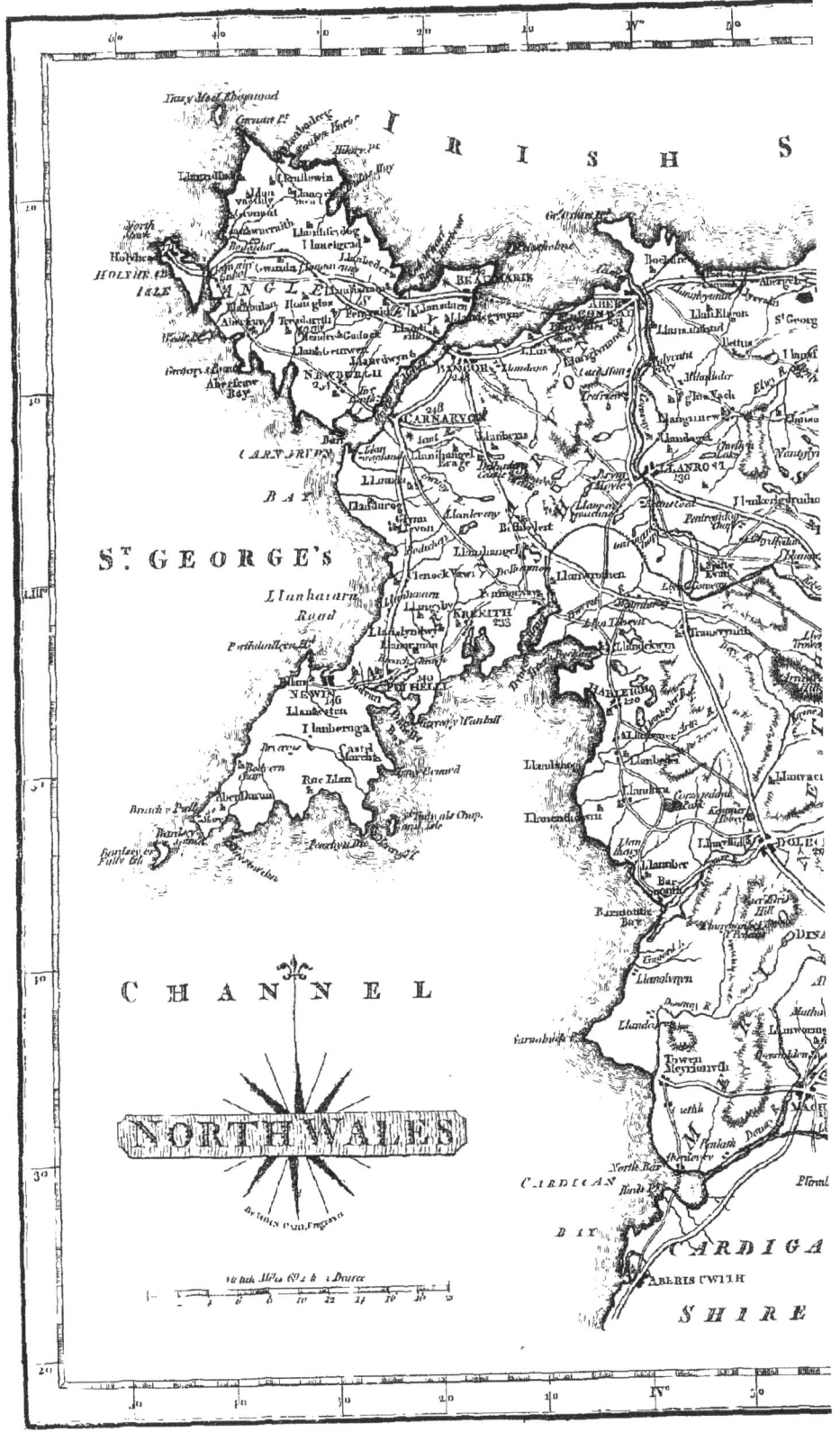

NORTH WALES

CONTAINS

ANGLESEY, CARNARVON, DENBIGH, FLINT, MERIONETH, and MONTGOMERY SHIRES.

ANGLESEY is an island at the north west part of this division, that was subdued and brought under the subjection of England by Edward I. It is in the province of Canterbury and diocese of Bangor, is 28 miles long, 13 broad, and about 80 in circumference, containing 180 square miles, or 115,200 acres, divided into 6 hundreds, and contains 74 parishes, with 2 market-towns, viz. Beaumaris, which sends one member to parliament, and is the principal town in the island; and Newburgh; but the village of Holyhead is the place from whence the Irish packets usually embark. North of Anglesey is the island of Skerries, whereon is a light-house. The principal rivers are the Menai and Keveny; on the coast Aberfraw Bay, Gregory Point, Wealt Island, North Stack, Holyhead Island, Carnar Point, Kemlyn Harbour, Hilary Point, Dulas Bay, and Red Wharf Bay and Harbour, with Priest Holme Island, and the Straits of Menai. It produces copper, mill and grind stones, red, yellow, and blue ocher, fine pastures, with plenty of corn and cattle. It sends 2 members to parliament, one for the county, and one as before-mentioned; pays one part of the land-tax, and provides 120 men to the national militia.

CARNARVONSHIRE is a maritime county, divided from Anglesey by the Straits of Menai. It lies in the province of Canterbury and the diocese of Bangor, is 48 miles long, 23 broad, and 150 in circumference, containing 430 square miles, or 275,200 acres, divided into 7 hundreds, has 68 parishes, one city, Bangor, the diocese of a bishop, and 5 market-towns, viz. Carnarvon, which gives the title of Marquis and Earl to the family of Brydges, and sends one member to parliament; Aberconway, Krekith, Pulhely, and Nevin. The principal rivers are the Conway, and the Seint; it has also several Lakes. The principal curiosities in this county are the numerous mountains, rocks, &c. the tops of which are 8 or 9 months in the year covered with snow. On the coasts are Traweth Mawr, Pulhely Bay, St Tudwell's Chapel and Morcrofs Isle, Ynys Gwiliin, Bardsey or Bully Isle and Sound, Porthdinlleyn Head, Llanhaiurn Road, Carnarvon Bay, and Great Orme's Head. It has a waterfall near Snowdon Peak, and Gaunhant 3 miles from Penmaen Mawr. Its products are timber, goats, fish, &c. It sends 2 members to parliament, one for the county, and one as before mentioned, pays one part of the land-tax, and provides 80 men to the national militia.

DENBIGHSHIRE is a maritime county, in the province of Canterbury, and the dioceses of St Asaph and Bangor, being 50 miles long, 20 broad, and 170 in circumference, containing 670 square miles, or 428,800 acres, divided into 12 hundreds, having 57 parishes, and 4 market-towns, viz. Denbigh, the county town, which sends one member to parliament, and gives the title of Earl to the Fielding family, Ruthin, which gives the title of Baron to the family of Yelverton, Wrexham and Llanroft. Its principal rivers are the Cluyd, Dee, Conway, Allen, Keriog, Kelyn, and Elwy. Its manufactures are those of gloves and flannels; and its products corn, horned cattle, and lead. The Vale of Cluyd is remarkably fertile and pleasant. This county is very mountainous, and abounds with Druidical monuments and British antiquities. It sends 2 members to parliament, one for the county, and one as already mentioned; pays one part of the land-tax, and provides 280 men to the national militia.

FLINTSHIRE

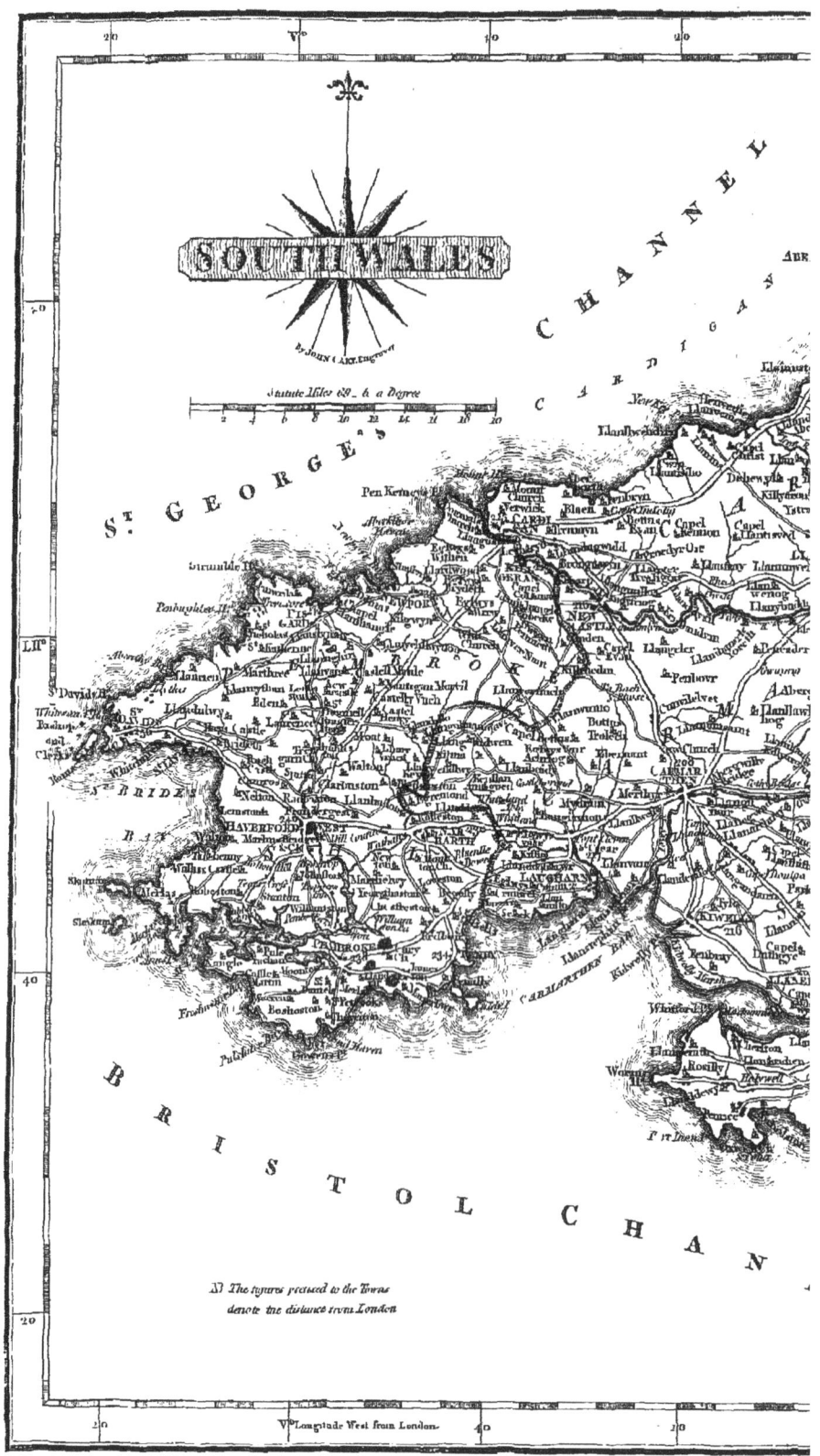

FLINTSHIRE is also a maritime county, which gives the title of Earl to the Prince of Wales; is in the province of Canterbury, and dioceses of St Asaph and Chester; it is 33 miles long, 11 broad, and 100 miles in circumference, containing 250 square miles, or 160,000 acres; divided into 5 hundreds, and has 28 parishes, with one city, St. Asaph, which is the see of a bishop, and gives the title of Viscount to the Ashburnham family; and has 2 market towns, viz Holywell, and Caerws. Flint, the county town, though it has no market, sends one member to parliament. The principal rivers are the Dee, Cluyd, Elwy, and Allen; the most remarkable places are the Dee's Mouth, the Cluyd's Mouth, and St Winifred's Well. It produces cattle, butter, honey, coal, and lead. It sends 2 members to parliament, one for the county, and one as above shewn; pays half of one part of the land-tax, and provides 120 men to the national militia.

MERIONETHSHIRE is another maritime county, in the province of Canterbury, and diocese of Bangor; it is 40 miles long, 36 broad, and 160 in circumference, containing 790 square miles, or 505,600 acres; divided into 6 hundreds, and has 37 parishes, with 4 market towns, viz Harleigh, Dolgele, Dinasmouthy, and Bala. Its principal rivers are the Dee, Douay, Avon, and Desunny. The most noted places on the coast are Traeth Bychan, Barmouth Bay, Sarnaouch Point, and North Bar; and inland are Dolgele Vale, Pemble Meer, and some very high mountains. It abounds with cattle, sheep, fish, and game; and its chief manufacture is Welsh Cottons. The soil of this county is rocky, has many British or Roman antiquities; sends one member only to parliament, and that for the county; pays half of one part of the land-tax, and supplies 80 men to the national militia.

MONTGOMERYSHIRE is an inland county, in the province of Canterbury, and dioceses of St. Asaph, Bangor, and Hereford. It is 40 miles long, 37 broad, and 170 in circumference, containing 860 square miles, or 550,400 acres; divided into 6 hundreds, and 47 parishes, with 6 market-towns, viz. Montgomery, the county town, which gives the title of Earl to the family of Herbert, and sends one member to parliament; Llanvilling, Welchpool, Newtown, Machynleth, and Llanydlos. The principal rivers are the Severn, Rayder, Tuigh, and Tanat, Verniew, and some smaller streams. It has numerous hills and mountains, which abound with antiquities of the Britons and Druids, plenty of fish and fowl, with a breed of large black cattle and horses, and lead. Its principal manufacture is flannel. It sends 2 members to parliament, one for the county, and one as before-mentioned; pays one part of the land-tax, and supplies 240 men to the national militia.

SOUTH WALES

CONTAINS

BRECKNOCK, CARDIGAN, CARMARTHEN, GLAMORGAN, PEMBROKE, and RADNOR SHIRES.

BRECKNOCKSHIRE is an inland county, in the province of Canterbury, and diocese of St David's, 33 miles long, 32 broad, and 120 miles in circumference, containing 590 square miles, or 377,600 acres, divided into 6 hundreds, having 61 parishes, and four market-towns, viz. Brecknock, the county town, which sends one member to parliament, Builth Hay, and Crickhowel. Its principal rivers are the Hodney, Wye, Usk, and the Yrvon, its manufactures are woollen stuffs and stockings, and its product, corn, pastures, cattle, otters, and river fish, with an abundance of fowl. It is very pleasant, but mountainous, and in the vallies fertile. It sends 2 members to parliament, one for the county, and one as above-mentioned; it pays one part of the land-tax, and provides 160 men to the national militia.

CARDIGANSHIRE is a maritime county, in the province of Canterbury, and diocese of St David's, 47 miles long, 20 broad, and 130 in circumference, containing 590 square miles, or 377,600 acres, divided into 5 hundreds, 64 parishes, and 6 market-towns, viz. Cardigan, the county town, which sends one member to parliament, and gives the title of Earl to the Brudenell family, Aberistwith, Tregaron, and Lanpiter or Llanbeder, Lanbadernvawr, and Llannurth. Its principal rivers are the Tavy, Rhidal, and Istwith. On its coast are Cardigan Island, Mount Herd, and Cardigan Bay, it has several lakes, and Rescob forest. It produces corn, plenty of cattle, game, with sea and river fish, has mines of lead, copper, and silver ore, and enjoys a milder air than any other county in Wales. It sends 2 members to parliament, one for the county, and one as above-mentioned, pays one part of the land-tax, and supplies 120 men to the national militia.

CARMARTHENSHIRE is a maritime county, in the province of Canterbury, and diocese of St David's, 48 miles long, 25 broad, and 150 in circumference, containing 800 square miles, or 512,000 acres, divided into 6 hundreds, and 87 parishes, with 8 market towns, viz. Carmarthen, the county town, which sends one member to parliament, and gives the title of Marquis to the family of Osborne, Kidwelly, Llandilovawr, Llanimdovery, Llangadoc, Llangharn, Newcastle, and Llanelly. The village of Browse gives the title of Baron to the families of Howard and Bulkeley, and that of Dinever the like honour to that of Cardonnel late Talbot. Its principal rivers are the Tavy, Cathy, Towy, Brane, and Gwilly. This county is well cloathed with wood, and feeds vast numbers of cattle, it abounds with fowl, fish, and game, it has coal and lead mines; and on the coast is Machanis Isle, Kidwelly Point, Llanstephen Point, Langharn Point, and Carmarthen Bay. It sends 2 members to parliament, one for the county, and one as above-mentioned; pays one part of the land-tax, and supplies 200 men to the national militia.

GLAMORGANSHIRE is a maritime county, in the province of Canterbury, and dioceses of Landaff and St. David's; is 50 miles long, 24 broad, and 145 in circumference, containing 660 square miles, or 422,400 acres, divided into 10 hundreds, having 118 parishes, one city, Landaff, which is the see of a bishop, and 8 market-towns, viz. Cardiffe, which sends one member to parliament, and gives the title of Baron to the families of Stewart and Herbert; Swansea, Caerfilly, Penrice, Neath, Bridgend, Llantrissent, and Cowbridge. The village of Hensol gives the title of Baron to the family of Talbot Chetwyn. Its principal rivers are the Taff, Rhymny, Ogmore, Avon, Cledaugh, and Tavy, it produces pastures, corn, pit-coal and culm, and lead ore. It is mountainous and cold in the north, but mild and fertile in the south. There are several ancient monuments in this county

imputed

imputed to the Romans and Britons, and on the coast are Sully Isle, Barry Isle, and Scalker Isle; with Breaksea Point, Nash Point, The Mumbles Point, Swansea Bay, Caswell Bay, Penarth Point, Oxwich Point, Port Inon Point, Wormshead, and Whitford Point. Also a warm spring, called Taye Well, and Swinter mineral spring. It sends 2 members to parliament, one of which is for the county, and one as before mentioned; pays one part of the land-tax, and provides 360 men to the national militia.

PEMBROKESHIRE is a maritime county, the south west extremity of Wales, and in a great part surrounded by the Irish sea; it is in the province of Canterbury, and diocese of St. David's, being 35 miles long, 29 broad, and 140 in circumference, containing 540 square miles, or 345,600 acres, divided into 7 hundreds, and 145 parishes, having one city, St. David's, the see of a bishop, and 8 market-towns, viz. Pembroke, the county town, which sends one member to parliament, and gives the title of Earl to the family of Herbert, Haverford West, which gives the title of Baron to the family of De la Poer, and sends one member to parliament, Tenby, Fishgard, Kilgarren, Newport, Nirbath, and Wiston. Its rivers are the Clethy, the Dougledye, and the Tavy, with several lesser streams; it produces corn, sheep, and cattle, fowls and fish, with coal mines and marl. On the coast are Tenby Point, St. Margaret's and Calely Isles, Stackpole Head, Broad Haven, St. Gowen's Point, Posheston Meer, Pulslater Bay, Head of Man, Freshwater Bay, Sheppy Isle, Milford Haven, St. Ann's Point, Merlas Bay, Skokum, Gasholm, and Skomai Isles, the Mer stone and Yarland Stone, Stock Rock, Dariston Haven, Dinas Man i, Bishop's Store, Bishop and Clerks Rocks, Ramsey Isle, Whitesand Bay, St. David's Head, Aberithy Bay, Abercastle, Penbughto Head, Strumble Head, Fisgard Bay, Newport Bay, Aberkibor Haven, and Pen Kemys Point. The air of the county is healthy, the soil fertile, and the coast abounds with wild fowl of various kinds seldom seen in other parts of Britain. It sends 3 members to parliament, one for the county, and two as above mentioned; pays one part of the land-tax, and supplies 160 men to the national militia.

RADNORSHIRE is an inland county, in the province of Canterbury, and dioceses of Hereford and St. David's, is 30 miles long, 25 broad, and 100 in circumference, containing 390 square miles, or 249,600 acres, divided into 6 hundreds, and 52 parishes, including 4 market-towns, viz. Radnor, or New Randor, the county town, which gives the title of Earl to the family of Stanley, and sends one member to parliament, Presteigna, Knighton, and Riadergovey. Its principal rivers are the Wye, Lug, Teine, Arrow, Somergill, Tame, and several small streams, and its product is cattle, sheep, horses, and cheese, and its only manufacture malt. On the Wye is a remarkable waterfall called Rhajadi-gry. It sends 2 members to parliament, viz. one for the county, and one as above shewn; pays one part of the land-tax, and provides 120 men to the national militia. It has an excellent mineral water at the village of Llandrindod.

Lightning Source UK Ltd.
Milton Keynes UK
UKOW07f1914240416

272888UK00004B/75/P